ON FEMALE BODY EXPERIENCE

STUDIES IN FEMINIST PHILOSOPHY
Cheshire Calhoun, *Series Editor*

Published in the series:

ON FEMALE BODY EXPERIENCE

"Throwing Like a Girl" and Other Essays

Iris Marion Young

OXFORD
UNIVERSITY PRESS

2005

OXFORD
UNIVERSITY PRESS

Oxford New York
Auckland Bangkok Buenos Aires Cape Town Chennai
Dar es Salaam Delhi Hong Kong Istanbul Karachi Kolkata
Kuala Lumpur Madrid Melbourne Mexico City Mumbai Nairobi
São Paulo Shanghai Singapore Taipei Tokyo Toronto

Copyright © 2005 by Oxford University Press, Inc.

Published by Oxford University Press, Inc.
198 Madison Avenue, New York, New York 10016

www.oup.com

Oxford is a registered trademark of Oxford University Press

Library of Congress Cataloging-in-Publication Data
Young, Iris Marion, 1949–
On female body experience : "Throwing like a girl" and other essays / Iris Marion Young.
p. cm.—(Studies in feminist philosophy)
Includes index.
ISBN-13 978-0-19-516193-9 (pbk.)
ISBN 0-19-516192-0; 0-19-516193-9 (pbk.)
1. Feminist theory. 2. Women—Psychology. 3. Women—Social Conditions. 4. Body,
Human—Social aspects. 5. Sex role. I. Title. II. Series

HQ1190 .Y679 2004
305.42'01—dc22   2004044842

2 3 4 5 6 7 8 9

Printed in the United States of America
on acid-free paper

For Morgen, again

Acknowledgments

All but one of these essays has been previously published, and I grate-fully acknowledge the editors of the journals and books in which they have appeared:

"Throwing Like a Girl: A Phenomenology of Feminine Body Com-portment, Motility, and Spatiality" was first published in *Human Stud-ies* 3 (1980): 137–56, and it is reprinted here with permission of Kluwer Academic Publishers.

"Pregnant Embodiment: Subjectivity and Alienation" appeared in *Journal of Medicine and Philosophy* 9.1 (January 1984): 45–62. It is reprinted with permission of Martin Scrivener.

A shorter version of "Women Recovering Our Clothes" appeared in *Postmodernism and Continental Philosophy*, ed. Hugh Silverman and Donn Welton (Albany: State University of New York Press, 1988), 144–52, and it is reprinted by permission. The advertisement from the Woolmark Company facing "Women Recovering Our Clothes" is re-printed from *Self* (Fall 1985).

A shorter version of "Breasted Experience: The Look and the Feel-ing" was published in *Medicine and Lived Body*, ed. Drew Leder and Mary Rawlinson (D. Reidel/Kluwer Academic Publishers, 1990); it is reprinted by permission.

All four of these articles were collected in Iris Marion Young, *Throw-ing Like a Girl and Other Essays in Feminist Philosophy and Female Body Experience* (Bloomington: Indiana University Press, 1990).

"House and Home: Feminist Variations on a Theme" was first pub-lished in Iris Marion Young, *Intersecting Voices: Dilemmas of Gender, Political Philosophy and Policy* (Princeton, N.J.: Princeton University Press, 1997); it is reprinted by permission.

"A Room of One's Own: Old Age, Extended Care, and Privacy" is a revised version of an essay published in *Privacies: Philosophical Evaluations*, ed. Beate Roessler (Stanford, Calif.: Stanford University Press, 2004); reprinted by permission.

"Lived Body vs. Gender: Reflections on Social Structure and Subjectivity" was first published in *Ratio: An International Journal of Analytic Philosophy* 15.4 (December 2002): 410–28; reprinted with permission of Blackwell Publishing.

I am grateful to Cheshire Calhoun for encouraging me to collect these essays, together with the previously unpublished "Menstrual Meditations," into a volume for this series.

Contents

ON FEMALE BODY EXPERIENCE

Introduction

Much has changed for women since I was a little girl in the 1950s in New York City. In many places the lives and spaces of women and men have become less separate, and women fill roles and appear in places that might have surprised my grandmother. For all that, the image of woman has not ceased being that of the Other: the surface that reflects fantasies and fears arising from our human being as vulnerable bodies. Just because images and expectations about women make us asymmetrically associated with sex, birth, age, and flesh, we have little voice to express our own point of view on this fleeting existence or on the social relations that position us.

The essays in this volume reflect on different aspects of women's everyday lived bodily experience. One of their purposes is simply expressive: to give words to meanings often unspoken, in ways that I hope evoke recognition and even a little bit of pleasure. Each of the essays also engages in social criticism; they expose mundane ways that actions and opportunities for women are unfairly constrained by social norms regulating body comportment and by the needs of people for bodily care. The essays thus take a feminist perspective, both as expressing sex- and gender-specific female subjectivity, and as claiming that women are not as free as we ought to be.

The composition of these essays spans more than twenty-five years of thinking about embodiment. I began work on the earliest, "Throwing Like a Girl," in 1977. The ink is barely dry on "Menstrual Meditations." When I began writing on themes of female embodiment, neither philosophical nor feminist-theoretical nor sociological literature contained many works engaged in such a project. In the discipline of philosophy in the United States, only scholars of existential phenomenology, the tradition from which my first work in this field arose, made body experience thematic. This rich and lively theoretical discussion, however, made little or no reference to sexual difference or gender. Sandra Bartky was the only philosopher I was aware of whose work aimed to bring ideas of existential phenomenology to analysis of women's gender-specific experience.

While feminist theorists often referred to facts and experiences of women's bodies, in these early years they had not yet developed theoretical methods for reflection on female embodiment. In the late 1970s and early 1980s American philosophers were only just beginning to notice Foucault's paradigm-shifting accounts of power. Shortly thereafter, the writing of theorists such as Julia Kristeva and Luce Irigaray gave feminist scholars new and often controversial vocabularies for articulating womanly experience.

In the succeeding decades, scholarly literature reflecting on female and male body experience from a feminist point of view has bloomed with hundreds of flowers. Important feminist writers have explored issues of embodiment, experience, and meaning using methods derived from continental philosophy. I have in mind scholars such as Christine Battersby, Susan Bordo, Judith Butler, Sonia Kruks, Dorothea Olkowski, Gail Weiss, and members of the "Australian school" of feminist philosophy such as Rosalind Diprose, Moira Gatens, and Elizabeth Grosz.

It is most natural that feminist concerns should have led scholars to uncover and challenge tendencies of Western philosophical and social-theoretical traditions to ignore or repress the significance of embodiment for thought, action, and feeling. Because much feminist reflection begins from the sociohistorical fact that women's bodily differences from men have grounded or served as excuses for structural inequalities, inquiry about the status and malleability of bodies in relation to social status is for us a matter of some urgency. Scholarship in women's studies deserves significant credit for leading critical social theory toward more systematic reflection on socialized bodies. In the decades since I began work in this field, moreover, exciting work on embodiment and society has blossomed more broadly in philosophy, sociology, literary studies, communication, and other disciplines.

My own reflections on embodied experience have benefited from these intellectual currents. Just because they have become so numerous and diverse, I have not tried to catalog or synthesize theories of embodiment here. I offer these essays as one set of overlapping inquiries about social meanings of female embodiment, in conversation with others. Nor have I attempted to revise the older essays included here in light of more recent concepts, distinctions, and arguments about gendered subjectivity or embodiment. If nothing else, the collection exhibits a trajectory of thinking of one idiosyncratic feminist critical theorist over several decades of the late twentieth and early twenty-first century; they may also reflect an evolution in the way a number of theorists have approached themes of gender and sexual difference. In the remainder of this introduction I shall explain some of what I mean by the title themes and briefly gesture toward the themes of the individual essays.

Female/Feminine Experience

In *Phenomenal Woman,* Christine Battersby distinguishes between the "female" and the "feminine" as a category for envisioning alternative human possibilities. Western metaphysics has postulated the idea of an autonomous individual subject, a self-enclosed ego that inhabits but is distinct from a body. Reflection on the existential qualities of female bodies, Battersby suggests, upsets most of the assumptions of this ontology—that selves are independent of one another, that their rational core stands at a distance from the pains and sufferings of vulnerable bodies. Battersby proposes a different philosophical framework arising from this female embodiment, from the experience of a body with the capacity to generate another body. This starting point, she suggests, acknowledges that the subject lives as flesh, and that there are inevitable dependencies between self and other. These in turn engender power inequalities that cannot be abolished but should be acknowledged if each of us is to receive due respect.[1]

Battersby is less specific about the category of the "feminine" about which she evinces suspicion. As I reconstruct this distinction, the "feminine" signifies a relational position in a dichotomy, masculine/feminine, where the first is more highly valued than the second, and where the second is partly defined as a lack with respect to the first. This dichotomy lines up with others that have a homologous hierarchical logic, such as mind/body, reason/passion, public/private, hard science/soft science, and dozens of other value-laden dichotomies whose discursive application has practical effects in personal lives, workplaces, media imagery, and politics, to name only a few social fields.

As contrasted with the female, and logically connected to this semiotic operation, I conceive the feminine also as a set of normatively disciplined expectations imposed on female bodies by male-dominated society. Among other things, these norms socially script caretaking work as belonging to women and the dispositions of caretaking as ill-fitting us for many other activities. Normative femininity detaches persons who fall under its disciplines from expressions or enactments of power and authority. Disciplines of the feminine, finally, aim to mask or subordinate the raw facts of embodiment, to make the body "pretty" by con-

---

1. Christine Battersby, *Phenomenal Woman: Feminist Metaphysics and the Patterns of Identity* (New York: Routledge, 1998).

straining fluid flesh, masking its organic smells with perfumes, painting skin, lips, eyes, and hair that have lost their nubile luster.

Battersby's distinction between the female and the feminine resonates with this book's title and helps situate its chapters. I take some issue, however, with the strength of the distinction as she seems to draw it. By means of this distinction, Battersby herself tends to set up something of a hierarchical dichotomy. "Female" is a more useful category than "feminine" for feminist theory, it seems, because the feminine is more hostage to hegemonic discourses. I think that distinguishing concepts of female and feminine in gendered social experience is both plausible and useful. The first refers more to living out materialities of bodies, while the second refers more to gendered social conventions. Nevertheless, I think that these two aspects of sexed and gendered experience are more ambiguously and problematically related than Battersby suggests. Experience and social structure often make the difference between them undecidable. I think that reflection on feminine meanings that are often devalued by dominant norms sometimes provides a basis for social criticism. Looking to either the female or the feminine for conceptual alternatives, however, risks reinscribing the very structures we aim to transform.

Some of the essays collected here reflect more on constraints and possibilities of the feminine, and some more on the ineluctable but nevertheless historically specific experiences of living in female bodies. "Throwing Like a Girl," for example, theorizes socially constructed habits of feminine body comportment in male-dominated society, and their implications for the sense of agency and power of persons who inhabit these body modalities. "Women Recovering Our Clothes" and "House and Home" also dwell on experiences and values traditionally associated with the feminine, both for the sake of exposing the oppressions they support and also in order to envision liberating possibilities in them.

"Pregnant Embodiment," "Breasted Experience," and "Menstrual Meditations," on the other hand, focus more on female experience. My interest is to explore the distinctive feelings and modalities of being-in-the-world that these aspects of embodiment produce. While many women never become pregnant or give birth, menstruating and having breasts are common to most women for a good part of their lives. Oddly, feminist scholars have thought systematically very little about these ordinary body experiences with which most women identify specifically as women, even though the concrete quality of these experiences varies greatly.

The Tradition of Existential Phenomenology

"Body experience" is another key term in my title. None of these essays takes bodies as objects or things to observe, study or explain. Rather, the essays aim to describe subjectivity and women's experience as lived and felt in the flesh. Thomas Csordas points out that when recent philosophy and social theory have thematized bodies, they have most often analyzed bodies or discourses about bodies as texts.[2] Foucault, for example, exposes and criticizes disciplinary discourses through which subjects operate on their own bodies. Feminist and queer theorists such as Judith Butler extend such analyses of discourses about normative bodies. Some students of media, to take a different kind of example, explore representations of bodies and their interactions in film, television, and popular magazines, using interpretive tools from deconstruction or psychoanalysis to theorize how such images interpellate and position their audiences.

Less articulated, according to Csordas, especially in recent decades, are critical theoretical interpretations of embodiment as a mode of being-in-the-world. The two theoretical approaches are complementary, he suggests, but not reducible one to the other. He argues that the imbalance should be corrected, and that more work should be done to theorize embodiment as lived. The essays collected here do both. They draw liberally on textual and discourse-analytic approaches to female bodies and feminine meanings, as well as on a large body of normative arguments from moral and political philosophy. The core task of all but the first, however, is to describe embodied being-in-the-world through modalities of sexual and gender difference.

As I noted above, when I began writing about female embodiment, existential phenomenology was the primary approach available to American philosophers for such a project. The earliest essay here reprinted, "Throwing Like a Girl," relies specifically on the theories of Maurice Merleau-Ponty and Simone de Beauvoir. Within the phenomenological tradition, Merleau-Ponty took the revolutionary step of theorizing consciousness itself as embodied. The subject who constitutes a world is always an embodied subject. Heidegger and Sartre had already moved away from the Husserlian quest for transcendental phenomenal essences toward conceptualizing being-in-the-world as situated. There is no situation, however, without embodied location and interaction. Conversely, the body as lived is always layered with social and historical meaning and is not some primitive matter prior to or underlying economic and political relations or cultural meanings. Simone de Beauvoir deepened this point by thematizing sexual difference as constitutive of much situated being-in-the-world.

More recent French philosophy criticized existential phenomenology on many grounds. Its concept of consciousness, even when embodied, assumes the subject as unitary and original to experience. The normative commitments of existential phenomenology express a naive humanism

---

2. Thomas J. Csordas, "Embodiment and Cultural Phenomenology," in *Perspectives on Embodiment: The Intersections of Nature and Culture*, ed. Gail Weiss and Honi Fern Haber (New York: Routledge, 1997), 143–62.

insufficiently aware of social plurality and the forms that power and repression take in well-intentioned liberal law and social criticism. After reading Lacan, Foucault, Derrida, Kristeva, Deleuze, Irigaray, and Bourdieu, we cannot be so innocent as to believe that phenomenology can discover a "pure" embodied experience prior to ideology and science.

Most of the essays in this book are influenced by these writers often called postmodern, and by their critical reaction to the existential phenomenological tradition. On the other side of this critique it seems to me that one can no longer say that phenomenology is a rigorous method, but more that it is an approach to inquiry.

It is notable that some Anglo-American philosophers and social theorists who for many years aligned themselves with these French postmodern thinkers have in recent years become more interested in the French phenomenologists. For some time now they have studied the work of Emmanuel Levinas, about whom Derrida says so much. More recently, Merleau-Ponty's philosophy seems to be gaining renewed interest. Recent feminist scholarship on Simone de Beauvoir's existentialism, moreover, has reevaluated her continuing contribution to feminist thought, and several writers now interpret her philosophical framework as closer to Merleau-Ponty's than to Jean-Paul Sartre's.[3]

One of the reasons for continuing scholarly attention to Beauvoir, Merleau-Ponty, and others in the tradition of existential phenomenology, I believe, is that this philosophy offers a unique approach to theorizing subjectivity. An existential phenomenological approach aims to speak from the point of view of the constituted subject's experience, in ways that complement but do not duplicate the observational or interpretive methods of Foucault, Butler, or Bourdieu.

Phenomenology, says Merleau-Ponty, "tries to give a direct description of our experience as it is, without taking account of its psychological origin and the causal explanation which the scientist, the historian or the sociologist may be able to provide."[4] In Merleau-Ponty's particular theorizing, the consciousness that constitutes its world is the body as lived in a tangible encounter with human and nonhuman others. The descriptive phenomenologist's task is to reveal the sense "where the paths of my various experiences intersect, and also where by own and other people's interact and engage each other like gears."[5]

Elizabeth Grosz argues that phenomenological description of lived body experience makes unique contributions to feminist philosophy,

3. See, for example, Toril Moi, *What Is a Woman?: And Other Essays* (New York: Oxford University Press, 1999); Debra B. Bergoffen, *Philosophy of Simone de Beauvoir: Gendered Phenomenologies, Erotic Generosities* (Albany: State University of New York, 1997); and Sonia Kruks, *Retrieving Experience: Subjectivity and Recognition in Feminist Politics* (Ithaca, N.Y.: Cornell University Press, 2001).

4. Maurice Merleau-Ponty, *The Phenomenology of Perception*, trans. Colin Smith (New York: Humanities Press, 1962), vii.

5. Ibid, viii.

alongside more psychoanalytic, deconstructionist, and ontological theories. She suggests that theorizing lived embodiment disrupts many dichotomies that structure more abstract thought—such as those distinguishing private and public, self and other, nature and culture. Grosz properly cautions against taking phenomenology to describe a foundational experience unconditioned by power and ideology. She argues, nevertheless, that "without some acknowledgment of the formative role of experience in the establishment of knowledges, feminism has no grounds from which to dispute patriarchal norms."[6]

Sonia Kruks likewise recommends phenomenological descriptions of lived body experience as an important resource for feminist projects of social criticism and transformation. Reflective inquiry that aims to express embodied being-in-the-world captures some of the feeling that can motivate social criticism and political organization. Descriptions of lived female and feminine experience can reveal reasons that differently situated women may have to sympathize with one another's embodied situation, while at the same time remaining sufficiently vague to allow for concrete variation.[7]

Order and Themes of the Essays

How do girls and women constitute their experienced world through their movement and orientation in places? What are some of the feelings of ambivalence, pleasure, power, shame, objectification, and solidarity that girls and women have about bodies, their shape, flows, and capacities? How do the things and people we touch and are touched by become a material support for or extension of ourselves? To the extent that women occupy relatively disadvantaged positions in gendered power and role structures, how, if at all, is our subordination embodied? These are the kinds of questions with which I approach themes and subjects of female experience in this volume. I have ordered them in the manner that seems thematically most sensible, rather than according to the chronology of their composition.

Thus the first essay of this book, "Lived Body vs. Gender," is one of the most recently written. It evaluates Toril Moi's arguments for abandoning the concept of gender for feminist theory and replacing it with the concept of lived body derived from existential phenomenology. I agree with Moi that lived body is a better concept than gender as a category theorizing subjectivity. I argue, however, that we need to retain and reposition a concept of gender for theorizing social structure. I begin

---

6. Elizabeth A. Grosz, *Volatile Bodies: Toward a Corporeal Feminism* (Bloomington, Ind.: Indiana University Press, 1994), 236–48.

7. Sonia Kruks, *Retrieving Experience: Subjectivity and Recognition in Feminist Politics* (Ithaca, N.Y.: Cornell University Press, 2001).

with this essay because it is the most methodological and programmatic in the volume. It reviews a history of theoretical debates in feminist theory in the last two decades and explains the meaning and function of the category of lived body. Thus this essay serves as a theoretical introduction to some of the concepts applied in the rest of the essays.

The next cluster of essays reflects on core elements of female body experience: movement in space, pregnancy, being breasted, menstruating. As mentioned above, "Throwing Like a Girl" describes experience and oppressions of feminine styles of comportment. Not all women necessarily express feminine motility and spatiality, which I describe as moving in a constricted space; some men do, moreover, though not many, and often only when working at it. Although there is something a bit dated about the way the essay expresses its feminist sentiments, I reprint it here because many teachers and students have told me that they continue to read the essay and find exciting the discussion it generates.

By no means all women become pregnant and give birth; some actively resist pressures to bear children either at certain times in their lives or for their entire lives. The very forces that would make childbearing normative for women, I suggest, also tend to rob those women who do choose to bear and birth children of the subjectivity of the experience. From the point of view of dominant discourse, pregnancy is a deviant condition, a temporary inconvenience instrumental to the social value of babies. "Pregnant Embodiment" takes a different perspective on pregnancy. What happens when we think of being pregnant as an intrinsic value, and describe it less as a process of producing a baby and more as a way of being-in-the-world with uniquely interesting characteristics? I take my main textual inspiration in this essay from some of Julia Kristeva's work, as well as from ideas of the women's health movement of the early 1980s.

The next two essays thematize aspects of female embodiment nearly universal to women, having breasts and menstruating. Women live each of these aspects of female embodiment in historically, culturally, and individually variable ways. While each essay tries to recognize such sociohistorical specificity, their level is too abstract to analyze these empirical differences. Both try to lay out some of the general meanings of female body experience and our encounter with normatively masculine institutions. "Breasted Experience" relies on Luce Irigaray's distinctions between a dominant Western specular ontology of solids and her vision of a tactile ontology of fluids. "Menstrual Meditations," the most recently written essay in this book, returns to the work of Simone de Beauvoir and also relies on the research of some remarkable contemporary feminist social scientists.

The final cluster of essays, on clothes, home, and old-age residences, explore aspects of everyday life gendered as feminine but which, I argue, harbor universalizable normative ideals. Both "Women Recovering Our

Clothes" and "House and Home: Feminist Variations on a Theme" apply a method I derive from Irigaray. They first describe a mode of existence in its femininity as constructed by patriarchal norms, and reflect on the devaluated position in which this puts women who learn to live as feminine. Then they flip the valuation and ask whether this position of feminine other can serve as a standpoint from which to criticize dominant social relations and generate alternative ideals. The last essay in the volume, "A Room of One's Own: Privacy, Old Age, and Nursing Homes," extends the social criticism begun in the essay on home to argue that nursing homes typically deny to frail old people one of the material bases of self.

While these essays take as their subject central aspects of women's experience, I do not claim that they represent a definitive account of female body experience. They are idiosyncratic even as I hope that they communicate with the thoughts and feelings of readers. Many additional themes and questions deserve our descriptive and analytical attention.

1

Lived Body vs. Gender:
Reflections on Social Structure
and Subjectivity

In her thorough and provocative essay "What Is a Woman?" Toril Moi argues that recent feminist and queer theorizing has brought us to the end of a constructivist gender rope.[1] While feminist theory of the 1970s found a distinction between sex and gender liberating for both theory and practice, subsequent feminist and queer critiques have rightly questioned the distinction. By destabilizing categories of both biological sex and gender identity, recent deconstructive approaches to feminist and queer theorizing have opened greater possibilities for thinking a plurality of intersecting identities and practices. Deconstructive challenge to the sex/gender distinction has increasingly abstracted from embodiment, however, at the same time that it has rendered a concept of gender virtually useless for theorizing subjectivity and identity. At this theoretical pass, Moi proposes that we throw over the concept of gender altogether and renew a concept of the lived body derived from existential phenomenology, as a means of theorizing sexual subjectivity without danger of either biological reductionism or gender essentialism.

Moi is not alone in proposing that feminist and queer theory question the usefulness of a concept of gender even more deeply than have deconstructive critiques, and I will refer to other recent writings that make similar points in the course of my discussion. I concentrate on Moi because her analysis of the evolution of our troubles with gender is so thorough, and because I find attractive her proposal that feminist and queer theory adopt a concept of the lived body to do the work that she argues that the category of gender does not do well. I find Moi's argu-

1. Toril Moi, "What Is a Woman?" in *What Is a Woman and Other Essays* (Oxford: Oxford University Press, 2001).

ment incomplete, however. While she is correct that gender is a problematic concept for theorizing subjectivity, there are or ought to be other aspects of feminist and queer theorizing that cannot do without a concept of gender. By reflecting on Moi's account of recent feminist and queer theorizing, we discover that these aspects, which concern social structure more than subjectivity and identity, have been relatively neglected. The oppression of women and people who transgress heterosexual norms occurs through systemic processes and social structures which need description that uses different concepts from those appropriate for describing subjects and their experience. Moi's proposal to reconstitute a concept of the lived body helps for the latter, but for the former we need a reconstituted concept of gender.

I. The Sex-Gender Distinction

Early feminist appropriations of what until then had been an obscure psychological distinction between gender, as referring to self-conception and behavior, and sex, as referring to anatomy and physiology, were very theoretically and politically productive. At this theoretical moment challenging the conviction that "biology is destiny" was an important feminist project. In order to argue for opening wider opportunities for women, we needed ways to conceptualize capacities and dispositions of members of both sexes that distanced behavior, temperament, and achievement from biological or natural explanations. A distinction between sex and gender served this purpose. Feminists could affirm that of course men and women are "different" in physique and reproductive function, while denying that these differences have any relevance for the opportunities members of the sexes should have or the activities that they should engage in. Such gender rules and expectations are socially constituted and socially changeable. Much of this early second-wave feminist theorizing invoked an ideal of equality for women that envisioned an end to gender. "Androgyny" named the ideal that many feminists theorized, a social condition in which biological sex would have no implications for a person's life prospects, or the way people treated one another (including, importantly, in the most consistent of these theories, one's choice of sex partners). These androgynous persons in the transformed liberated society would have no categorically distinct forms of dress, comportment, occupations, propensities toward aggression or passivity, associated with their embodiment. We would all be just people with various bodies.[2]

2. For one statement of the androgynous ideal, see Ann Ferguson, "Androgyny as an Ideal for Human Development," in *Sexual Democracy: Women, Oppression, and Revolution* (Westview, Conn.: Allen and Unwin, 1991).

This appeal to an ideal of androgyny was short lived. Some of the turning-point texts of feminist theory in the late 1970s and early 1980s turned instead to accounts of the social and psychological specificities of femininely gendered identity and social perspective derived from gender roles. While not at all explained by biological distinctions between men and women, nevertheless there are deep social divisions of masculine and feminine gendered dispositions and experience which have implications for the psychic lives of men and women, their interactions with one another, their dispositions to care for children or exercise authority. Nancy Chodorow, Carol Gilligan, Nancy Hartsock, and others developed theories of feminine gender identities as expressing a general structure of subjectivity and social standpoint in significant ways defining the lives and possibilities of most women.[3]

No sooner had such a general account of feminine gender identity emerged than it came under attack as "essentialist." These accounts assume mothering as defining the experience of most women. They fail to inquire about the differences that race or class positioning make to caring practices, and they assume that women are or wish to be in relationships with men. They extrapolate from the historical specificity of twentieth-century affluent urban nuclear families and occupational structures, ignoring historical and cross-cultural specifications in the organization of family and work. Although the criticisms were not always voiced in the fairest way, most feminist theorists took their points to heart.

Queer theory broke into this dissolution of gender theory in the person of writers such as Diana Fuss and Judith Butler. Because Moi focuses on Butler's subversion of the sex-gender distinction, and I will support Moi's conclusion in specific respects, I will follow Moi in this focus.

In *Gender Trouble,* Butler questioned the motive of feminist theory to seek a theory of gender identity. Feminists believe they need such a general theory of gender, she argued, in order to know what is the subject of feminist politics. Feminism has no meaning as a specific transformative social movement, it is thought, without an account of the "agent" of change, the subject to be liberated; that subject is "woman," and "gender" is the concept that displays what a woman is. As gendered, "women" are distinct from the biological sex, female. Butler argued, however, that the feminist distinction between sex and gender nevertheless retains a binarism of stable categorical complementarity between male and female, which reproduces a logic of heterosexual normativity. The very distinction between sex and gender ought to be put

---

3. Nancy Chodorow, *The Reproduction of Mothering: Psychoanalysis and the Sociology of Gender* (Berkeley: University of California Press, 1978); Carol Gilligan, *In a Different Voice* (Cambridge: Harvard University Press, 1982); Nancy C. M. Hartsock, *Money, Sex, and Power: Toward a Feminist Historical Materialism* (Boston; Longman, 1983).

in question in order to challenge any reliance on a distinction between nature and culture, or any conception that subjects have inner lives to which an idea of stable gender identity corresponds. Gender is nothing other than a social performative. The discursive rules of normative heterosexuality produce gendered performances that subjects reiterate and cite; the sexing of bodies themselves derives from such performatives. In this process of reiterated gender performance some persons become constituted as abject, outside the heterosexual binary. Radical politics, then, consists in troubling the gender binaries and playing with gender citation.

In response to the critical reaction of some commentators that her theory of gender as performance makes bodies and sexual identity simply a product of discourse, in *Bodies That Matter* Butler argues that the materiality of sexed bodies is itself socially constituted. She insists that such production of bodies is not "idealist," and that a valuation of "materialism" over "idealism" itself relies on a questionable binary logic.

Moi does not refute Butler's arguments, which she takes to be cogent, given their terms and methods. She argues nevertheless that ideals of subjectivity and sexuality have become increasingly abstract in this train of theorizing that begins with the sex-gender distinction and ends deconstructing a material-ideal dichotomy. It is not clear at this point what lived problems the theory addresses or how the concepts help people understand and describe their experience. Butler successfully calls into question the logic of the sex-gender distinction, yet her theorizing never goes beyond these terms and remains tied to them. This line of critique, Moi argues, calls for throwing off the idea of gender altogether as useful for understanding subjectivity and identity. Queer theory and practice bend gender meanings, aiming to loosen them from the normative polarities of hegemonic masculinity and femininity. Moi suggests that queer and feminist theorists should make a break with gender altogether.

II. The Lived Body

For an alternative to the categories of sex and gender, Moi proposes to return to the framework of existential phenomenology on which Simone de Beauvoir relies.[4] The central category for this theoretical approach is

4. Sonia Kruks gives a reading of the existentialism of Simone de Beauvoir that aims to respond to contemporary conundrums of "identity politics" in feminist theory. She too proposes to understand Beauvoir as developing a concept of the lived body useful for feminist theory, and she argues that interpretations of Beauvoir have failed to appreciate the extent to which she was influenced by Maurice Merleau-Ponty's concept of the lived body; see Kruks, "Freedoms That Matter: Subjectivity and Situation in the Work of Beauvoir, Sartre, and Merleau-Ponty," in *Retrieving Experience: Subjectivity and Recognition in Feminist Politics* (Ithaca, N.Y.: Cornell University Press, 2001), 27–51. Debra B. Bergoffen also recommends a return to Simone de Beauvoir as a way out of conundrums of

that of the *lived body*. A reconstituted concept of the lived body, Moi argues, would offer feminists an idea that can serve the function we have wanted from the sex-gender categorization, without bringing its problems.

The lived body is a unified idea of a physical body acting and experiencing in a specific sociocultural context; it is body-in-situation. For existentialist theory, *situation* denotes the produce of *facticity* and *freedom*. The person always faces the material facts of her body and its relation to a given environment. Her bodily organs have certain feeling capacities and function in determinate ways; her size, age, health, and training make her capable of strength and movement in relation to her environment in specific ways. Her skin has a particular color, her face determinate features, her hair particular color and texture, all with their own aesthetic properties. Her specific body lives in a specific context—crowded by other people, anchored to the earth by gravity, surrounded by buildings and streets with a unique history, hearing particular languages, having food and shelter available, or not, as a result of culturally specific social processes that make specific requirements on her to access them. All these concrete material relations of a person's bodily existence and her physical and social environment constitute her *facticity*.

The person, however, is an actor; she has an ontological freedom to construct herself in relation to this facticity. The human actor has specific projects, things she aims to accomplish, ways she aims to express herself, make her mark on the world, transform her surroundings and relationships. Often these are projects she engages in jointly with others. *Situation,* then, is the way that the facts of embodiment, social and physical environment, appear in light of the projects a person has. She finds that her movements are awkward in relation to her desire to dance. She sees the huge city with its thousand-year history as an opportunity for learning about her ancestors. "To claim that the body is a situation is to acknowledge that the meaning of a woman's body is bound up with the way she uses her freedom" (Moi, "Woman," 65).

How does Moi propose that the idea of the lived body might replace that of gender, and the distinction between sex and gender? Like the category of sex, that of the lived body can refer to the specific physical facts of bodies, including sexual and reproductive differentiation. "Woman" and "man" name the physical facticity of certain bodies, some with penises, others with clitorises and breasts, each with differing experiences of desire and sexual feeling. A category of lived body, moreover, need not make sexual difference dimorphous; some bodies have

gender theorizing to which recent feminist and queer theories have come. See Bergoffen, "Simone de Beauvoir: Disrupting the Metonymy of Gender," in *Resistance, Flight, Creation: Feminist Enactments of French Philosophy*, ed. Dorothea Olkowski (Ithaca, N.Y.: Cornell University Press, 2000), 97–119.

physical traits like those of men in certain respects, those of women in others. People experience their desires and feeling in diverse ways that do not neatly correlate with sexual dimorphism or heterosexual norms. As a lived body, moreover, perceptual capacities and motility are not distinct from association with sexual specificity; nor is size, bone structure or skin color. Most important for the proposal Moi makes, the concept of the lived body, unlike the concept of sex, is not biologistic. It does not refer to an objectivist scientific account that generalizes laws of physiology and function. A scientific approach to bodies proceeds at a significantly higher level of abstraction than does a description of bodies as lived. The idea of the lived body thus can bring the physical facts of different bodies into theory without the reductionist and dichotomous implications of the category of "sex."

The idea of the lived body, moreover, refuses the distinction between nature and culture that grounds a distinction between sex and gender. The body as lived is always enculturated: by the phonemes a body learns to pronounce at a very early age, by the clothes the person wears that mark her nation, her age, her occupational status, and in what is culturally expected or required of women. The body is enculturated by habits of comportment distinctive to interactional settings of business or pleasure; often they are specific to locale or group. Contexts of discourse and interaction position persons in systems of evaluation and expectations which often implicate their embodied being; the person experiences herself as looked at in certain ways, described in her physical being in certain ways, she experiences the bodily reactions of others to her, and she reacts to them. The diverse phenomena that have come under the rubric of "gender" in feminist theory can be redescribed in the idea of lived body as some among many forms of bodily habitus and interactions with others that we enact and experience. In such redescription we find that Butler is right in at least this respect: it is a mystification to attribute the ways of being associated with the category "gender" to some inner core of identity of a subject, whether understood as "natural" or acquired.

In a recent essay Linda Nicholson similarly proposes that feminist and queer theory focus on the sociohistorical differentiation of bodies as lived, rather than maintain a distinction between biological sex and embodiment and gender as historically variable. To the extent that this distinction between sex and gender remains, feminist theory continues a "biological foundationalism," as distinct from biological reductionism. The study of sexuality, reproduction, and the roles assigned to men and women should consist in reading bodies themselves and not presume a nature/culture distinction that considers gender as "merely cultural."[5]

5. Linda Nicholson, "Interpreting Gender," in *The Play of Reason: From the Modern to the Postmodern* (Ithaca, N.Y.: Cornell University Press, 1999), 53–76.

The idea of the lived body thus does the work the category "gender" has done, but better and more. It does this work better because the category of the lived body allows description of the habits and interactions of men with women, women with women, and men with men in ways that can attend to the plural possibilities of comportment, without necessary reduction to the normative heterosexual binary of "masculine" and "feminine." It does more because it helps avoid a problem generated by use of ascriptive general categories such as "gender," "race," "nationality," "sexual orientation," to describe the constructed identities of individuals, namely the additive character that identities appear to have under this description. If we conceptualize individual identities as constituted by the diverse group identities—gender, race, class, sexual orientation, and so on—there seems to be a mystery about both how persons are individualized, and how these different group identities combine in the person. With the idea of the lived body there is no such puzzle. Each person is a distinctive body, with specific features, capacities, and desires that are similar to and different from those of others in determinate respects. She is born in a particular place and time, is raised in a particular family setting, and all these have specific sociocultural histories that stand in relation to the history of others in particular ways. What we call categories of gender, race, ethnicity, etc., are shorthand for a set of structures that position persons, a point to which I will return. They are not properly theorized as general group identities that add together to constitute individual identities. The individual person lives out her unique body in a sociohistorical context of the behavior and expectations of others, but she does not have to worry about constituting her identity from a set of generalized "pop-beads" strung together.[6]

By means of a category of the lived body, then, "one can arrive at a highly historicized and concrete understanding of bodies and subjectivity without relying on the sex-gender distinction that Butler takes as axiomatic" (Moi, "Woman," 46). The idea of the lived body recognizes that a person's subjectivity is conditioned by sociocultural facts and the behavior and expectations of others in ways that she has not chosen. At the same time, the theory of the lived body says that each person takes up and acts in relation to these unchosen facts in her own way.

> To consider the body as a situation . . . is to consider both the fact of being a specific kind of body and the meaning that concrete body has for the situated individual. This is not the equivalent of either sex or gender. The same is true for "lived experience" which encompasses our experience of all kinds of situations (race, class, nationality, etc.) and is a far more wide-ranging concept than the highly psychologizing concept of gender identity. (Moi, "Woman," 81)

6. See Elizabeth Spelman, *Inessential Woman: Problems of Exclusion in Feminist Thought* (Boston: Beacon Press, 1988).

III. Is the Lived Body Enough?

Toril Moi argues that a concept of the lived body serves feminist theoretical purposes better than a concept of gender. She defines those purposes as providing a theory of subjectivity and the body, and providing an understanding of what it means to be a woman or man in a particular society ("Woman," 4, 36, 14). Feminist theory, she says, ought to become a project of dispelling confusions concerning bodies, sex, sexuality, sexual difference, and the power relations among women and men, heterosexuals and homosexuals (120). This last phrase about power relations is extremely vague. Depending on how it is specified, the scope of theorizing power relations might fall beyond what I take as Moi's major emphasis in defining the tasks of feminist theory. She defines this theory as focusing on subjectivity, who one is as an agent, the attributes and capacities one has for experience, the relations with others that contribute to one's sense of self. In the essay I referred to earlier, Linda Nicholson also seems to consider that the theoretical function a concept of gender has meant to serve is one of theorizing self-identity and the social constitution of the human character.

Recent discussions questioning the stability of gender and the adequacy of a sex-gender distinction well reveal dilemmas and increasing abstraction into which feminist and queer theory have been forced or to which they have had to respond. These problems with a concept of gender have surfaced at least partly because gender aims to be a general category, but subjectivity is always particular. Moi's appropriation of the concept of the lived body offers more refined tools for theorizing sexed subjectivity, and the experience of differently situated men and women, than does the more blunt category of gender. Agreeing with this means dispensing with gender altogether, however, only if the projects of feminist and queer theories consist only in theorizing subjectivity. But I think they are not. The debates about gender and essentialism that Moi aims to bring to a close with her arguments have, I think, tended to narrow the interests of feminists and queer theorists to issues of experience, identity, and subjectivity. Her discussion clears the way for asking whether other aspects of a project for feminist and queer theory have been obscured by these debates, for which a resituated concept of gender might still be needed. In the remaining pages of this essay I want to suggest that a concept of gender is important for theorizing social structures and their implications for the freedom and well being of persons.

As I understand them, feminist and queer theory consist not only in giving account of the meaning of the lives of women and men in all their relational and sexual diversity. Nor are they only about analyzing how discourses construct subjects and the stereotypical or defamatory aspects of some of these discourses that contribute to the suffering of some men and women who fall on the wrong side of normalizing processes. Feminist and queer theories are also projects of social criticism. These are

theoretical efforts to identify certain wrongful harms or injustices, locate and explain their sources in institutions and social relations, and
propose directions for institutionally oriented action to change them.
This latter set of tasks requires the theorist to have an account not only
of individual experience, subjectivity, and identity, but also of social
structures.

In other writings I have articulated a concept of social structure specifically directed at the project of giving an institutional account of
sources of injustice in response to the dilemmas that emerge from claiming that individuals share group identities.[7] Structures denote the confluence of institutional rules and interactive routines, mobilization of
resources, and physical structures, which constitute the historical givens
in relation to which individuals act, and which are relatively stable over
time. Structures also connote the wider social outcomes that result from
the confluence of many individual actions within given institutional relations, whose collective consequences often do not bear the mark of any
person or group's intention.

Alexander Wendt distinguishes two levels of kinds of structure, micro
and macro levels. Micro structures refer to structural analysis of interaction. The patterning of practices and interactive routines, the rules which
actors implicitly and explicitly follow and the resources and instruments
they mobilize in their interactions can all be regarded as structured. Gender structures are very important to interactions at this micro level. In
recommending that feminist social theory complement attention to subjectivity and identity with renewed attention to social structures, however, I am more concerned with what Wendt refers to as the macro level,
which involves "multiply realizable outcomes."[8] That is to say, social
theory that wishes to understand and criticize the constraints on individuals and groups that render them relatively unfree and limited in their
opportunities in relation to others need to have a picture of large-scale
systemic outcomes of the operations of many institutions and practices
which produce outcomes that constrain some people in specific ways at
the same time that they enable others. Macro structures depend on
micro-level interactions for their production and reproduction, according to Wendt, but their form and the ways they constrain and enable
cannot be reduced to effects of particular interactions.

Social structures position individuals in relations of labor and production, power and subordination, desire and sexuality, prestige and status.

7. See my *Inclusion and Democracy* (Oxford: Oxford University Press, 2000), especially chapter 3; see also "Equality of Whom? Social Groups and Judgments of Injustice,"
Journal of Political Philosophy 9.1 (March 2001): 1–18. There I build a definition of
social structures by drawing primarily on ideas of Peter Blau, Anthony Giddens, and Jean-
Paul Sartre.

8. Alexander Wendt, *Social Theory and International Relations* (Cambridge: Cambridge University Press, 2000), chapter 4.

The way a person is positioned in structures is as much a function of how other people treat him or her within various institutional settings as of the attitude a person takes to himself or herself. Any individual occupies multiple positions in structures, and these positionings become differently salient depending on the institutional setting and the position of others there.

From the point of view of critical social theory, the main reason to care about structures is in order to have an account of the constitution and causes of social inequality. Some people encounter relative constraints in their freedom and material well-being as the cumulative effect of the possibilities of their social positions, as compared with others who in their social positions have more options or easier access to benefits. Social groups defined by caste, class, race, age, ethnicity, and, of course, gender, name subjective identities less than axes of structural inequality. They name structural positions whose occupants are privileged or disadvantaged in relation to one another due to the adherence of actors to institutional rules and norms and the pursuit of their interests and goals within institutions. A structural account offers a way of understanding inequality of opportunity, oppression and domination, that does not seek individualized perpetrators but rather considers most actors complicit in its production, to a greater or lesser degree.

Nancy Folbre conceptualizes such issues of social inequality in terms she calls "structures of constraint."[9] Structures of constraint include sets of asset distributions, rules, norms, and preferences that afford more freedom and opportunity for benefits to some than others. Constraints define the range of options available to individuals, or the costs of pursuing some options rather than others: time and money as basic assets. Legal rules function as important constraints, but so do culture norms. They impose a "price" on nonconformity. Preferences can be constraints when they conflict with one another. A configuration of particular assets, rules, norms, and preferences creates the constraints that define what we call social groups based on gender, class, race, age, and so on. Thus membership in the group called "women" is the product of a loose configuration of different structural factors.

To describe and explain some of the structures and processes that effect differential opportunities and privileges in contemporary society, I suggest, we cannot do without a concept of gender. Feminist and queer theories need conceptual tools to describe the rules and practices of institutions that presume differing roles for men and women, and/or presume that men and women are coupled with each other in intimate relations. We need tools for understanding how and why certain patterns in the allocation of tasks or status recognition remain persistent in ways that limit the options of many women and of most people whose sexual and

9. Nancy Folbre, *Who Pays for the Kids? Gender and the Structures of Constraint* (New York: Routledge, 1994), especially chapter 2.

intimate choices deviate from heterosexual norms. An important conceptual shift occurs, however, when we understand the concept of gender as a tool for theorizing structures more than subjects. We no longer need to ascribe a single or shared gender identity to men and women.

My own effort to respond to critiques of early feminist theories of gender turned in this direction of theorizing gender as an attribute of social structures more than of persons. In "Gender as Seriality: Thinking about Women as a Social Collective," I draw on a concept from Sartre's later philosophy, his idea of a series.[10] Gender, I suggest there, is best understood as a particular form of the social positioning of lived bodies in relation to one another within historically and socially specific institutions and processes that have material effects on the environment in which people act and reproduce relations of power and privilege among them. On this account, what it means to say that individual persons are "gendered" is that we all *find ourselves* passively grouped according to these structural relations, in ways too impersonal to ground identity. There I proposed that there are two basic axes of gender structures: a sexual division of labor and normative heterosexuality. Here I will take a lead from Bob Connell and add to these a third axis, gendered hierarchies of power.[11]

The structuring of work and occupations by gender is a basic aspect of all modern societies (and many premodern societies), with far-reaching consequences for the lives of individuals and the constraints and opportunities they face. The core of a gendered division of labor in modern societies is the division between "private" and "public" work. An aspect of the basic structure of these societies is that the work of caring—for persons, their bodily needs, their emotional well being, and the maintenance of their dwellings—takes place primarily in unpaid labor in private homes. While recent decades have seen some changes in the allocation of their work between men and women, it is still the case that this unpaid caring and household work falls primarily to women. The operations of the entire society depend on the regular performance of this work, yet it goes relatively unnoticed and little valued. The persons to whom this work is assigned have less time and energy to devote to other tasks and activities than do those who do less of it. This gendered division of labor persists apparently because people collectively do not wish to organize broadly funded public services that take more collective responsibility for care work. Despite many significant changes in gender ideas and ideology in contemporary societies, there has been little change in this basic division of labor. Indeed, neo-liberal economic policies

10. In I. M. Young, *Intersecting Voices: Dilemmas of Gender, Political Philosophy, and Policy* (Princeton, N.J.: Princeton University Press, 1997).

11. R. W. Connell, *Gender and Power* (Stanford, Calif.: Stanford University Press, 1987).

across the globe have had the effect of retrenching this division where it may have loosened.

Feminist social and political theory in the last twenty years has documented dozens of ways that this gendered structure constrains the opportunities of those persons doing unpaid care work, mostly women.[12] They work longer hours than others and are rendered dependent on other people for provision of their needs, which makes them vulnerable to poverty or abuse. Feminist researchers have also documented how this basic structure underlies occupational divisions in public paid work according to gender. When occupations involve caring they tend to become female-gendered. Because many women arrange their public work lives in relation to caring responsibilities, only a relatively small number of occupations welcome them, which helps keep wages low in those occupations. The structuring of both private and public work along these lines exhibits gendered hierarchies of status and power, not to mention financial reward.

It might be thought that these structural consequences of a sexual division of labor describe Western industrial societies primarily. Theorized at the right level of categorical generality, however, similar structures describe much about many less developed countries, especially in urban life. As some feminist scholars of development have argued, for example, both government policy and the policies of international organizations such as the International Monetary Fund implicitly rely on the assumption that unpaid domestic labor is infinitely expandable, and that household caretakers are available to take up the slack in meeting the needs of their family members when food subsidies are slashed, school fees go up, or health clinics are closed.

A structural account of the sexual division of labor, that is, does not assume that this division of labor has the same content across societies. It is a theoretical framework that asks whether there are tasks and occupations usually performed by members of one sex or the other, and/or whether the social norms and cultural products of the society tend to represent certain tasks or occupations as more appropriately performed by members of one sex or the other. For any society, both today and in the past, the answer is usually yes, but there is nevertheless considerable variation among them in *which* occupations are sex-associated, the ideologies often legitimating these associations, how many tasks are sex-typed, and what implications this sexual division of labor has for the distribution of resources among persons, their relative status, and the constraints and opportunities that condition their lives.

12. Nancy Folbre's book, cited above, is an excellent analysis of the operations of these constraints in several countries in Europe, Asia, and Latin America, as well as the United States.

A second axis of gender structuring in our society is normative het-erosexuality. This structuring consists in the diverse institutional and ideological facts that privilege heterosexual coupling. These include the form and implications of many legal institutions, many rules and policies of private organizations in allocating positions and benefits, the structur-ing of schooling and mainstream media to accord with these institutions, as well as the assumptions many people make in their everyday interac-tions with others. Together such social facts make structures with differ-ential consequences on the lives of different men and women, and which sometimes produce serious suffering or wrongful limitations on free-dom. The system of normative heterosexuality significantly constrains the lives of men and women, with all their varying sexual and desiring inclinations, motivating some to adjust their lives in ways they believe will bring them material reward and acceptance, and others to carve out lives in the interstices of social relations where their desires and projects do not fit, or openly to rebel.

Cheshire Calhoun argues that lesbian and gay subordination is differ-ent in form from the structural constraints on the lives of women or people of color, for example. Whereas structures of female subordina-tion or institutionalized racism confine people perceived as belonging to certain categories as having certain places or positions, Calhoun argues that persons who transgress heterosexual norms have no legitimized place at all in political citizenship, civil society, or private spheres. Struc-tures of normative heterosexuality constrain lesbians and gay men by enforcing their invisibility.[13]

Institutionalized valuations of particular associations of maleness or masculinity condition hierarchies of power in ways that constrain the possible actions of many people seem quite resistant to change. Positions and practices of institutionalized and organized violence are most impor-tant here—military and police forces, prison systems, etc. In general, the structuring of state institutions, corporations, and other bureaucracies according to hierarchies of decision making authority and status affords some people significant privileges and freedom—and these are usually men—at the same time that they limit, constrain, and subordinate oth-ers, including most women and many men. Gendered hierarchies of power intersect with a sexual division of labor and normative heterosex-uality in many ways to reproduce a sense of entitlement of men to wom-en's service and an association of heterosexual masculinity with force and command.

When describing social structures as gendered, it is not necessary to make generalizations about men and women nor is it necessary to reduce varying gender structures to a common principle. A gendered occupa-tional division of labor may strongly code certain occupations as female

13. Cheshire Calhoun, *Feminism, the Family, and the Politics of the Closet: Lesbian and Gay Displacement* (Oxford: Oxford University Press, 2000).

and others as male, and these codings may have far-reaching implications for the power, prestige, and material reward incumbents of each enjoy. Nothing follows from this, however, about what most men or most women do for a living. Recognizing the structures of normative heterosexuality may well result in theorizing plural understandings of gender, varying rules and practices that make expectations on men and women regarding sexual interaction, relation of adults and children, social aesthetics, relationship of persons to workplace roles, and so on— rules that do not share a common logic and in some respects may be in tension with one another. Structures of a gendered hierarchy of power differentiate men from one another according to social roles and dispositions and do not simply differentiate men and women. The most important thing about the analysis is to understand how the rules, relations, and their material consequences produce privileges for some people that underlie an interest in their maintenance at the same time that they limit options of others, cause relative deprivations in their lives, or render them vulnerable to domination and exploitation.

In this essay I have agreed with Toril Moi's proposal that the existential phenomenological category of the lived body is a richer and more flexible concept than gender for theorizing the socially constituted experience of women and men than concepts of either sex or gender. The lived body is particular in its morphology, material similarities, and differences from other bodies. I have argued, moreover, that this proposal should not mean dispensing with a category of gender, but rather confining its use to analysis of social structures for the purposes of understanding certain specific relations of power, opportunity, and resource distribution. An obvious question arises at this point, as to the relation of lived bodies to these structures.

Another reason that turning to a concept of lived body may be productive for feminist and queer theory is precisely that it can offer a way of articulating how persons live out their positioning in social structures along with the opportunities and constraints they produce. I do not have the space here to develop the framework for such articulation, and I will offer only a few lines toward a sketch.

Gender structures, I said above, are historically given and condition the action and consciousness of individual persons. They precede that action and consciousness. Each person experiences aspects of gender structures as facticity, as sociohistorical givens with which she or he must deal. Every person faces the question of what to wear, for example, and clothing options and conventions derive from multiple structures of profit seeking, class and occupational distinction, income distribution, heterosexual normativity, and spaces and expectations of occasions and activities and the possibilities of conformity and transgression they bring. However limited the choices or the resources to enact them, each person takes up the constrained possibilities that gender structures offer in their own way, forming their own habits as variations on those possibilities, or actively trying to resist or refigure them. Gender as structured is also lived through individual bodies, always as personal experiential response and not as a set of attributes that individuals have in common.

Pierre Bourdieu's concept of the *habitus* offers one interpretation of how generalized social structures are produced and reproduced in the movement and interaction of bodies. Especially in his understanding of gender structures, however, Bourdieu's understanding of the relation of social structures to actors and experience conceptualizes these structures too rigidly and ahistorically.[14] It may be more fruitful to draw on a theory of the lived body like that of Maurice Merleau-Ponty but connect it more explicitly than he does to how the body lives out its positions in social structures of the division of labor, hierarchies of power, and norms of sexuality.[15] Under the influence of such a theory of how bodies live out their structured positioning, moreover, one might find that a deconstructive gender theory such as Judith Butler's appears not as a theory of the determination or constitution of gendered subjects, but as a theory of the variable movements of habituated bodies reacting to, reproducing, and modifying structures.

14. See for example, Pierre Bourdieu, *The Logic of Practice*, trans. Richard Nice (Stanford, Calif.: Stanford University Press, 1990), especially chapters 3 and 4. Toril Moi herself explores the implications of Bourdieu's theory for feminist theory; see "Appropriating Bourdieu: Feminist Theory and Pierre Bourdieu's Sociology of Culture," chapter 3 of *What Is a Woman?*. Bourdieu's book, *La Domination masculine* (Paris: Editions du Seuil, 1998), assumes that he can generalize about gender structures largely from his observations of Kabylic society in North Africa.

15. Nick Crossley argues that a reconstruction of Merleau-Ponty's theory of sociality and habit can serve social theory better than Bourdieu's concept of *habitus* because Merleau-Ponty's conceptualization gives more place to freedom and individual difference. See Crossley, "The Phenomenological Habitus and Its Construction," *Theory and Society* 30 (2001): 81–120; see also Crossley's "Habitus, Agency, and Change: Engaging with Bourdieu," paper presented at "Philosophy of the Social Science," Czech Academy of Sciences, Prague, May 2001.

2

Throwing Like a Girl:
A Phenomenology of Feminine Body
Comportment, Motility, and Spatiality

In discussing the fundamental significance of lateral space, which is one of the unique spatial dimensions generated by the human upright posture, Erwin Straus pauses at "the remarkable difference in the manner of throwing of the two sexes" (157).[1] Citing a study and photographs of young boys and girls, he describes the difference as follows:

> The girl of five does not make any use of lateral space. She does not stretch her arm sideward; she does not twist her trunk; she does not move her legs, which remain side by side. All she does in preparation for throwing is to lift her right arm forward to the horizontal and to bend the forearm backward in a pronate position. . . . The ball is released without force, speed, or accurate aim. . . . A boy of the same age, when preparing to throw, stretches his right arm sideward and backward; supinates the forearm; twists, turns and bends his trunk; and moves his right foot backward. From this stance, he can support his throwing almost with the full

This essay was first presented at a meeting of the Mid-West Division of the Society for Women in Philosophy (SWIP) in October 1977. Versions of the essay were subsequently presented at a session sponsored by SWIP at the Western Division meetings of the American Philosophical Association, April 1978, and at the third annual Merleau-Ponty Circle meeting, Duquesne University, September 1978. Many people in discussions at those meetings contributed gratifying and helpful responses. I am particularly grateful to Professors Sandra Bartky, Claudia Card, Margaret Simons, J. Davidson Alexander, and William McBride for their criticisms and suggestions. Final revisions of the essay were completed while I was a fellow in the National Endowment for the Humanities Fellowship in Residence for College Teachers program at the University of Chicago.

1. Erwin W. Straus, "The Upright Posture," *Phenomenological Psychology* (New York: Basic Books, 1966), 137–65. References to particular pages are indicated in the text.

strength of his total motorium. . . . The ball leaves the hand with considerable acceleration; it moves toward its goal in a long flat curve. (157–60)[2]

Though he does not stop to trouble himself with the problem for
long, Straus makes a few remarks in the attempt to explain this "remarkable difference." Since the difference is observed at such an early
age, he says, it seems to be "the manifestation of a biological, not an
acquired, difference" (157). He is somewhat at a loss, however, to specify the source of the difference. Since the feminine style of throwing is
observed in young children, it cannot result from the development of
the breast. Straus provides further evidence against the breast by pointing out that "it seems certain" that the Amazons, who cut off their right
breasts, "threw a ball just like our Betty's, Mary's and Susan's" (158).
Having thus dismissed the breast, Straus considers the weaker muscle
power of the girl as an explanation of the difference but concludes that
the girl should be expected to compensate for such relative weakness
with the added preparation of reaching around and back. Straus explains the difference in style of throwing by referring to a "feminine
attitude" in relation to the world and to space. The difference for him
is biologically based, but he denies that it is specifically anatomical. Girls
throw in a way different from boys because girls are "feminine."

What is even more amazing than this "explanation" is the fact that a
perspective that takes body comportment and movement as definitive
for the structure and meaning of human lived experience devotes no
more than an incidental page to such a "remarkable difference" between
masculine and feminine body comportment and style of movement, for
throwing is by no means the only activity in which such a difference
can be observed. If there are indeed typically "feminine" styles of body
comportment and movement, this should generate for the existential
phenomenologist a concern to specify such a differentiation of the modalities of the lived body. Yet Straus is by no means alone in his failure to describe the modalities, meaning, and implications of the difference between "masculine" and "feminine" body comportment and
movement.

A virtue of Straus's account of the typical difference of the sexes in
throwing is that he does not explain this difference on the basis of physical attributes. Straus is convinced, however, that the early age at which

2. Studies continue to be performed that arrive at similar observations. See, for example, Lolas E. Kalverson, Mary Ann Robertson, M. Joanne Safrit, and Thomas W. Roberts,
"Effect of Guided Practice on Overhand Throw Ball Velocities of Kindergarten Children,"
Research Quarterly (American Alliance for Health, Physical Education, and Recreation)
48 (May 1977): 311–18. The study found that boys achieved significantly greater velocities than girls did. See also F. J. J. Buytendijk's remarks in *Woman: A Contemporary View*
(New York: Newman Press, 1968), 144–45. In raising the example of throwing, Buytendijk is concerned to stress, as am I in this essay, that the important thing to investigate is
not the strictly physical phenomenon, but rather the manner in which each sex projects
her or his Being-in-the-world through movement.

the difference appears shows that it is not an acquired difference, and thus he is forced back onto a mysterious "feminine essence" in order to explain it. The feminist denial that the real differences in behavior and psychology between men and women can be attributed to some natural and eternal feminine essence is perhaps most thoroughly and systematically expressed by Beauvoir. Every human existence is defined by its *situation;* the particular existence of the female person is no less defined by the historical, cultural, social, and economic limits of her situation. We reduce women's condition simply to unintelligibility if we "explain" it by appeal to some natural and ahistorical feminine essence. In denying such a feminine essence, however, we should not fall into that "nominalism" that denies the real differences in the behavior and experiences of men and women. Even though there is no eternal feminine essence, there is "a common basis which underlies every individual female existence in the present state of education and custom."[3] The situation of women within a given sociohistorical set of circumstances, despite the individual variation in each woman's experience, opportunities, and possibilities, has a unity that can be described and made intelligible. It should be emphasized, however, that this unity is specific to a particular social formation during a particular epoch.

Beauvoir proceeds to give such an account of the situation of women with remarkable depth, clarity, and ingenuity. Yet she also, to a large extent, fails to give a place to the status and orientation of the woman's body as relating to its surroundings in living action. When Beauvoir does talk about the woman's bodily being and her physical relation to her surroundings, she tends to focus on the more evident facts of a woman's physiology. She discusses how women experience the body as a burden, how the hormonal and physiological changes the body undergoes at puberty, during menstruation and pregnancy, are felt to be fearful and mysterious, and she claims that these phenomena weigh down the woman's existence by tying her to nature, immanence, and the requirements of the species at the expense of her own individuality.[4] By largely ignoring the situatedness of the woman's actual bodily movement and orientation to its surroundings and its world, Beauvoir tends to create the impression that it is woman's anatomy and physiology *as such* that at least in part determine her unfree status.[5]

3. Simone de Beauvoir, *The Second Sex* (New York: Vintage Books, 1974), xxxv. See also Buytendijk, 175–76.

4. See Beauvoir, *The Second Sex,* chapter 1, "The Data of Biology."

5. Shulasmith Firestone claims that Beauvoir's account served as the basis of her own thesis that the oppression of women is rooted in nature and thus to be overcome requires the transcendence of nature itself. See *The Dialectic of Sex* (New York: Bantam Books, 1970). Beauvoir would claim that Firestone is guilty of desituating woman's situation by pinning a source on nature as such. That Firestone would find inspiration for her thesis in Beauvoir, however, indicates that perhaps de Beauvoir has not steered away from causes in "nature" as much as is desirable.

This essay seeks to begin to fill a gap that thus exists in both existential phenomenology and feminist theory. It traces in a provisional way some of the basic modalities of feminine body comportment, manner of moving, and relation in space. It brings intelligibility and significance to certain observable and rather ordinary ways in which women in our society typically comport themselves and move differently from the ways that men do. In accordance with the existentialist concern with the situatedness of human experience, I make no claim to the universality of this typicality of the bodily comportment of women and the phenomenological description based on it. The account developed here claims only to describe the modalities of feminine bodily existence for women situated in contemporary advanced industrial, urban, and commercial society. Elements of the account developed here may or may not apply to the situation of woman in other societies and other epochs, but it is not the concern of this essay to determine to which, if any, other social circumstances this account applies.

The scope of bodily existence and movement with which I am concerned here is also limited. I concentrate primarily on those sorts of bodily activities that relate to the comportment or orientation of the body as a whole, that entail gross movement, or that require the enlistment of strength and the confrontation of the body's capacities and possibilities with the resistance and malleability of things. The kind of movement I am primarily concerned with is movement in which the body aims to accomplish a definite purpose or task. There are thus many aspects of feminine bodily existence that I leave out of this account. Most notable of these is the body in its sexual being. Another aspect of bodily existence, among others, that I leave unconsidered is structured body movement that does not have a particular aim—for example, dancing. Besides reasons of space, this limitation of subject is based on the conviction, derived primarily from Merleau-Ponty, that it is the ordinary purposive orientation of the body as a whole toward things and its environment that initially defines the relation of a subject to its world. Thus a focus upon ways in which the feminine body frequently or typically conducts itself in such comportment or movement may be particularly revelatory of the structures of feminine existence.[6]

Before entering the analysis, I should clarify what I mean here by "feminine" existence. In accordance with Beauvoir's understanding, I

6. In his discussion of the "dynamics of feminine existence," Buytendijk focuses precisely on those sorts of motions that are aimless. He claims that it is through these kinds of expressive movements—e.g., walking for the sake of walking—and not through action aimed at the accomplishment of particular purposes that the pure image of masculine or feminine existence is manifest (*Woman: A Contemporary View*, 278–79). Such an approach, however, contradicts the basic existentialist assumption that Being-in-the-world consists in projecting purposes and goals that structure one's situatedness. While there is certainly something to be learned from reflecting upon feminine movement in noninstru-

take "femininity" to designate not a mysterious quality or essence that all women have by virtue of their being biologically female. It is, rather, a set of structures and conditions that delimit the typical *situation* of being a woman in a particular society, as well as the typical way in which this situation is lived by the women themselves. Defined as such, it is not necessary that *any* women be "feminine"—that is, it is not necessary that there be distinctive structures and behavior typical of the situation of women.[7] This understanding of "feminine" existence makes it possible to say that some women escape or transcend the typical situation and definition of women in various degrees and respects. I mention this primarily to indicate that the account offered here of the modalities of feminine bodily existence is not to be falsified by referring to some individual women to whom aspects of the account do not apply, or even to some individual men to whom they do.

The account developed here combines the insights of the theory of the lived body as expressed by Merleau-Ponty and the theory of the situation of women as developed by Beauvoir. I assume that at the most basic descriptive level, Merleau-Ponty's account of the relation of the lived body to its world, as developed in *The Phenomenology of Perception,* applies to any human existence in a general way. At a more specific level, however, there is a particular style of bodily comportment that is typical of feminine existence, and this style consists of particular *modalities* of the structures and conditions of the body's existence in the world.[8]

As a framework for developing these modalities, I rely on Beauvoir's account of woman's existence in patriarchal society as defined by a basic tension between immanence and transcendence.[9] The culture and society in which the female person dwells defines woman as Other, as the inessential correlate to man, as mere object and immanence. Woman is thereby both culturally and socially denied the subjectivity, autonomy, and creativity that are definitive of being human and that in patriarchal society are accorded the man. At the same time, however, because she is a human existence, the female person necessarily is a subjectivity and transcendence, and she knows herself to be. The female person who

---

mental activity, given that accomplishing tasks is basic to the structure of human existence, it serves as a better starting point for investigation of feminine motility. As I point out at the end of this essay, a full phenomenology of feminine existence must take account of this noninstrumental movement.

7. It is not impossible, moreover, for men to be "feminine" in at least some respects, according to the above definition.

8. On this level of specificity there also exist particular modalities of masculine motility, inasmuch as there is a particular style of movement more or less typical of men. I will not, however, be concerned with those in this essay.

9. See Beauvoir, *The Second Sex,* chapter 21, "Woman's Situation and Character."

enacts the existence of women in patriarchal society must therefore live a contradiction: as human she is a free subject who participates in transcendence, but her situation as a woman denies her that subjectivity and transcendence. My suggestion is that the modalities of feminine bodily comportment, motility, and spatiality exhibit this same tension between transcendence and immanence, between subjectivity and being a mere object.

Section I offers some specific observations about bodily comportment, physical engagement with things, ways of using the body in performing tasks, and bodily self-image, which I find typical of feminine existence. Section II gives a general phenomenological account of the modalities of feminine bodily comportment and motility. Section III develops these modalities further in terms of the spatiality generated by them. Finally, in section IV, I draw out some of the implications of this account for an understanding of the oppression of women as well as raise some further questions about feminine being-in-the-world that require further investigation.

I

The basic difference that Straus observes between the way boys and girls throw is that girls do not bring their whole bodies into the motion as much as the boys do. They do not reach back, twist, move backward, step, and lean forward. Rather, the girls tend to remain relatively immobile except for their arms, and even the arms are not extended as far as they could be. Throwing is not the only movement in which there is a typical difference in the way men and women use their bodies. Reflection on feminine comportment and body movement in other physical activities reveals that these also are frequently characterized, much as in the throwing case, by a failure to make full use of the body's spatial and lateral potentialities.

Even in the most simple body orientations of men and women as they sit, stand, and walk, one can observe a typical difference in body style and extension. Women generally are not as open with their bodies as are men in their gait and stride. Typically, the masculine stride is longer proportional to a man's body than is the feminine stride to a woman's. The man typically swings his arms in a more open and loose fashion than does a woman and typically has more up and down rhythm in his step. Though we now wear pants more than we used to and consequently do not have to restrict our sitting postures because of dress, women still tend to sit with their legs relatively close together and their arms across their bodies. When simply standing or leaning, men tend to keep their feet farther apart than do women, and we also tend more to keep our hands and arms touching or shielding our bodies. A final indicative difference is the way each carries books or parcels; girls and women most often carry books embraced to their chests, while boys and men swing them along their sides.

The approach that people of each sex take to the performance of physical tasks that require force, strength, and muscular coordination is frequently different. There are indeed real physical differences between men and women in the kind and limit of their physical strength. Many of the observed differences between men and women in the performance of tasks requiring coordinated strength, however, are due not so much to brute muscular strength as to the way each sex *uses* the body in approaching tasks. Women often do not perceive themselves as capable of lifting and carrying heavy things, pushing and shoving with significant force, pulling, squeezing, grasping, or twisting with force. When we attempt such tasks, we frequently fail to summon the full possibilities of our muscular coordination, position, poise, and bearing. Women tend not to put their whole bodies into engagement in a physical task with the same ease and naturalness as men. For example, in attempting to lift something, women more often than men fail to plant themselves firmly and make their thighs bear the greatest proportion of the weight. Instead, we tend to concentrate our effort on those parts of the body most immediately connected to the task—the arms and shoulders—rarely bringing the power of the legs to the task at all. When turning or twisting something, to take another example, we frequently concentrate effort in the hand and wrist, not bringing to the task the power of the shoulder, which is necessary for its efficient performance.[10]

The previously cited throwing example can be extended to a great deal of athletic activity. Now, most men are by no means superior athletes, and their sporting efforts display bravado more often than genuine skill and coordination. The relatively untrained man nevertheless engages in sport generally with more free motion and open reach than does his female counterpart. Not only is there a typical style of throwing like a girl, but there is a more or less typical style of running like a girl, climbing like a girl, swinging like a girl, hitting like a girl. They have in common first that the whole body is not put into fluid and directed motion, but rather, in swinging and hitting, for example, the motion is concentrated in one body part; and second that the woman's motion tends not to reach, extend, lean, stretch, and follow through in the direction of her intention.

For many women as they move in sport, a space surrounds us in imagination that we are not free to move beyond; the space available to our movement is a constricted space. Thus, for example, in softball or

10. It should be noted that this is probably typical only of women in advanced industrial societies, where the model of the bourgeois woman has been extended to most women. It would not apply to those societies, for example, where most people, including women, do heavy physical work. Nor does this particular observation, of course, hold true in our own society for women who do heavy physical work.

volleyball women tend to remain in one place more often than men do, neither jumping to reach nor running to approach the ball. Men more often move out toward a ball in flight and confront it with their own countermotion. Women tend to wait for and then *react* to its approach, rather than going forth to meet it. We frequently respond to the motion of a ball coming toward us as though it were coming *at* us, and our immediate bodily impulse is to flee, duck, or otherwise protect ourselves from its flight. Less often than men, moreover, do women give self-conscious direction and placement to their motion in sport. Rather than aiming at a certain place where we wish to hit a ball, for example, we tend to hit it in a "general" direction.

Women often approach a physical engagement with things with timidity, uncertainty, and hesitancy. Typically, we lack an entire trust in our bodies to carry us to our aims. There is, I suggest, a double hesitation here. On the one hand, we often lack confidence that we have the capacity to do what must be done. Many times I have slowed a hiking party in which the men bounded across a harmless stream while I stood on the other side warily testing my footing on various stones, holding on to overhanging branches. Though the others crossed with ease, I do not believe it is easy for *me,* even though once I take a committed step I am across in a flash. The other side of this tentativeness is, I suggest, a fear of getting hurt, which is greater in women than in men. Our attention is often divided between the aim to be realized in motion and the body that must accomplish it, while at the same time saving itself from harm. We often experience our bodies as a fragile encumbrance, rather than the medium for the enactment of our aims. We feel as though we must have our attention directed upon our bodies to make sure they are doing what we wish them to do, rather than paying attention to what we want to do *through* our bodies.

All the above factors operate to produce in many women a greater or lesser feeling of incapacity, frustration, and self-consciousness. We have more of a tendency than men do to greatly underestimate our bodily capacity.[11] We decide beforehand—usually mistakenly—that the task is beyond us and thus give it less than our full effort. At such a halfhearted level, of course, we cannot perform the tasks, become frustrated, and fulfill our own prophecy. In entering a task we frequently are self-conscious about appearing awkward and at the same time do not wish to appear too strong. Both worries contribute to our awkwardness and frustration. If we should finally release ourselves from this spiral and really give a physical task our best effort, we are greatly surprised indeed

11. See A. M. Gross, "Estimated versus Actual Physical Strength in Three Ethnic Groups," *Child Development* 39 (1968): 283–90. In a test of children at several different ages, at all but the youngest age level, girls rated themselves lower than boys rated themselves on self-estimates of strength, and as the girls grow older, their self-estimates of strength become even lower.

at what our bodies can accomplish. It has been found that women more often than men underestimate the level of achievement they have reached.[12]

None of the observations that have been made thus far about the way women typically move and comport their bodies applies to all women all of the time. Nor do those women who manifest some aspect of this typicality do so in the same degree. There is no inherent, mysterious connection between these sorts of typical comportments and being a female person. Many of them result, as will be developed later, from lack of practice in using the body and performing tasks. Even given these qualifications, one can nevertheless sensibly speak of a general feminine style of body comportment and movement. The next section will develop a specific categorical description of the modalities of the comportment and movement.

II

The three modalities of feminine motility are that feminine movement exhibits an *ambiguous transcendence,* an *inhibited intentionality,* and a *discontinuous unity* with its surroundings. A source of these contradictory modalities is the bodily self-reference of feminine comportment, which derives from the woman's experience of her body as a *thing* at the same time that she experiences it as a capacity.

1. In his *Phenomenology of Perception,*[13] Merleau-Ponty takes as his task the articulation of the primordial structures of existence, which are prior to and the ground of all reflective relation to the world. In asking how there can be a world for a subject, Merleau-Ponty reorients the entire tradition of that questioning by locating subjectivity not in mind or consciousness, but in the *body.* Merleau-Ponty gives to the lived body the ontological status that Sartre, as well as "intellectualist" thinkers before him, attribute to consciousness alone: the status of transcendence as being for itself. It is the body in its orientation toward and action upon and within its surroundings that constitutes the initial meaning-giving act (121, 146–47). The body is the first locus of intentionality, as pure presence to the world and openness upon its possibilities. The most primordial intentional act is the motion of the body orienting itself with respect to and moving within its surroundings. There is a world for a

12. See Marguerite A. Cifton and Hope M. Smith, "Comparison of Expressed Self-Concept of Highly Skilled Males and Females Concerning Motor Performance," *Perceptual and Motor Skills* 16 (1963): 199–201. Women consistently underestimated their level of achievement in skills such as running and jumping far more often than men did.

13. Maurice Merleau-Ponty, *The Phenomenology of Perception,* trans. Colin Smith (New York: Humanities Press, 1962). All references to this work are noted in parentheses in the text.

subject just insofar as the body has capacities by which it can approach, grasp, and appropriate its surroundings in the direction of its intentions.

While feminine bodily existence is a transcendence and openness to the world, it is an *ambiguous transcendence,* a transcendence that is at the same time laden with immanence. Now, once we take the locus of subjectivity and transcendence to be the lived body rather than pure consciousness, all transcendence is ambiguous because the body as natural and material is immanence. But it is not the ever-present possibility of any lived body to be passive, to be touched as well as touching, to be grasped as well as grasping, which I am referring to here as the ambiguity of the transcendence of the feminine lived body. The transcendence of the lived body that Merleau-Ponty describes is a transcendence that moves out from the body in its immanence in an open and unbroken directedness upon the world in action. The lived body as transcendence is pure fluid action, the continuous calling-forth of capacities that are applied to the world. Rather than simply beginning in immanence, feminine bodily existence remains in immanence or, better, is *overlaid* with immanence, even as it moves out toward the world in motions of grasping, manipulating, and so on.

In the previous section, I observed that a woman typically refrains from throwing her whole body into a motion and rather concentrates motion in one part of the body alone, while the rest of the body remains relatively immobile. Only part of the body, that is, moves out toward a task, while the rest remains rooted in immanence. I also observed earlier that a woman frequently does not trust the capacity of her body to engage itself in physical relation to things. Consequently, she often lives her body as a burden, which must be dragged and prodded along and at the same time protected.

2. Merleau-Ponty locates intentionality in motility (110–12); the possibilities that are opened up in the world depend on the mode and limits of the bodily "I can" (137, 148). Feminine existence, however, often does not enter bodily relation to possibilities by its own comportment toward its surroundings in an unambiguous and confident "I can." For example, as noted earlier, women frequently tend to posit a task that would be accomplished relatively easily once attempted as beyond their capacities before they begin it. Typically, the feminine body underuses its real capacity, both as the potentiality of its physical size and strength and as the real skills and coordination that are available to it. Feminine bodily existence is an *inhibited intentionality,* which simultaneously reaches toward a projected end with an "I can" and withholds its full bodily commitment to that end in a self-imposed "I cannot."[14]

14. Much of the work of Seymour Fisher on various aspects of sex differences in body image correlates suggestively with the phenomenological description developed here. It is difficult to use his conclusions as confirmation of that description, however, because there

An uninhibited intentionality projects the aim to be accomplished and connects the body's motion toward that end in an unbroken directedness that organizes and unifies the body's activity. The body's capacity and motion structure its surroundings and project meaningful possibilities of movement and action, which in turn call the body's motion forth to enact them: "To understand is to experience the harmony between what we aim at and what is given, between the intention and the performance" (144; see also 101, 131, and 132). Feminine motion often severs this mutually conditioning relation between aim and enactment. In those motions that when properly performed require the coordination and directedness of the whole body upon some definite end, women frequently move in a contradictory way. Their bodies project an aim to be enacted but at the same time stiffen against the performance of the task. In performing a physical task the woman's body does carry her toward the intended aim, often not easily and directly, but rather circuitously, with the wasted motion resulting from the effort of testing and reorientation, which is a frequent consequence of feminine hesitancy.

For any lived body, the world appears as the system of possibilities that are correlative to its intentions (131). For any lived body, moreover, the world also appears to be populated with opacities and resistances correlative to its own limits and frustrations. For any bodily existence, that is, an "I cannot" may appear to set limits to the "I can." To the extent that feminine bodily existence is an inhibited intentionality, however, the same set of possibilities that appears to be correlative to its intentions also appears to be a system of frustrations correlative to its hesitancies. By repressing or withholding its own motile energy, feminine bodily existence frequently projects an "I can" and an "I cannot" with respect to the very same end. When the woman enters a task with inhibited intentionality, she projects the possibilities of that task—thus projects an "I *can*"—but projects them merely as the possibilities of "someone," and not truly *her* possibilities—and thus projects an "*I* cannot."

3. Merleau-Ponty gives to the body the unifying and synthesizing function that Kant locates in transcendental subjectivity. By projecting an aim toward which it moves, the body brings unity to and unites itself with its surroundings; through the vectors of its projected possibilities it sets things in relation to one another and to itself. The body's movement

---

is something of a speculative aspect to his reasoning. Nevertheless, I shall refer to some of these findings with that qualification in mind.

One of Fisher's findings is that women have a greater anxiety about their legs than men do, and he cites earlier studies with the same results. Fisher interprets such leg anxiety as being anxiety about motility itself, because in body conception and body image the legs are the body parts most associated with motility. See Fisher, *Body Experience in Fantasy and Behavior* (New York: Appleton-Century Crofts, 1970), 537. If his findings and his interpretation are accurate, this tends to correlate with the sort of inhibition and timidity about movement that I am claiming is an aspect of feminine body comportment.

and orientation organizes the surrounding space as a continuous extension of its own being (143). Within the same act in which the body synthesizes its surroundings, moreover, it synthesizes itself. The body synthesis
is immediate and primordial. "I do not bring together one by one the
parts of my body; this translation and this unification are performed
once and for all within me: they are my body itself" (150).

The third modality of feminine bodily existence is that it stands in
discontinuous unity with both itself and its surroundings. I remarked
earlier that in many motions that require the active engagement and
coordination of the body as a whole in order to be performed properly,
women tend to locate their motion in part of the body only, leaving the
rest of the body relatively immobile. Motion such as this is discontinuous with itself. The part of the body that is transcending toward an aim
is in relative disunity from those that remain immobile. The undirected
and wasted motion that is often an aspect of feminine engagement in a
task also manifests this lack of body unity. The character of the inhibited
intentionality whereby feminine motion severs the connection between
aim and enactment, between possibility in the world and capacity in the
body, itself produces this discontinuous unity.

According to Merleau-Ponty, for the body to exist as a transcendent
presence to the world and the immediate enactment of intentions, it cannot exist as an *object* (123). As subject, the body is referred not onto
itself, but onto the world's possibilities. "In order that we may be able
to move our body towards an object, the object must first exist for it,
our body must not belong to the realm of the 'in-itself'" (139). The
three contradictory modalities of feminine bodily existence—ambiguous
transcendence, inhibited intentionality, and discontinuous unity—have
their root, however, in the fact that for feminine existence the body
frequently is both subject and object for itself at the same time and in
reference to the same act. Feminine bodily existence is frequently not a
pure presence to the world because it is referred onto *itself* as well as
onto possibilities in the world.[15]

Several of the observations of the previous section illustrate this self-
reference. It was observed, for example, that women have a tendency to
take up the motion of an object coming *toward* them as coming *at* them.
I also observed that women tend to have a latent and sometimes conscious fear of getting hurt, which we bring to a motion. That is, feminine
bodily existence is self-referred in that the woman takes herself to be the

15. Fisher finds that the most striking difference between men and women in their
general body image is that women have a significantly higher degree of what he calls
"body prominence," awareness of and attention to the body. He cites a number of different studies that have the same results. The explanation Fisher gives for this finding is that
women are socialized to pay attention to their bodies, to prune and dress them, and to
worry about how they look to others. Fisher, *Body Experience in Fantasy and Behavior*,
524–25. See also Fisher, "Sex Differences in Body Perception," *Psychological Monographs*
78 (1964), no. 14.

object of the motion rather than its originator. Feminine bodily existence is also self-referred to the extent that a woman is uncertain of her body's capacities and does not feel that its motions are entirely under her control. She must divide her attention between the task to be performed and the body that must be coaxed and manipulated into performing it. Finally, feminine bodily existence is self-referred to the extent that the feminine subject posits her motion as the motion that is *looked at.* In section IV, we will explore the implications of the basic fact of the woman's social existence as the object of the gaze of another, which is a major source of her bodily self-reference.

In summary, the modalities of feminine bodily existence have their root in the fact that feminine existence experiences the body as a mere thing—a fragile thing, which must be picked up and coaxed into movement, a thing that exists as *looked at and acted upon.* To be sure, any lived body exists as a material thing as well as a transcending subject. For feminine bodily existence, however, the body is often lived as a thing that is other than it, a thing like other things in the world. To the extent that a woman lives her body as a thing, she remains rooted in immanence, is inhibited, and retains a distance from her body as transcending movement and from engagement in the world's possibilities.

III

For Merleau-Ponty there is a distinction between lived space, or phenomenal space, and objective space, the uniform space of geometry and science in which all positions are external to one another and interchangeable. Phenomenal space arises out of motility, and lived relations of space are generated by the capacities of the body's motion and the intentional relations that that motion constitutes. "It is clearly in action that the spatiality of our body is brought into being and an analysis of one's own movement should enable us to arrive at a better understanding" (102, cf. 148, 149, 249). In this account, if there are particular modalities of feminine bodily comportment and motility, it must follow that there are also particular modalities of feminine spatiality. Feminine existence lives space as *enclosed* or confining, as having a *dual* structure, and the woman experiences herself as *positioned* in space.

1. There is a famous study that Erik Erikson performed several years ago in which he asked several male and female preadolescents to construct a scene for an imagined movie out of some toys. He found that girls typically depicted indoor settings, with high walls and enclosures, while boys typically constructed outdoor scenes. He concluded that females tend to emphasize what he calls "inner space," or enclosed space, while males tend to emphasize what he calls "outer space," or a spatial orientation that is open and outwardly directed. Erikson's interpretation of these observations is psychoanalytical: girls depict "inner space" as

the projection of the enclosed space of their wombs and vaginas; boys depict "outer space" as a projection of the phallus.[16] I find such an explanation wholly unconvincing. If girls do tend to project an enclosed space and boys to project in open and outwardly directed space, it is far more plausible to regard this as a reflection of the way members of each sex live and move their bodies in space.

In the first section, I observed that women tend not to open their bodies in their everyday movements, but tend to sit, stand, and walk with their limbs close to or closed around them. I also observed that women tend not to reach, stretch, bend, lean, or stride to the full limits of their physical capacities, even when doing so would better accomplish a task or motion. The space, that is, that is *physically* available to the feminine body is frequently of greater radius than the space that she uses and inhabits. Feminine existence appears to posit an existential enclosure between herself and the space surrounding her, in such a way that the space that belongs to her and is available to her grasp and manipulation is constricted and the space beyond is not available to her movement.[17] A further illustration of this confinement of feminine lived space is the observation already noted that in sport, for example, women tend not to move out and meet the motion of a ball, but rather tend to stay in one place and react to the ball's motion only when it has arrived within the space where she is. The timidity, immobility, and uncertainty that frequently characterize feminine movement project a limited space for the feminine "I can."

2. In Merleau-Ponty's account, the body unity of transcending performance creates an immediate link between the body and the outlying space. "Each instant of the movement embraces its whole space, and particularly the first which, by being active and initiative, institutes the link between a here and a yonder" (140). In feminine existence, however, the projection of an enclosed space severs the continuity between a "here" and a "yonder." In feminine existence there is a *double spatiality,* as the space of the "here" is distinct from the space of the "yonder." A distinction between space that is "yonder" and not linked with my own body possibilities and the enclosed space that is "here," which I inhabit with my bodily possibilities, is an expression of the discontinuity between aim and capacity to realize the aim that I have articulated as the

16. Erik H. Erikson, "Inner and Outer Space: Reflections on Womanhood," *Daedelus* 3 (1964): 582–606. Erikson's interpretation of his findings is also sexist. Having in his opinion discovered a particular significance that "inner space," which he takes to be space *within* the body, holds for girls, he goes on to discuss the womanly "nature" as womb and potential mother, which must be made compatible with anything else the woman does.

17. Another of Fisher's findings is that women experience themselves as having more clearly articulated body *boundaries* than men do. More clearly than men do, they distinguish themselves from their spatial surroundings and take a distance from them. See Fisher, *Body Experience in Fantasy and Behavior, 528.*

meaning of the tentativeness and uncertainty characterizing the inhibited intentionality of feminine motility. The space of the "yonder" is a space in which feminine existence projects possibilities in the sense of understanding that "someone" could move within it, but not I. Thus the space of the "yonder" exists for feminine existence, but only as that which she is looking into, rather than moving in.

3. The third modality of feminine spatiality is that feminine existence experiences itself as *positioned in* space. For Merleau-Ponty, the body is the original subject that constitutes space; there would be no space without the body (102, 142). As the origin and subject of spatial relations, the body does not occupy a position coequal and interchangeable with the positions occupied by other things (143, 247–49). Because the body as lived is not an *object,* it cannot be said to exist *in* space as water is *in* the glass (139–40). "The word 'here' applied to my body does not refer to a determinate position in relation to other positions or to external coordinates, but the laying down of the first coordinates, the anchoring of the active body in an object, the situation of the body in the face of its tasks" (100).

Feminine spatiality is contradictory insofar as feminine bodily existence is both spatially constituted and a constituting spatial subject. Insofar as feminine existence lives the body as transcendence and intentionality, the feminine body actively constitutes space and is the original coordinate that unifies the spatial field and projects spatial relations and positions in accord with its intentions. But to the extent that feminine motility is laden with immanence and inhibited, the body's space is lived as constituted. To the extent, that is, that feminine bodily existence is self-referred and thus lives itself as an *object,* the feminine body does exist *in* space. In section I, I observed that women frequently react to motions, even our own motions, as though we are the object of a motion that issues from an alien intention, rather than taking ourselves as the subject of motion. In its immanence and inhibition, feminine spatial existence is *positioned* by a system of coordinates that does not have its origin in a woman's own intentional capacities. The tendency for the feminine body to remain partly immobile in the performance of a task that requires the movement of the whole body illustrates this characteristic of feminine bodily existence as rooted *in place.* Likewise does the tendency of women to wait for an object to come within their immediate bodily field, rather than move out toward it.

Merleau-Ponty devotes a great deal of attention to arguing that the diverse senses and activities of the lived body are synthetically related in such a way that each stands in a mutually conditioning relation with all the others. In particular, visual perception and motility stand in a relation of reversability; an impairment in the functioning of one, for example, leads to an impairment in the functioning of the other (133–37). If we assume that reversability of visual perception and motility, the previous account of the modalities of feminine motility and the spatiality that arises from them suggests that visual space will have its own modalities as well.

Numerous psychological studies have reported differences between the sexes in the character of spatial perception. One of the most frequently discussed of these conclusions is that females are more often "field-dependent." That is, it has been claimed that males have a greater capacity for lifting a figure out of its spatial surroundings and viewing relations in space as fluid and interchangeable, whereas females have a greater tendency to regard figures as embedded within and fixed by their surroundings.[18] The above account of feminine motility and spatiality gives some theoretical intelligibility to these findings. If feminine body spatiality is such that the woman experiences herself as rooted and enclosed, on the reversability assumption it would follow that visual space for feminine existence also has its closures of immobility and fixity. The objects in visual space do not stand in a fluid system of potentially alterable and interchangeable relations correlative to the body's various intentions and projected capacities. Rather, they too have their own *places* and are anchored in their immanence.

IV

The modalities of feminine bodily comportment, motility, and spatiality that I have described here are, I claim, common to the existence of women in contemporary society to one degree or another. They have their source, however, in neither anatomy nor physiology, and certainly not in a mysterious feminine essence. Rather, they have their source in the particular *situation* of women as conditioned by their sexist oppression in contemporary society.

Women in sexist society are physically handicapped. Insofar as we learn to live out our existence in accordance with the definition that patriarchal culture assigns to us, we are physically inhibited, confined, positioned, and objectified. As lived bodies we are not open and unambiguous transcendences that move out to master a world that belongs to

18. The number of studies with these results is enormous. See Eleanor E. Maccoby and Carol N. Jacklin, *The Psychology of Sex Differences* (Palo Alto, Calif.: Stanford University Press, 1974), 91–98. For a number of years psychologists used the results from tests of spatial ability to generalize about field independence in general, and from that to general "analytic" ability. Thus it was concluded that women have less analytical ability than men do. More recently, however, such generalizations have been seriously called into question. See, for example, Julia A. Sherman, "Problems of Sex Differences in Space Perception and Aspects of Intellectual Functioning," *Psychological Review* 74 (1967): 290–99. She notes that while women are consistently found to be more field-dependent in spatial tasks than men are, on nonspatial tests measuring field independence, women generally perform as well as men do.

us, a world constituted by our own intentions and projections. To be sure, there are actual women in contemporary society to whom all or part of the above description does not apply. Where these modalities are not manifest in or determinative of the existence of a particular woman, however, they are definitive in a negative mode—as that which she has escaped, through accident or good fortune, or, more often, as that which she has had to overcome.

One of the sources of the modalities of feminine bodily existence is too obvious to dwell upon at length. For the most part, girls and women are not given the opportunity to use their full bodily capacities in free and open engagement with the world, nor are they encouraged as much as boys are to develop specific bodily skills.[19] Girls' play is often more sedentary and enclosing than the play of boys. In school and after-school activities girls are not encouraged to engage in sport, in the controlled use of their bodies in achieving well-defined goals. Girls, moreover, get little practice at "tinkering" with things and thus at developing spatial skill. Finally, girls are not often asked to perform tasks demanding physical effort and strength, while as the boys grow older they are asked to do so more and more.[20]

The modalities of feminine bodily existence are not merely privative, however, and thus their source is not merely in lack of practice, though this is certainly an important element. There is a specific positive style of feminine body comportment and movement, which is learned as the girl comes to understand that she is a girl. The young girl acquires many subtle habits of feminine body comportment—walking like a girl, tilting her head like a girl, standing and sitting like a girl, gesturing like a girl, and so on. The girl learns actively to hamper her movements. She is told that she must be careful not to get hurt, not to get dirty, not to tear her clothes, that the things she desires to do are dangerous for her. Thus she develops a bodily timidity that increases with age. In assuming herself to be a girl, she takes herself to be fragile. Studies have found that young children of both sexes categorically assert that girls are more likely to get hurt than boys are,[21] and that girls ought to remain close to home,

19. Nor are girls provided with example of girls and women being physically active. See Mary E. Duquin, "Differential Sex Role Socialization toward Amplitude Appropriation," *Research Quarterly* (American Alliance for Health, Physical Education, and Recreation) 48 (1977): 188–92. A survey of textbooks for young children revealed that children are thirteen times more likely to see a vigorously active man than a vigorously active woman and three times more likely to see a relatively active man than a relatively active woman.

20. Sherman, "Problems of Sex Differences," argues that it is the differential socialization of boys and girls in being encouraged to "tinker," explore, etc., that accounts for the difference between the two in spatial ability.

21. See L. Kolberg, "A Cognitive-Developmental Analysis of Children's Sex-Role Concepts and Attitudes," in *The Development of Sex Differences*, ed. E. E. Maccoby (Palo Alto, Calif.: Stanford University Press, 1966), 101.

while boys can roam and explore.[22] The more a girl assumes her status as feminine, the more she takes herself to be fragile and immobile and the more she actively enacts her own body inhibition. When I was about thirteen, I spent hours practicing a "feminine" walk, which was stiff and closed, and rotated from side to side.

Studies that record observations of sex differences in spatial perception, spatial problem-solving, and motor skills have also found that these differences tend to increase with age. While very young children show virtually no differences in motor skills, movement, spatial perception, etc., differences seem to appear in elementary school and increase with adolescence. If these findings are accurate, they would seem to support the conclusion that it is in the process of growing up as a girl that the modalities of feminine bodily comportment, motility, and spatiality make their appearance.[23]

There is, however, a further source of the modalities of feminine bodily existence that is perhaps even more profound than these. At the root of those modalities, I have stated in the previous section, is the fact that the woman lives her body as *object* as well as subject. The source of this is that patriarchal society defines woman as object, as a mere body, and that in sexist society women are in fact frequently regarded by others as objects and mere bodies. An essential part of the situation of being a woman is that of living the ever-present possibility that one will be gazed upon as a mere body, as shape and flesh that presents itself as the potential object of another subject's intentions and manipulations, rather than as a living manifestation of action and intention.[24] The source of this objectified bodily existence is in the attitude of others regarding her, but the woman herself often actively takes up her body as a mere thing. She gazes at it in the mirror, worries about how it looks to others, prunes it, shapes it, molds and decorates it.

This objectified bodily existence accounts for the self-consciousness of the feminine relation to her body and resulting distance she takes from her body. As human, she is a transcendence and subjectivity and cannot live herself as mere bodily object. Thus, to the degree that she does live herself as mere body, she cannot be in unity with herself but must take a distance from and exist in discontinuity with her body. The

---

22. Lenore J. Weitzman, "Sex Role Socialization," in *Woman: A Feminist Perspective,* ed. Jo Freeman (Palo Alto, Calif.: Mayfield Publishing Co., 1975), 111–12.

23. Maccoby and Jacklin, *The Psychology of Sex Differences,* 93–94.

24. The manner in which women are objectified by the gaze of the Other is not the same phenomenon as the objectification by the Other that is a condition of self-consciousness in Sartre's account. See *Being and Nothingness,* trans. Hazel E. Barnes (New York: Philosophical Library, 1956), part 3. While the basic ontological category of being for others is objectified for itself, the objectification that women are subject to is being regarded as a mere in itself. On the particular dynamic of sexual objectification, see Sandra Bartky, "Psychological Oppression," in *Philosophy and Women,* ed. Sharon Bishop and Marjories Weinzweig (Belmont, Calif.: Wadsworth Publishing Co., 1979), 33–41.

objectifying regard that "keeps her in her place" can also account for the spatial modality of being positioned and for why women frequently tend not to move openly, keeping their limbs closed around themselves. To open her body in free, active, open extension and bold outward-directedness is for a woman to invite objectification.

The threat of being seen is, however, not the only threat of objectification that the woman lives. She also lives the threat of invasion of her body space. The most extreme form of such spatial and bodily invasion is the threat of rape. But we daily are subject to the possibility of bodily invasion in many far more subtle ways as well. It is acceptable, for example, for women to be touched in ways and under circumstances that it is not acceptable for men to be touched, and by persons—i.e., men—whom it is not acceptable for them to touch.[25] I would suggest that the enclosed space that has been described as a modality of feminine spatiality is in part a defense against such invasion. Women tend to project an existential barrier closed around them and discontinuous with the "over there" in order to keep the other at a distance. The woman lives her space as confined and closed around her, at least in part as projecting some small area in which she can exist as a free subject.

This essay is a prolegomenon to the study of aspects of women's experience and situation that have not received the treatment they warrant. I would like to close with some questions that require further thought and research. This essay has concentrated its attention upon the sorts of physical tasks and body orientation that involve the whole body in gross movement. Further investigation into woman's bodily existence would require looking at activities that do not involve the whole body and finer movement. If we are going to develop an account of the woman's body experience in situation, moreover, we must reflect on the modalities of a woman's experience of her body in its sexual being, as well as upon less task-oriented body activities, such as dancing. Another question that arises is whether the description given here would apply equally well to any sort of physical task. Might the kind of task, and specifically whether it is a task or movement that is sex-typed, have some effect on the modalities of feminine bodily existence? A further question is to what degree we can develop a theoretical account of the connection between the modalities of the bodily existence of women and other aspects of our existence and experience. For example, I have an intuition that the general lack of confidence that we frequently have about our cognitive or leadership abilities is traceable in part to an original doubt of our body's capacity. None of these questions can be dealt with properly, however, without first performing the kind of guided observation and data collection that my reading has concluded, to a large degree, is yet to be performed.

25. See Nancy Henley and Jo Freeman, "The Sexual Politics of Interpersonal Behavior," in Freeman, *Woman: A Feminist Perspective*, 391–401.

3

Pregnant Embodiment:
Subjectivity and Alienation

The library card catalog contains dozens of entries under the heading "pregnancy": clinical treatises detailing signs of morbidity; volumes cataloging studies of fetal development, with elaborate drawings; or popular manuals in which physicians and others give advice on diet and exercise for the pregnant woman. Pregnancy does not belong to the woman herself. It is a state of the developing fetus, for which the woman is a container; or it is an objective, observable process coming under scientific scrutiny; or it becomes objectified by the woman herself as a "condition" in which she must "take care of herself." Except, perhaps, for one insignificant diary, no card appears listing a work that, as Kristeva puts it, is "concerned with the subject, the mother as the site of her proceedings."[1]

We should not be surprised to learn that discourse on pregnancy omits subjectivity, for the specific experience of women has been absent from most of our culture's discourse about human experience and history. This essay considers some of the experiences of pregnancy from the pregnant subject's viewpoint. Through reference to diaries and literature, as well as phenomenological reflection on the pregnant experience, I seek to let women speak in their own voices.

Section I describes some aspects of bodily existence unique to pregnancy. The pregnant subject, I suggest, is decentered, split, or doubled in several ways. She experiences her body as herself and not herself. Its inner movements belong to another being, yet they are not other, because her body boundaries shift and because her bodily self-location is focused on her trunk in addition to her head. This split subject appears

---

1. Julia Kristeva, "Motherhood According to Giovanni Bellini," in *Desire in Language* (New York: Columbia University Press, 1980), 237.

in the eroticism of pregnancy, in which the woman can experience an innocent narcissism fed by recollection of her repressed experience of her own mother's body. Pregnant existence entails, finally, a unique temporality of process and growth in which the woman can experience herself as split between past and future.

This description of the lived pregnant body both develops and partially criticizes the phenomenology of bodily existence found in the writings of Straus, Merleau-Ponty, and several other existential phenomenologists. It continues the radical undermining of Cartesianism that these thinkers inaugurated, but it also challenges their implicit assumptions of a unified subject and sharp distinction between transcendence and immanence. Pregnancy, I argue, reveals a paradigm of bodily experience in which the transparent unity of self dissolves and the body attends positively to itself at the same time that it enacts its projects.

Section II reflects on the encounter of the pregnant subject with the institutions and practices of medicine. I argue that within the present organization of these institutions and practices, women usually find such an encounter alienating in several respects. Medicine's self-identification as the curing profession encourages others as well as the woman to think of her pregnancy as a condition that deviates from normal health. The control over knowledge about the pregnancy and birth process that the physician has through instruments, moreover, devalues the privileged relation she has to the fetus and her pregnant body. The fact that in the contemporary context the obstetrician is usually a man reduces the likelihood of bodily empathy between physician and patient. Within the context of authority and dependence that currently structures the doctor-patient relation, moreover, coupled with the use of instruments and drugs in the birthing process, the pregnant and birthing woman often lacks autonomy within these experiences.

Before proceeding, it is important to note that this essay restricts its analysis to the specific experience of women in technologically sophisticated Western societies. The analysis presupposes that pregnancy can be experienced for its own sake, noticed, and savored. This entails that the pregnancy be chosen by the woman, either as an explicit decision to become pregnant or at least as choosing to be identified with and positively accepting of it. Most women in human history have not chosen their pregnancies in this sense. For the vast majority of women in the world today, and even for many women in this privileged and liberal society, pregnancy is not an experience they choose. So I speak in large measure for an experience that must be instituted and for those pregnant women who have been able to take up their situation as their own.

I

The unique contribution of Straus, along with Merleau-Ponty and certain other existential phenomenologists, to the Western philosophical tradition has consisted in locating consciousness and subjectivity in the body itself. This move to situate subjectivity in the lived body jeopardizes dualistic metaphysics altogether. There remains no basis for preserving the mutual exclusivity of the categories subject and object, inner and outer, I and world. Straus puts it this way:

> The meaning of "mine" is determined in relation to, in contraposition to, the world, the Allon, to which I am nevertheless a party. The meaning of "mine" is not comprehensible in the unmediated antithesis of I and not-I, own and strange, subject and object, constituting I and constituted world. Everything points to the fact that separateness and union originate in the same ground.[2]

As Sarano has pointed out, however, antidualist philosophers still tend to operate with a dualist language, this time distinguishing two forms of experiencing the body itself, as subject and as object, both transcending freedom and mere facticity.[3] Reflection on the experience of pregnancy, I shall show, provides a radical challenge even to this dualism that is tacitly at work in the philosophers of the body.

To the extent that these existential phenomenologists preserve a distinction between subject and object, they do so at least partly because they assume the subject as a unity. In the *Phenomenology of Perception,* for example, Merleau-Ponty locates the "intentional arc" that unifies experience in the body, rather than in an abstract constituting consciousness. He does not, however, abandon the idea of a unified self as a condition of experience.

> There must be, then, corresponding to this open unity of the world, an open and indefinite unity of subjectivity. Like the world's unity, that of the I is invoked rather than experienced each time I perform an act of perception, each time I reach a self-evident truth, and the universal I is the background against which these effulgent forms stand out: it is through one present thought that I achieve the unity of all my thoughts.[4]

Merleau-Ponty's later work, as well as more recent French philosophy, however, suggests that this transcendental faith in a unified subject as a condition of experience may be little more than ideology.[5] The work of Lacan, Derrida, and Kristeva suggests that the unity of the self is itself a project, a project sometimes successfully enacted by a moving and often contradictory subjectivity. I take Kristeva's remarks about pregnancy as a starting point:

2. Erwin Straus, *Psychiatry and Philosophy* (New York: Springer-Verlag, 1969), 29.

3. J. Sarano, *The Meaning of the Body,* trans. James H. Farley (Philadelphia: Westminster Press, 1966), 62–63.

4. Maurice Merleau-Ponty, *Phenomenology of Perception,* trans. Colin Smith (New York: Humanities Press, 1962), 406.

5. See Rosalind Coward and John Ellis, *Language and Materialism* (London: Routledge and Kegan Paul, 1977).

> Pregnancy seems to be experienced as the radical ordeal of the splitting of the subject: redoubling up of the body, separation and coexistence of the self and another, of nature and consciousness, of physiology and speech.[6]

We can confirm this notion of pregnancy as split subjectivity even outside the psychoanalytic framework that Kristeva uses. Reflection on the experience of pregnancy reveals a body subjectivity that is decentered, myself in the mode of not being myself.

As my pregnancy begins, I experience it as a change in my body; I become different from what I have been. My nipples become reddened and tender; my belly swells into a pear. I feel this elastic around my waist, itching, this round, hard middle replacing the doughy belly with which I still identify. Then I feel a little tickle, a little gurgle in my belly. It is my feeling, my insides, and it feels somewhat like a gas bubble, but it is not; it is different, in another place, belonging to another, another that is nevertheless my body.

The first movements of the fetus produce this sense of the splitting subject; the fetus's movements are wholly mine, completely within me, conditioning my experience and space. Only I have access to these movements from their origin, as it were. For months only I can witness this life within me, and it is only under my direction of where to put their hands that others can feel these movements. I have a privileged relation to this other life, not unlike that which I have to my dreams and thoughts, which I can tell someone but which cannot be an object for both of us in the same way. Adrienne Rich reports this sense of the movements within me as mine, even though they are another's.

> In early pregnancy, the stirring of the fetus felt like ghostly tremors of my own body, later like the movements of a being imprisoned within me; but both sensations were *my* sensations, contributing to my own sense of physical and psychic space.[7]

Pregnancy challenges the integration of my body experience by rendering fluid the boundary between what is within, myself, and what is outside, separate. I experience my insides as the space of another, yet my own body.

> Nor in pregnancy did I experience the embryo as decisively internal in Freud's terms, but rather, as something inside and of me, yet becoming hourly and daily more separate, on its way to becoming separate from me and of itself. . . .
>
> Far from existing in the mode of "inner space," women are powerfully and vulnerably attuned both to "inner" and "outer" because for us the two are continuous, not polar.[8]

6. Julia Kristeva, "Women's Time," trans. Alice Jardine and Harry Blake, *Signs: Journal of Women in Culture and Society* 7 (1981): 31; cf. Kristeva, "Motherhood According to Giovanni Bellini," 238.

7. Adrienne Rich, *Of Woman Born* (New York: W. W. Norton, 1976), 47.

8. Rich, *Of Woman Born*, 47–48.

The birthing process entails the most extreme suspension of the bodily distinction between inner and outer. As the months and weeks progress, increasingly I feel my insides, strained and pressed, and increasingly feel the movement of a body inside me. Through pain and blood and water this inside thing emerges between my legs, for a short while both inside and outside me. Later I look with wonder at my mushy middle and at my child, amazed that this yowling, flailing thing, so completely different from me, was there inside, part of me.

The integrity of my body is undermined in pregnancy not only by this externality of the inside, but also by the fact that the boundaries of my body are themselves in flux. In pregnancy I literally do not have a firm sense of where my body ends and the world begins. My automatic body habits become dislodged; the continuity between my customary body and my body at this moment is broken.[9] In pregnancy my prepregnant body image does not entirely leave my movements and expectations, yet it is with the pregnant body that I must move. This is another instance of the doubling of the pregnant subject.

I move as if I could squeeze around chairs and through crowds as I could seven months before, only to find my way blocked by my own body sticking out in front of me—but yet not me, since I did not expect it to block my passage. As I lean over in my chair to tie my shoe, I am surprised by the graze of this hard belly on my thigh. I do not anticipate my body touching itself, for my habits retain the old sense of my boundaries. In the ambiguity of bodily touch, I feel myself being touched and touching simultaneously, both on my knee and my belly.[10] The belly is other, since I did not expect it there, but since I feel the touch upon it, it is me.[11]

Existential phenomenologists of the body usually assume a distinction between transcendence and immanence as two modes of bodily being. They assume that insofar as I adopt an active relation to the world, I am not aware of my body for its own sake. In the successful enactment of my aims and projects, my body is a transparent medium.[12] For several of these thinkers, awareness of my body as weighted material, as physical, occurs only or primarily when my instrumental relation to the world breaks down, in fatigue or illness.

The transformation into the bodily as physical always means discomfort and malaise. The character of husk, which our live bodiness here increas-

9. See Merleau-Ponty, *Phenomenology of Perception*, 82.

10. On the ambiguity of touch, see Merleau-Ponty, 93; see also Straus, *Psychiatry and Philosophy*, 46.

11. Straus discusses an intentional shift between the body as "other" and as self; see *The Primary World of the Senses* (London: Free Press, 1963), 370.

12. Merleau-Ponty, *Phenomenology of Perception*, 138–39.

ingly assumes, shows itself in its onerousness, bringing heaviness, burden, weight.[13]

Being brought to awareness of my body for its own sake, these thinkers assume, entails estrangement and objectification.

> If, suddenly, I am no longer indifferent to my body, and if I suddenly give my attention to its functions and processes, then my body as a whole is objectified, becomes to me an other, a part of the outside world. And though I may also be able to feel its inner processes, I am myself excluded.[14]

Thus the dichotomy of subject and object appears anew in the conceptualization of the body itself. These thinkers tend to assume that awareness of my body in its weight, massiveness, and balance is always an alienated objectification of my body, in which I am not my body and my body imprisons me. They also tend to assume that such awareness of my body must cut me off from the enactment of my projects; I cannot be attending to the physicality of my body and using it as the means to the accomplishment of my aims.

Certainly there are occasions when I experience my body only as a resistance, only as a painful otherness preventing me from accomplishing my goals. It is inappropriate, however, to tie such a negative meaning to all experience of being brought to awareness of the body in its weight and materiality. Sally Gadow has argued that in addition to experiencing the body as a transparent mediator for our projects or an objectified and alienated resistance or pain, we also at times experience our bodily being in an aesthetic mode. That is, we can become aware of ourselves as body and take an interest in its sensations and limitations for their own sake, experiencing them as a fullness rather than as a lack.[15] While Gadow suggests that both illness and aging can be experiences of the body in such an aesthetic mode, pregnancy is most paradigmatic of such experience of being thrown into awareness of one's body. Contrary to the mutually exclusive categorization between transcendence and immanence that underlies some theories, the awareness of my body in its bulk and weight does not impede the accomplishing of my aims.

This belly touching my knee, this extra part of me that gives me a joyful surprise when I move through a tight place, calls me back to the matter of my body even as I move about accomplishing my aims. Pregnant consciousness is animated by a double intentionality: my subjectivity splits between awareness of myself as body and awareness of my

---

13. Hans Plugge, "Man and His Body," in *The Philosophy of the Body,* ed. Stuart Spicker (Chicago: Quadrangle Books, 1970), 298.

14. Straus, *Primary World of the Senses,* 245.

15. Sally Gadow, "Body and Self: A Dialectic," *Journal of Medicine and Philosophy* 5 (1980): 172–85.

aims and projects. To be sure, even in pregnancy there are times when I am so absorbed in my activity that I do not feel myself as body, but when I move or feel the look of another I am likely to be recalled to the thickness of my body.

I walk through the library stacks searching for the *Critique of Dialectical Reason;* I feel the painless pull of false contractions in my back. I put my hand on my belly to notice its hardening, while my eyes continue their scanning. As I sit with friends listening to jazz in a darkened bar, I feel within me the kicking of the fetus, as if it follows the rhythm of the music. In attending to my pregnant body in such circumstances, I do not feel myself alienated from it, as in illness. I merely notice its borders and rumblings with interest, sometimes with pleasure, and this aesthetic interest does not divert me from my business.

This splitting focus both on my body and my projects has its counterpart in the dual location I give to myself on my body. Straus suggests that in everyday instrumental actions of getting about our business, comprehending, observing, willing, and acting, the "I" is located phenomenologically in our head. There are certain activities, however, of which dancing is paradigmatic, where the "I" shifts from the eyes to the region of the trunk. In this orientation that Straus calls "pathic" we experience ourselves in greater sensory continuity with the surroundings.[16]

The pregnant subject experiences herself as located in the eyes and trunk simultaneously, I suggest. She often experiences her ordinary walking, turning, sitting as a kind of dance, movement that not only gets her where she is going, but also in which she glides through space in an immediate openness. She is surprised sometimes that this weighted solidity that she feels herself becoming can still move with ease.

Pregnancy roots me to the earth, makes me conscious of the physicality of my body not as an object, but as the material weight that I am in movement. The notion of the body as a pure medium of my projects is the illusion of a philosophy that has not quite shed the Western philosophical legacy of humanity as spirit.[17] Movement always entails awareness of effort and the feeling of resistance. In pregnancy this fact of existence never leaves me. I am an actor transcending through each moment to further projects, but the solid inertia and demands of my body call me to my limits not as an obstacle to action, but only as a fleshy relation to the earth.[18] As the months proceed, the most ordinary efforts of human existence, such as sitting, bending, and walking, which I for-

16. See Erwin Straus, "Forms of Spatiality," in *Phenomenological Psychology* (New York: Basic Books), especially 11–12.

17. See Elizabeth V. Spelman, "Woman as Body: Ancient and Contemporary Views," *Feminist Studies* 8 (1982): 109–23.

18. On the relation of body to ground, see R. M. Griffith, "Anthropology: Man-a-foot," in *Philosophy of the Body,* 273–92; see also Stuart Spicker, "Terra Firma and Infirma Species: From Medical Philosophical Anthropology to Philosophy of Medicine," *Journal of Medicine and Philosophy* 1 (1976): 104–35.

merly took for granted, become apparent as the projects they themselves are. Getting up, for example, increasingly becomes a task that requires my attention.[19]

In the experience of the pregnant woman, this weight and materiality often produce a sense of power, solidity, and validity. Thus, whereas our society often devalues and trivializes women, regards women as weak and dainty, the pregnant woman can gain a certain sense of self-respect.

> This bulk slows my walking and makes my gestures and my mind more stately. I suppose if I schooled myself to walk massively the rest of my life, I might always have massive thoughts.[20]

There was a time when the pregnant woman stood as a symbol of stately and sexual beauty.[21] While pregnancy remains an object of fascination, our own culture harshly separates pregnancy from sexuality. The dominant culture defines feminine beauty as slim and shapely. The pregnant woman is often not looked upon as sexually active or desirable, even though her own desires and sensitivity may have increased. Her male partner, if she has one, may decline to share in her sexuality, and her physician may advise her to restrict her sexual activity. To the degree that a woman derives a sense of self-worth from looking "sexy" in the manner promoted by dominant cultural images, she may experience her pregnant body as being ugly and alien.

Though the pregnant woman may find herself desexualized by others, at the same time she may find herself with a heightened sense of her own sexuality. Kristeva suggests that the pregnant and birthing woman renews connection to the repressed, preconscious, presymbolic aspect of existence. Instead of being a unified ego, the subject of the paternal symbolic order, the pregnant subject straddles the spheres of language and instinct. In this splitting of the subject, the pregnant woman recollects a primordial sexual continuity with the maternal body, which Kristeva calls "juissance."[22]

The pregnant woman's relation to her body can be an innocent narcissism. As I undress in the morning and evening, I gaze in the mirror for long minutes, without stealth or vanity. I do not appraise myself, ask whether I look good enough for others, but like a child take pleasure

---

19. Straus's essay "The Upright Posture" well expresses the centrality of getting up and standing up to being a person; see *Phenomenological Psychology*, 137–65.

20. Ann Lewis, *An Interesting Condition* (Garden City, N.Y.: Doubleday, 1950), 83. When I began reading for this essay I was shocked at how few texts I found of women speaking about their pregnancies; this book is a rare gem in that regard.

21. Rich discusses some of the history of views of pregnancy and motherhood; see *Of Woman Born*, chapter 4.

22. Kristeva, "Motherhood According to Giovanni Bellini," 242. Marianne Hirsch makes a useful commentary in "Mothers and Daughters," *Signs* 7 (1981): 200–222.

in discovering new things in my body. I turn to the side and stroke the
taut flesh that protrudes under my breasts.

Perhaps the dominant culture's desexualization of the pregnant body
helps make possible such self-love when it happens. The culture's separation of pregnancy and sexuality can liberate her from the sexually
objectifying gaze that alienates and instrumentalizes her when in her
nonpregnant state. The leer of sexual objectification regards the woman
in pieces, as the possible object of a man's desire and touch.[23] In pregnancy the woman may experience some release from this alienating gaze.
The look focusing on her belly is one not of desire, but of recognition.
Some may be repelled by her, find her body ridiculous, but the look that
follows her in pregnancy does not alienate her, does not instrumentalize
her with respect to another's desire. Indeed, in this society, which still
often narrows women's possibilities to motherhood, the pregnant
woman often finds herself looked at with approval.

> As soon as I was visibly and clearly pregnant, I felt, for the first time in
> my adolescent and adult life, not-guilty. The atmosphere of approval in
> which I was bathed—even by strangers in the street, it seemed—was like
> an aura I carried with me, in which doubts, fears, misgivings, met with
> absolute denial. This is what women have always done.[24]

In classical art this "aura" surrounding motherhood depicts repose. The
dominant culture projects pregnancy as a time of quiet waiting. We refer
to the woman as "expecting," as though this new life were flying in
from another planet and she sat in her rocking chair by the window,
occasionally moving the curtain aside to see whether the ship is coming.
The image of uneventful waiting associated with pregnancy reveals
clearly how much the discourse of pregnancy leaves out the subjectivity
of the woman. From the point of view of others pregnancy is primarily
a time of waiting and watching, when nothing happens.

For the pregnant subject, on the other hand, pregnancy has a temporality of movement, growth, and change. The pregnant subject is not
simply a splitting in which the two halves lie open and still, but a dialectic. The pregnant woman experiences herself as a source and participant
in a creative process. Though she does not plan and direct it, neither
does it merely wash over her; rather, she *is* this process, this change.
Time stretches out, moments and days take on a depth because she experiences more changes in herself, her body. Each day, each week, she
looks at herself for signs of transformation.

> Were I to lose consciousness for a month, I could still tell that an apprecia-
> ble time had passed by the increased size of the fetus within me. There is
> a constant sense of growth, of progress, of time, which, while it may be

23. See Sandra Bartky, "On Psychological Oppression," in *Philosophy and Women,*
ed. Bishop and Weinzweig (Belmont, Calif.: Wadsworth Publishing Co., 1979), 330–41.
24. Rich, *Of Woman Born,* 6.

wasted for you personally, is still being used, so that even if you were to do nothing at all during those nine months, something would nevertheless be accomplished and a climax reached.[25]

For others the birth of an infant may be only a beginning, but for the birthing woman it is a conclusion as well. It signals the close of a process she has been undergoing for nine months, the leaving of this unique body she has moved through, always surprising her a bit in its boundary changes and inner kicks. Especially if this is her first child she experiences the birth as a transition to a new self that she may both desire and fear. She fears a loss of identity, as though on the other side of the birth she herself became a transformed person, such that she would "never be the same again."

Finally her "time" comes, as is commonly said. During labor, however, there is no sense of growth and change, but the cessation of time. There is no intention, no activity, only a will to endure. I only know that I have been lying in this pain, concentrating on staying above it, for a long time because the hands of the clock say so or the sun on the wall has moved to the other side of the room.

> Time is absolutely still. I have been here forever. Time no longer exists. Always, Time holds steady for birth. There is only this rocketing, this labor.[26]

II

Feminist writers often use the concept of alienation to describe female existence in a male-dominated society and culture.[27] In this section I argue that the pregnant subject's encounter with obstetrical medicine in the United States often alienates her from her pregnant and birthing experience. Alienation here means the objectification or appropriation by one subject of another subject's body, action, or product of action, such that she or he does not recognize that objectification as having its origins in her or his experience. A subject's experience or action is alienated when it is defined or controlled by a subject who does not share one's assumptions or goals. I will argue that a woman's experience in pregnancy and birthing is often alienated because her condition tends to be defined as a disorder, because medical instruments objectify internal processes in such a way that they devalue a woman's experience of those

25. Lewis, *An Interesting Condition*, 78.

26. Phyllis Chesler, *With Child: A Diary of Motherhood* (New York: Thomas Y. Crowell, 1979).

27. Ann Foreman, *Femininity as Alienation* (London: Pluto Press, 1977); Sandra Bartky, "Narcissism, Femininity, and Alienation," *Social Theory and Practice* 8 (1982): 127–43.

processes, and because the social relations and instrumentation of the medical setting reduce her control over her experience.

Through most of the history of medicine its theoreticians and practitioners did not include the reproductive processes of women within its domain. Once women's reproductive processes came within the domain of medicine, they were defined as diseases. Indeed, by the mid–nineteenth century, at least in Victorian England and America, being female itself was symptomatic of disease. Medical writers considered women to be inherently weak and psychologically unstable, and the ovaries and uterus to be the cause of a great number of diseases and disorders, both physical and psychological.[28]

Contemporary obstetricians and gynecologists usually take pains to assert that menstruation, pregnancy, childbirth, and menopause are normal body functions that occasionally have a disorder. The legacy that defined pregnancy and other reproductive functions as conditions requiring medical therapy, however, has not been entirely abandoned.

Rothman points out that even medical writers who explicitly deny that pregnancy is a disease view normal changes associated with pregnancy, such as lowered hemoglobin, water retention, and weight gain, as "symptoms" requiring "treatment" as part of the normal process of prenatal care.[29] Though 75 percent to 88 percent of pregnant women experience some nausea in the early months, some obstetrical textbooks refer to this physiological process as a neurosis that "may indicate resentment, ambivalence and inadequacy in women ill-prepared for motherhood."[30] Obstetrical teaching films entitled Normal Delivery depict the use of various drugs and instruments, as well as the use of paracervical block and the performance of episiotomy.[31]

A continued tendency on the part of medicine to treat pregnancy and childbirth as dysfunctional conditions derives first from the way medicine defines its purpose. Though medicine has extended its domain to include many bodily and psychological processes that ought not to be conceptualized as illness or disease—such as child development, sexuality, and aging, as well as women's reproductive functions—medicine continues to define itself as the practice that seeks cure for disease. E. D. Pellegrino and D. C. Thomasma, for example, define the goal of medicine as "the relief of perceived lived body disruption" and "organic restoration to a former or better state of perceived health or well-being."

When a patient consults a physician, he or she does so with one specific purpose in mind: to be healed, to be restored and made whole, i.e., to be

28. Barbara Ehrenreich and Deirdre English, For Her Own Good (Garden City, N.Y.: Doubleday, 1978), chapters 2 and 3.

29. Barbara Katz Rothman, "Women, Health, and Medicine," in Women: A Feminist Perspective, ed. Jo Freeman (Palo Alto, Calif.: Mayfield Publishing Co., 1979), 27–40.

30. Quoted in Gena Corea, The Hidden Malpractice: How American Medicine Treats Women as Patients and Professionals (New York: William Morrow, 1977), 76.

31. Rothman, "Women, Health, and Medicine," 36.

relieved of some noxious element in physical or emotional life which the patient defines as disease—a distortion of the accustomed perception of what is a satisfactory life.[32]

These are often not the motives that prompt pregnant women to seek the office of the obstetrician. Yet because medicine continues to define itself as the curing profession, it can tend implicitly to conceptualize women's reproductive processes as disease or infirmity.

A second conceptual ground for the tendency within gynecological and obstetrical practice to approach menstruation, pregnancy, and menopause as "conditions" with "symptoms" that require "treatment" lies in the implicit male bias in medicine's conception of health. The dominant model of health assumes that the normal, healthy body is unchanging. Health is associated with stability, equilibrium, a steady state. Only a minority of persons, however, namely adult men who are not yet old, experience their health as a state in which there is no regular or noticeable change in body condition. For them a noticeable change in their bodily state usually does signal a disruption or dysfunction. Regular, noticeable, sometimes extreme change in bodily condition, on the other hand, is an aspect of the normal bodily functioning of adult women. Change is also a central aspect of the bodily existence of healthy children and healthy old people, as well as some of the so-called disabled. Yet medical conceptualization implicitly uses this unchanging adult male body as the standard of all health.

This tendency of medical conceptualization to treat pregnancy as disease can produce alienation for the pregnant woman. She often has a sense of bodily well-being during her pregnancy and often has increased immunity to common diseases such as colds and flu. As we saw in the previous section, moreover, she often has a bodily self-image of strength and solidity. Thus, while her body may signal one set of impressions, her entrance into the definitions of medicine may lead her to the opposite understanding. Even though certain discomforts associated with pregnancy, such as nausea, flatulence, and shortness of breath, can happen in the healthiest of woman, her internalization of various discussions of the fragility of pregnancy may lead her to define such experience as signs of weakness.

Numerous criticisms of the use of instruments, drugs, surgery, and other methods of intervention in obstetrical practice have been voiced in recent years.[33] I do not wish to reiterate them here, nor do I wish to

32. E. D. Pellegrino and D. C. Thomasma, *A Philosophical Basis of Medical Practice* (New York: Oxford University Press, 1981), 122; earlier quotes from 76 and 72, respectively.

33. Suzanne Arms, *Immaculate Deception: A New Look at Women and Childbirth in America* (Boston: Houghton Mifflin, 1975); D. Haire, "The Cultural Warping of Childbirth," *Environmental Child Health*,19 (1973): 171–91; and Adele Laslie, "Ethical Issues in Childbirth," *Journal of Medicine and Philosophy* 7 (1982): 179–96.

argue that the use of instruments and drugs in pregnancy and childbirth is usually inappropriate or dangerous. The instrumental and intervention orientation that predominates in contemporary obstetrics, however, can contribute to a woman's sense of alienation in at least two ways.

First, the normal procedures of the American hospital birthing setting render the woman considerably more passive than she need be. Most hospitals, for example, do not allow the woman to walk around even during early stages of labor, despite the fact that there is evidence that moving around can lessen pain and speed the birthing process. Routine breaking of the amniotic sac enforces this bed confinement. Women usually labor and deliver in a horizontal or near-horizontal position, reducing the influence of gravity and reducing the woman's ability to push. The use of intravenous equipment, monitors, and pain-relieving drugs all inhibit a woman's capacity to move during labor.

Second, the use of instruments provides a means of objectifying the pregnancy and birth that alienates a woman because it negates or devalues her own experience of those processes. As the previous section described, at a phenomenological level the pregnant woman has a unique knowledge of her body processes and the life of the fetus. She feels the movements of the fetus, the contractions of her uterus, with an immediacy and certainty that no one can share. Recently invented machines tend to devalue this knowledge. The fetal-heart sensor projects the heartbeat of the six-week-old fetus into the room so that all can hear it in the same way. The sonogram is receiving increasing use to follow the course of fetal development. The fetal monitor attached during labor records the intensity and duration of each contraction on white paper; the woman's reports are no longer necessary for charting the progress of her labor. Such instruments transfer some control over the means of observing the pregnancy and birth process from the woman to the medical personnel. The woman's experience of these processes is reduced in value, replaced by more objective means of observation.

Alienation within the context of contemporary obstetrics can be further produced for the pregnant woman by the fact that the physician attending her is usually a man. Humanistic writers about medicine often suggest that a basic condition of good medical practice is that the physician and patient share the lived-body experience.[34] If the description of the lived-body experience of pregnancy in the previous section is valid, however, pregnancy and childbirth entail a unique body subjectivity that is difficult to empathize with unless one is or has been pregnant. Since the vast majority of obstetricians are men, then, this basic condition of therapeutic practice usually cannot be met in obstetrics. Physicians and pregnant women are thereby distanced in their relationship, perhaps more than others in the doctor-patient relation. The sexual asymmetry

34. Pellegrino and Thomasma, *A Philosophical Basis of Medical Practice*, 114.

between physician and patient also produces a distance because it must be desexualized. Prenatal checkups follow the same procedure as gynecological examinations, requiring an aloof matter-of-factness in order to preclude attaching sexual meaning to them.[35]

There is a final alienation the woman experiences in the medical setting, which drives from the relations of authority and subordination that usually structure the doctor-patient relation in contemporary medical practice. Many writers have noted that medicine has increasingly become an institution with broad social authority on a par with the legal system or even organized religion.[36] The relationship between doctor and patient is usually structured as superior to subordinate. Physicians often project an air of fatherly infallibility and resist having their opinions challenged; the authoritarianism of the doctor-patient relations increases as the social distance between them increases.[37]

This authority that the physician has over any patient is amplified in gynecology and obstetrics by the dynamic of gender hierarchy. In a culture that still generally regards men as being more important than women and gives men authority and power over women in many institutions, the power the doctor has over the knowledge and objectification of her body processes, as well as his power to direct the performance of her office visits and her birthing, are often experienced by her as another form of male power over women.[38]

Philosophers of medicine have pointed out that the concept of health is much less a scientific concept than a normative concept referring to human well-being and the good life.[39] I have argued that there exists a male bias in medicine's concept of health insofar as the healthy body is understood to be the body in a steady state. This argument suggests that medical culture requires a more self-consciously differentiated under-

35. J. Emerson, "Behavior in Private Places: Sustaining Definitions of Reality in Gynecological Examinations," in *Recent Sociology,* ed. H. Dreitzen, no. 2 (London: Macmillan, 1970), 74–97.

36. See E. Friedson, *The Profession of Medicine* (New York: Dodd and Mead Co., 1970); Irving K. Zola, "Medicine as an Institution of Social Control," *Sociological Review* 2 (1972): 487–504; and Janice Raymond, "Medicine as Patriarchal Religion," *Journal of Medicine and Philosophy* 7 (1982): 197–216.

37. See G. Ehrenreich and J. Ehrenreich, "Medicine and Social Control," in *The Cultural Crisis of Modern Medicine,* ed. John Erenreich (New York: Monthly Review Press, 1979), 1–28.

38. See B. Kaiser and K. Kaiser, "The Challenge of the Women's Movement to American Gynecology," *American Journal of Obstetrics and Gynecology* 120 (1974): 652–61.

39. Pellegrino and Thomasma, *A Philosophical Basis of Medical Practice,* 74–76; see also Tristram Engelhardt, "Human Well-Being and Medicine: Some Basic Value Judgments in the Biomedical Sciences," in *Science, Ethics and Medicine,* ed. Engelhardt and Daniel Callahan (Hastings-on-Hudson, N.Y.: Ethics and the Life Sciences, 1976), 120–39; and Caroline Whitbeck, "A Theory of Health" in *Concepts of Health and Disease: Interdisciplinary Perspectives,* ed. Arthur L. Caplan, Tristram Engelhardt, and James J. McCartney (Reading, Mass.: Addison-Wesley, 1981), 611–26.

standing of health and disease.[40] Contemporary culture has gone to a certain extent in the direction of developing distinct norms of health and disease for the aged, the physically impaired, children, and hormonally active women. Such developments should be encouraged, and medical theorists and practitioners should be vigilant about tendencies to judge physical difference as deviance.

Moreover, to overcome the potentialities for alienation that I have argued exist in obstetrical practices, as well as other medical practices, medicine must shed its self-definition as primarily concerned with curing. Given that nearly all aspects of human bodily life and change have come within the domain of medical institutions and practices, such a definition is no longer appropriate. There are numerous life states and physical conditions in which a person needs help or care, rather than medical or surgical efforts to alter, repress, or speed a body process. The birthing woman certainly needs help in her own actions, being held, talked to, coached, dabbed with water, and having someone manipulate the emergence of the infant. Children, old people, and the physically impaired often need help and care though they are not diseased. Within current medical and related institutions there exist professionals who perform these caring functions. They are usually women, usually poorly paid, and their activities are usually seen as complementing and subordinate to the direction of activities such as diagnostic tests, drug therapies, and surgical therapies performed by the physicians, usually men. The alienation experienced by the pregnant and birthing woman would probably be lessened if caring were distinguished from curing and took on a practical value that did not subordinate it to curing.

Postscript, November 2003

"Pregnant Embodiment" was first published in 1983. Despite the enormous technological changes that have taken place in the United States and elsewhere that affect the experience of pregnancy and childbirth, I have left the text in its original form. The basic description of pregnant embodiment remains valid, I believe, as does the analysis of alienation of this subjectivity under the gaze of medicine. At least one technologically induced change in the experience of pregnancy, however, deserves an afterword comment. Description of the experience of pregnancy in this essay does not take into account the influence of sonogram technology, which arguably has altered the experience of pregnant women and their partners in significant ways. It is now routine for obstetricians to order one or more sonogram images after the fetus is large enough to distin-

---

40. Arlene Dallery, "Illness and Health: Alternatives to Medicine," in *Phenomenology in a Pluralistic Context: Selected Studies in Phenomenology and Existentialism,* ed. E. Schrag and W. L. McBride (Albany: State University of New York Press, 1983), 167–76.

guish features through its use. The sonogram projects an image of the developing fetus. Pregnant women, their partners and others who view the image often speak of the thrill of first seeing it. I have met more than one proud father who carries around a print of the image of a two-month-old fetus to show to his friends and colleagues.

The frequency of the routine use of sonogram in American obstetrical practice does not change the basic analysis of this paper. Indeed, it reinforces that analysis. This essay has two parts that describe a tension in the experience of pregnancy and childbirth for the woman who lives them. On the one hand, she *is* a pregnant person; it is she and only she who lives this growing body and moves within it. She and only she has a privileged relation of *feeling* with the developing fetus. The pregnant woman feels the weight, position, and motion of the fetus as part of herself yet not herself. Others have access to feeling this developing life only by contact with and through her.

On the other hand, however, the second section of the essay describes the conversion of this subjective experience into objective entities that can be observed by anyone with the proper instruments. These objectified observables come to be defined as the authoritative knowledge of the process of gestation and the state of the fetus, and thereby the pregnant woman's privileged insider knowledge comes to be devalued. In the last twenty years in the United States, as well as many other advanced industrial societies, this objectifying process has accelerated, I suggest. Sonogram technology makes it possible for anyone to experience fetal movement by looking at the same projected image. The pregnant woman's experience of that image is just the same as anyone else's who views it. This shared and shareable experience of the fetus tends to have more status as "reality" than the feelings only she can report. It is no accident, it seems to me, that this authoritative reality comes to those who witness it by way of *vision*. Sonogram technology has revolutionized the experience of pregnancy and expectant parenting by putting a visual representation of the fetus at the center, in the context of a modern epistemological system that has always given priority to the visual over the tactile or even the oral.

See Yourself in Wool.
ANNE KLEIN II

4

Women Recovering Our Clothes

"See yourself in wool." Yes, I would like that. I see myself in that wool, heavy, thick, warm, swinging around my legs in rippling caresses. And who might I be? An artist, perhaps, somewhat well established, thinking of my next series. Or maybe I will be a lecturer coming off the airplane, greeted by my colleagues, who will host me at a five-star restaurant. Or perhaps I'm off to meet my new lover, who will greet me face to face and stroke my wool.

But who's this coming up behind me? Bringing me down to his size? Don't look back, I can't look back, his gaze is unidirectional, he sees me but I can't see him. But no—I am seeing myself in wool seeing him see me. Is it that I cannot see myself without seeing myself being seen? So I need him there to unite me and my image of myself? Who does he think I am?

So I am split. I see myself, and I see myself being seen. Might such a split express a woman's relation to clothes, to images of clothes, to images of herself in clothes, whoever she imagines herself to be? Can we separate the panels? I wonder if there's a way we can get him out of the picture.

Matting: Is This a Frame-Up?

In her monumental book *Seeing through Clothes,* Ann Hollander argues that the meaning of clothes is conditioned by pictorial images. Throughout the modern period, Western artists have depicted and sanctified clothing images, associating clothes with kinds of personages and situations. This representation of clothes freezes the conventional into the natural, and people measure women in their clothes in relation to the natural aesthetic created by clothing images.[1]

For most of the modern period, this thesis about the relation of the experience of clothing to images of clothing applied only to those classes able to buy artworks or invited to places where they are displayed. As Stuart and Elizabeth Ewen discuss, however, the mid–nineteenth century witnessed a revolutionary proletarianization of the image with the invention of cheap methods of color printing. By the early twentieth century it would seem that the experience of clothing, especially women's experience of clothing, is saturated with the experience of images of women in clothing—in advertising drawings and photographs, catalogs, and film.[2]

Hollander cites the historical specificity of twentieth-century women's clothing standards and images conditioned by cinema. The nineteenth century held an image of women's demeanor as statuesque, immobile, hiding or hobbling the limbs. The twentieth century, by contrast, emphasizes the mobility of women in clothes—the exhibition of legs, skirts, and pants that do not so much inhibit movement. Images of clothes show women on the move—striding down the street, leaping with excitement, running on the sands, leaning over a desk. If she is standing still, her hair or skirt or scarf flies with the wind. Contemporary images of women's clothes capture a single movement in a narrative whose beginning and end lie outside the frame.[3]

In wearing our clothes, Hollander suggests, we seek to fashion ourselves in the mode of the dominant pictorial aesthetic. In this project the mirror provides us a means of representation. In the mirror we see not the "bare facts," but a clothed image reverberating the dominant magazine and film images of us in our clothes. Contemporary urban life provides countless opportunities for us to see ourselves—in hotel and theater lobbies, in restaurants and powder rooms, in train stations and store windows.[4] I love to walk down a city street when I feel well dressed and to catch sight of my moving image in a store window, trying not to see myself seeing myself. I imagine myself in a movie, freely swinging down the street in happy clothes, on my way. The mirror gives me pictures, and the pictures in magazines and catalogs give me reflections of identities in untold but signified stories. The feminist question is: *Whose* imagination conjures up the pictures and their meanings?

1. Ann Hollander, *Seeing through Clothes* (New York: Viking Press, 1978).
2. Stuart Ewen and Elizabeth Ewen, *Channels of Desire: Mass Images and the Shaping of American Consciousness* (New York: McGraw-Hill, 1982).
3. Hollander, *Seeing through Clothes*, 345–52.
4. Hollander, *Seeing through Clothes*, 391–416.

Panel I: Reflections on Snow White's Mirror

Our experience of clothes derives from film in more than a merely asso-
ciative way, Maureen Turim suggests, but also through producing the
implicit narrative imagination of our clothes.

> Films not only expose new fashions to a mass audience, they not only
> provide the fashion industry with a glittering showcase; because we see
> those fashions within a narrative context, films also invest fashions with
> unconscious attachments, connotations. This process, the narration of
> fashion, means more than the association of a style with a given story or
> fiction. It is a process that fuses the unconscious effects of film experience
> with the very lines and colors of clothing designs.[5]

My question is: How shall I describe a woman's pleasure in clothes?
If I live my identification with the clothing images through my experience of film narrative, it may not be too wild to explore our pleasure in
clothes through feminist film theory. Following a Lacanian framework,
feminist film theorists have developed an account of a female experience
of pleasure in the objectified female body within a patriarchal order.
The story goes something like this.[6]

Subjectivity is crucially constituted by relations of looking. Through
active looking the subject acquires a sense of subject set off against objects. Through looking at an image of himself in the mirror, the subject
gains a sense of narcissistic identification with a totalized motor being
misrepresented as a unity. In the phallocratic order, however, this subject who takes pleasure in looking at objects other than himself and who
takes pleasure in looking at totalized images of himself is a male subject.
The phallocratic order splits looking into active and passive moments.
The gaze is masculine, and that upon which it gazes is feminine. Women
are only lack, the other that shores up the phallic subject, the object that
gives power and unified identity to men's looking. If women are to
achieve any subjectivity it can only be through adopting this position of
the male subject who takes pleasure in the objectification of women.

In film the activity of looking has two aspects—a voyeuristic and a
fetishistic—and film positions women's bodies in relation to both sorts
of looking. Voyeuristic looking takes a distance from the object of its
gaze, from which it is absent and elsewhere. From this distance the object of the gaze cannot return or reciprocate the gaze; the voyeur's look

5. Maureen Turim, "Fashion Shapes: Film, the Fashion Industry, and the Image of
Women," *Socialist Review* 13.5 (September–October 1983): 86.

6. I derive my account of the male gaze and film from the following works: Turim,
"Fashion Shapes"; Laura Mulvey, "Visual Pleasure and Narrative Cinema," *Screen* 16.3
(Autumn 1975): 6–18; Annette Kuhn, *Women's Pictures: Feminism and Cinema* (London:
Routledge and Kegan Paul, 1982), 47–65; and E. Ann Kaplan, *Women and Film: Both
Sides of the Camera* (New York: Methuen, 1983), 23–35.

is judgmental, holding power over the guilty object of the gaze by offering punishment or forgiveness. In fetishistic looking, on the other hand, the subject finds his likeness in the object, represented as the unity of the phallus. In film both voyeuristic and fetishistic looking deny the threatening difference of the female, either judging her lacking and guilty or turning her body or parts of her body into an icon in which the subject finds himself, his phallus.

Women also watch films and enjoy them. What, in this account, makes women's pleasure in films possible? Only identification with the male subject. I quote Ann Kaplan:

> Why do we find our objectification and surrender pleasurable? . . . Such pleasure is not surprising if we consider the shape of the girl's Oedipal crisis. . . . The girl is forced to turn away from the illusory unity with the Mother in the prelinguistic realm and has to enter the symbolic world which involves subject and object. Assigned the place of object (lack), she is the recipient of male desire, passively appearing rather than acting. Her sexual pleasure in this position can thus be constructed only around her own objectification. Furthermore, given the male structuring around sadism, the girl may adopt a corresponding masochism. . . . We could say that in locating herself in fantasy in the erotic, the woman places herself as either passive recipient of male desire or, at one remove, as *watching* a woman who is passive recipient of male desires and sexual actions.[7]

I cannot deny that these analyses apply to our experience of clothes, to our experience of images of women in clothes. The voyeuristic gaze is often implicit or explicit in magazine advertising for clothes, and it is easy to find the language of guilt and imperfection attached to the clothed woman. Sandra Bartky describes how women internalize the objectifying gaze of what she calls the "fashion-beauty complex," a gaze that deprecates and evaluates a woman's body.

> I must exist perpetually at a distance from my physical self, fixed at this distance in a permanent posture of disapproval. Thus, insofar as the fashion-beauty complex shapes one of the introjected subjects for whom I exist as object, I sense myself as deficient. Nor am I able to control in any way those images which give rise to the criteria by which those deficiencies appear . . . All the projections of the fashion-beauty complex have this in common: they are images of *what* I *am not*.[8]

Good clothes, new clothes, this year's clothes will cover up my flaws, straighten me out, measure me up to the approving eye.

Maureen Turim discusses how within the matrix of film imagery women's clothing fashions fetishize the female body. Through what she calls the "slit aesthetic," clothing cuts play fabric off against bare skin,

---

7. Kaplan, *Women and Film,* 26.

8. Sandra Bartky, "Narcissism, Femininity, and Alienation," *Social Theory and Practice* 8.2 (Summer 1982): 136.

turning the body or body parts into fetishes. Sweaters cut low in front or back, bathing suits and lingerie cut high on the hip, cutouts in midriff at the waist, skirt slits or short skirts, cutoff pants—all pattern the clothing cut to focus on bare flesh, and frequently the cuts also direct attention to the fetishized neck, breasts, stomach, genitals, thighs, calves, ankles.[9] The slit aesthetic creates the image of the sexy clothed body, an image of phallic female power. We women sometimes respond to this image with desire, the desire to be that sexy woman.

It's all true, I guess; at least I cannot deny it: In clothes I seek to find the approval of the transcending male gaze; in clothing I seek to transform myself into a bewitching object that will capture his desire and identity. When I leaf through magazines and catalogs I take my pleasure from imagining myself perfected and beautiful and sexual for the absent or mirrored male gaze. I take pleasure in these images of female bodies in their clothes because my own gaze occupies the position of the male gaze insofar as I am a subject at all. I will not deny it, but it leaves a hollowness in me. If I simply affirm this, I must admit that for me there is no subjectivity that is not his, that there is no specifically female pleasure I take in clothes.[10]

But I remember the hours that Suzanne and I played with paper dolls, cutting, drawing, coloring, trading their clothes, stacks of their clothes in shoe boxes. Suzanne and I talked about the clothes, and we dressed up the dolls for their activities—going to work or on vacation, visiting each other or going on shopping trips; yes, they went on dates, too, though I don't remember any men paper dolls. I remember playing paper dolls with Suzanne, and I want to be loyal to her.

Panel II: Through the Looking Glass

Luce Irigaray's book *Speculum of the Other Woman*[11] concerns how Western culture expresses a masculine desire and has silenced and repressed a specifically female desire. The masculine discourse that receives expression in Western ontology conceives being in solid objects, self-identical, one and the same thing, to be observed, measured, passed

9. Turim, "Fashion Shapes," 86–89.

10. Kim Sawchuck, for one, agrees that feminist literature criticizing fashion is a primary commodifier of women, a major source of the reproduction of women's oppression in patriarchal capitalism; she argues, however, that such accounts are usually too monolothic and one-sided, tending "to fall within the trap of decoding all social relations within patriarchy and capitalism as essentially repressive and homogeneous in its effects" (56). "A Tale of Inscription/Fashion Statements," *Canadian Journal of Political and Social Theory* 9.1–2 (1987): 56.

11. Luce Irigaray, *Speculum of the Other Woman*, trans. Gillian C. Gill (Ithaca, N.Y.: Cornell University Press, 1985).

around from hand to hand in the relations of commodity exchange that bind the male social contract. In patriarchal society woman is the supreme object, the possession that complements his subjectivity. In the patriarchal discourse of Western culture, Irigaray suggests, woman serves as the mirror for masculine subjectivity and desire. She reflects back to him his self, as the mother who engendered him or the wife who serves him and gives him his image in a child. The male-gaze theory I have summarized illustrates this function of femininity as the mirror in which man sees himself reflected. The institutions of patriarchy contribute to enhancing male subjectivity by organizing women's desire and action to be identified with his, desiring to make herself into a beautiful object for his gaze, finding her pleasure in his satisfaction.

The subversion of patriarchy, then, according to Irigaray, requires that women speak our desire, not as it has been formed in the interests of men but from and for ourselves. Speaking for ourselves to one another from our own female flesh and imagination, our creation of a different voice can pierce the smug universality of transcendental subjectivity. I am not sure what Irigaray means by our lips speaking together, but for me it means a discovery, recovery, and invention of women's culture. We can mine traditionally female social practices and experiences and find in them specific ways that we as women relate to one another and to ourselves, female-specific intrinsic values. There is no question that there are race, class, and sexuality differences in women's relations to one another, and in this women's culture women most often relate to women of the same race or class identification as themselves. Still, I have often found it easiest to bridge such difference between myself and another woman by talking about elements of women's culture—often clothes.

The project of speaking such women's culture does not deny women's oppression and that structures of femininity support that oppression. But if we have always been agents, we have also expressed our desire and energy in positive symbols and practices. Irigaray suggests that whereas patriarchal masculine desire is obsessed with identifiable objects that can be seen, women's desire is plural, fluid, and interested more in touch than in sight. She links a phallocentric logic of identity with property, the propensity to draw borders, count and measure, and keep hold of one's own; when the goods (women) get together, she suggests, they might speak different relationships. As I recover our clothes, or perhaps cut them out of whole cloth, I shall follow these lines.

Patriarchal fashion folds create a meticulous paradigm of the woman well dressed for the male gaze, then endows with guilt the pleasure we might derive for ourselves in these clothes. Misogynist mythology gloats in its portrayal of women as frivolous body decorators. Well-trained to meet the gaze that evaluates us for our finery, for how well we show him off, we then are condemned as sentimental, superficial, duplicitous, because we attend to and sometimes learn to love the glamorous arts.[12] The male gazers paint us gazing at ourselves at our toilet, before the table they call a vanity. In their own image, the male mythmakers can imagine only narcissistic pleasures. Outside this orbit of self-reference, I find three pleasures we take in clothes: touch, bonding, and fantasy.

But for whom do I speak in this "we"? For women. But how can I speak for women? This question expresses a dilemma. Patriarchal domination requires the subversion of its authority by the speaking of a specifically female desire beyond its power to know. But there cannot be a woman's desire; the very project of feminist subversion leads us to the dissolution of such universals. When I speak, then, for whom do I speak? For myself, of course. But this is politics, not autobiography, and I speak from my own experience, which I claim resonates with that of other women. My own experience is particular and limited, and it is possible that it most resonates among white, middle-class, heterosexual professional women in late capitalist society. At least I can claim to speak only for the experience of women like me. I believe that some of the experience I express resonates with that of other women, but that is for them to say. The differences among women do not circumscribe us within exclusive categories, but the only way we can know our similarities and differences is by each of us expressing our particular experience. I offer, then, this expression of women's pleasure in clothes.

Touch

Irigaray suggests that masculine desire expresses itself through visual metaphors, that the experience of seeing, gazing, is primary in a masculine aesthetic. Sight is the most distancing of the senses, in which the subject stands separate and against the object, which is other, there. A patriarchal seeing, however, according to Irigaray, separates only in order to know the objects, to master them with the mind's eye and thereby find in the objects the reflection of the subject's brilliance.

Feminine desire, Irigaray suggests, moves through the medium of touch more than sight. Less concerned with identifying things, comparing them, measuring them in their relations to one another, touch immerses the subject in fluid continuity with the object, and for the touching subject the object touched reciprocates the touching, blurring the border between self and other. By touch I do mean that specific sense of skin on matter, fingers on texture. But I also mean an orientation to sensuality as such that includes all senses. Thus we might conceive a mode of vision, for example, that is less a gaze, distanced from and mastering its object, but an immersion in light and color. Sensing as

---

12. Sawchuck, "A Tale of Inscription/Fashion Statements," 58.

touching is within, experiencing what touches it as ambiguous, continuous, but nevertheless differentiated.

When I "see" myself in wool it's partly the wool itself that attracts me, its heavy warmth and textured depth. Some of the pleasure of clothes is the pleasure of fabric and the way the fabric hangs and falls around the body. Straight skirts with slits may give thigh for the eye, but the skirt in all its glory drapes in flowing folds that billow when you twirl. History documents the measurement of nobility and grace through fabric. Women have been imprisoned by this history, have been used as mannequins to display the trappings of wealth.

But feminine experience also affords many of us a tactile imagination, the simple pleasure of losing ourselves in cloth. We wander through yard-goods stores, stroke the fabrics hanging off the bolts, pull them out to appraise the patterns, imagine how they might be best formed around the body or the chair or on the windows.

Some of our clothes we love for their own sake, because their fabric and cut and color charm us and relate to our bodies in specific ways— because, I almost want to say, they love us back. Those wool-blend pinstriped elephant-bottom pants that held a crease so well and flopped so happily around my ankles. The green herringbone wool blazer I made with my own hands and, after the lining fell apart, I sadly gave it to my sister because the new lining was too small. The wine-red-print full-sleeved smooth rayon blouse, gathered at the shoulders to drape lightly over my chest. Many of our clothes never attain this privileged status of the beloved, perhaps because our motives for having most of them are so extrinsic: to be in style or to give our face the most flattering color, to be cost-effective, or to please others. Some we love with passion or tenderness, though, and we are sad or angry when they become damaged or go out of fashion.

Bonding

The dedication of Diane Keury's marvelous movie *Peppermint Soda,* about two teenage sisters in a Paris lycée, reads: "To my sister, who still hasn't given me back my orange sweater."

Clothes often serve for women in this society as threads in the bonds of sisterhood. Women often establish rapport with one another by remarking on their clothes, and doing so often introduces a touch of intimacy or lightness into serious or impersonal situations. When we are relaxing with one another, letting down our guard or just chatting, we often talk about clothes: what we like and what we can't stand, how difficult it is to get this size or that fabric, how we feel when we wear certain kinds of clothes or why we don't wear others. We often feel that women will understand the way clothes are important to us and that men will not. Other women will understand the anxieties, and they will understand the subtle clothing aesthetic. We take pleasure in discussing the arts of scarf tying and draping, the rules and choices of mix and match. Women often have stories to tell about their clothes—and even more often about their jewelry—that connect these items they wear to other women who once wore them, and we often bond with one another by sharing these stories.

Often we share the clothes themselves. Girls often establish relations of intimacy by exchanging clothes; sisters and roommates raid each other's closets, sometimes unpermitted; daughters' feet clomp around in their mothers' shoes. I love my sweater, and in letting you wear it you wear an aspect of me, but I do not possess it, since you can wear it. Or I go into a fit of rage upon discovering that you have gone out in my favorite blouse, for in doing so you have presumed to take my place. As the clothes flow among us, so do our identities; we do not keep hold of ourselves, but share.

In these relations my clothes are not my *property*, separate things with identifiable value that I might bring to market and thus establish with others relations of commodity exchange that would keep a strict accounting of our transactions. I do not possess my clothes; I live with them. And in relating to other women though our clothes we do not just exchange; we let or do not let each other into our lives.

Women often bond with each other by shopping for clothes. Many a lunch hour is spent with women in twos and threes circulating through Filene's Basement, picking hangers off the racks and together entering the mirror-walled common dressing room. There they chat to one another about their lives and self-images as they try on outfits—the events coming up for which they might want new clothes, their worry about getting a cut that will not emphasize the tummy. Women take care of one another in the dressing room, often knowing when to be critical and discouraging and when to encourage a risky choice or an added expense. Women buy often enough on these expeditions, but often they walk out of the store after an hour of dressing up with no parcels at all; the pleasure was in the choosing, trying, and talking, a mundane shared fantasy.

Fantasy

Women take pleasure in clothes, not just in wearing clothes, but also in looking at clothes and looking at images of women in clothes, because they encourage fantasies of transport and transformation. We experience our clothes, if Hollander is right, in the context of the images of clothes from magazines, film, TV, that draw us into situations and personalities that we can play at.

Implicitly feminist critics of media images of women have tended to assimilate all images of women in advertising into the pornographic: that such images position women as the object of a male gaze. Clothing ads are split, however (occasionally visually, as we have seen, which creates a complex and oppressive irony), between positioning women as object and women as subject. Clothing images are not always the authoritative mirror that tells who's the fairest of them all, but the entrance to a wonderland of characters and situations.

Roland Barthes analyzes the rhetoric of fashion magazines to show how they evoke such fantasy. In using Barthes's ideas to describe women's experience of clothes, I no doubt will tear them from their systematic fabric. Only a man, I think, would have presumed to present *The Fashion System* between two covers.[13] Barthes is a self-conscious theoretician of ideology, aware that no theoretician transcends the ideology he analyzes. At the close of *The Fashion System* he writes:

> There remains a word to be said about the situation of the analyst confronted with, or rather, *within* the systematic universe he has just dealt with; not only because it would be akin to bad faith to consider the analyst as alien to this universe, but also because the semiological project provides the analyst with the formal means to incorporate himself into the system he reconstitutes. (292)

Here is the sensitive theoretician, withdrawing from the authority of the transhistorical gaze precisely in relation to a universe from which he *is* alien, one that speaks a rhetoric not addressed to him. For all his reflexive attention to history and social context, Barthes never remarks on the position of the Fashion analyst as a man.

I don't know that this surprising silence makes his analysis unsatisfactory, or more unsatisfactory than it would otherwise be. Barthes offers wonderfully evocative discussions of the meaning of the rhetoric of fashion magazines that I think express the pleasure of fantasy that clothes can give women. Fashion, he says, offers women a double dream of identity and play—indeed, the invitation to play with identities (255–56). The fantasies I have as I leaf through the magazine or click the hangers on the rack, or put on the outfit in the dressing room, may be fleeting and multiple possibilities of who I might be, character types I try on, situations in which I place myself imaginatively. I see myself in wool, but in the mode of another (or several others) in transforming possibilities, all without the real-life anxiety of having to decide who I am.

> Yet, in the vision of Fashion, the ludic motif does not involve what might be called the vertigo effect: it multiplies the person without any risk of her losing herself, insofar as, for Fashion, clothing is not play but the *sign* of play. (256–57; cf. 260–61)

This fantasy of multiple and changing identities without the anxiety of losing oneself is possible because Fashion creates unreal identities in utopian places. In our clothing fantasies we are not the voyeuristic gaze

---

13. Roland Barthes, *The Fashion System,* trans. Matthew Ward and Richard Howard (New York: Hill and Wang, 1983); page references are given in the text.

before whom the narrative reel unfolds, because the pictures come to us only with the feeling of a narrative, not with narrative itself. Clothing ads, catalogs, music videos, etc., present images of situations, clips of possible narratives, but without any thread and temporality. "The doing involved in Fashion is, as it were, abortive: its subject is torn by a representation of essences at the moment of acting: to display the being of doing, without assuming its reality" (249; cf. 253, 262, 266). Fashion images are vague, open—a woman walking on a street, sitting on a patio, leaning on a bed, climbing up a rock. The variables in the formulae can be filled in with any number of concrete narrative values, and our pleasure in the fantasy of clothes is partly imagining ourselves in those possible stories, entering unreality. The very multiplicity and ambiguity of the fantasy settings evoked by clothes and by fashion imagery of these clothes contributes to such pleasure.[14]

There is a certain freedom involved in our relation to clothes, an active subjectivity not represented in the male-gaze theory. Here I draw on Sartre but not his gaze theory. In *The Psychology of Imagination*, Sartre proposes imaginary consciousness as a modality of freedom.[15] An image is consciousness of an unreal object. In imagining, I am aware of an unreal object and aware that the object is unreal. The pleasure of imagining derives from just this unreality, for the unreal object has no facticity, no givenness that constrains us, no brute physicality that freedom must deal with or face the consequences. The unreal object has no aspects not presented to me in the image, no "other side" that transcends my apprehension, as does the perceived object. The image gives the affective dimensions of a person or situation, what it feels like to be or to see them, without their material context and consequences. The freedom of the imaginary object lies in the fact that there is nothing in the object that has not been put there by imaginary consciousness.

Part of the pleasure of clothes for many of us consists of allowing ourselves to fantasize with images of women in clothes, and in desiring to become an image, unreal, to enter an intransitive, playful utopia. There are ways of looking at oneself in the mirror that do not appraise oneself before the objectifying gaze, but rather desubstantialize oneself, turn oneself into a picture, an image, an unreal identity. In such fantasy we do not seek to be somebody else. Fantasizing is not wishing, hoping, or planning; it has no future. The clothing image provides the image of situations without any situatedness; there is an infinite before and after; thus the images are open at both ends to an indefinite multitude of possible transformations.

14. See Steve Neal, "Sexual Difference in Cinema—Issues of Fantasy, Narrative, and the Look," in "Sexual Difference," ed. Robert Young, special issue of *Oxford Literary Review* 8.1–2 (1986): 123–32.

15. Jean-Paul Sartre, *The Psychology of the Imagination* (New York: Philosophical Library, 1948).

One of the privileges of femininity in rationalized instrumental culture is an aesthetic freedom, the freedom to play with shape and color on the body, to don various styles and looks, and through them exhibit and imagine unreal possibilities. Women often actively indulge in such theatrical imagining, which is largely closed to the everyday lives of men or which they live vicariously through the clothes of women. Such female imagination has liberating possibilities because it subverts, unsettles the order of respectable, functional rationality in a world where that rationality supports domination. The unreal that wells up through imagination always creates the space for a negation of what is, and thus the possibility of alternatives.[16]

In the context of patriarchal consumer capitalism, however, such liberating aspects of clothing fantasy are intertwined with oppressing moments. Perhaps such ambiguity characterizes all mass culture that succeeds in tapping desire. To the degree that feminine fashion fantasy serves as an escape from and complement to bureaucratic scientific rationality for everyone, women's bodies and imaginations are the instruments of a cultural need.

The fantasy of fashion, moreover, often has specifically exploitative and imperialist aspects. Fashion imagery may be drawn indiscriminately from many places and times, and the clothes themselves come from all over the world, usually sewn by very poorly paid women. The fashion fantasies level and dehistoricize these times and places, often contributing to the commodification of an exotic Third World at the same time that they obscure the real imperialism and exploitation that both the fantasies and realities of clothes enact.[17]

It may not be possible to extricate the liberating and valuable in women's experience of clothes from the exploitative and oppressive, but there is reason to try. We can speak of the touch and bonding that move in the shadows, hidden from the light of the phallocentric gaze, and criticize the capitalist imperialist fantasies even as we make up our own.

16. See Herbert Marcuse, *The Aesthetic Dimension* (Boston: Beacon Press, 1978).

17. See Julia Emberly, "The Fashion Apparatus and the Deconstruction of Postmodern Subjectivity," *Canadian Journal of Political and Social Theory* 11.1–2 (1987): 38–50.

5

Breasted Experience:

The Look and the Feeling

The chest, the house of the heart, is an important center of a person's being. I may locate my consciousness in my head, but my self, my existence as a solid person in the world, starts from my chest, from which I feel myself rise and radiate.[1] At least in Euro-American culture, it is to

I am grateful to Sandra Bartky, Lucy Candib, Drew Leder, and Francine Rainone for helpful comments on an earlier version of this paper. Thanks to Nancy Irons for research help.

Considering the vast explosion of women's-studies literature in the past two decades, there is an amazing absence of writing about women's experience of breasts, and some of what little there is does not arise from feminist sensibility. One wants to explain why it is that feminists have not written about breasts, even when there is a great deal of writing about sexuality, mothering, the body, and medical interactions with women's bodies. Why this silence about breasts, especially when if you tell women you are writing about women's breasted experience, they begin to pour out stories of their feelings about their breasts? Women are interested in talking about their breasted bodies and interested in listening to one another. But we almost never do it in conversation, let alone in writing.

In the darkness of my despair about women's own breast censorship, I uncovered a gold mine: Daphna Ayalah and Isaac Weinstock, *Breasts: Women Speak about Their Breasts and Their Lives* (New York: Summit Books, Simon and Schuster, 1979). This is a collection of photographs of the breasts, with accompanying experiential accounts, of fifty women. Ayalah and Weinstock asked all the women the same set of questions about growing up, sexuality, aging, birthing and nursing, and so on. Thus while each woman's story is her own and told in her own words, the stories can be compared. The authors were careful to interview different kinds of women: old, young, and middle-aged; women of color as well as white women; women who have and have not had children; lesbians as well as straight women; models; call girls; etc. This is an extraordinary book, and many of the generalizations I make about women's experience in this paper are derived from my reading of it.

1. Erwin Straus locates the self as consciousness phenomenologically in the head but mentions the chest or trunk as an important location of the self in movement and a sense

my chest, not my face, that I point when I signify myself. In Hindu philosophy of the body the chest is not the only center, but it has the integrative power among them.[2]

Structurally, a person's chest can be more or less open, more tight or relaxed, and this often expresses a person as being withdrawn from or open to the world and other people.[3] People who sit and stand straight, chest out, shoulders back, feel ready to meet the world in action, and others judge them as upright, active, open. A person stoop-shouldered, bent, closed around this center appears to be withdrawn, depressed, oppressed, or tired.

If the chest is a center of a person's sense of being-in-the-world and identity, men and women have quite different experiences of being in the world. When a woman places her hand over her heart, it lies on and between her breasts. If her chest is the house of her being, from which radiates her energy to meet the world, her breasts are also entwined with her sense of herself. How could her breasts fail to be an aspect of her identity, since they emerge for her at that time in her life when her sense of her own independent identity is finally formed?[4] For many women, if not all, breasts are an important component of body self-image; a woman may love them or dislike them, but she is rarely neutral.

In our culture that focuses to the extreme on breasts, a woman, especially in those adolescent years but also through the rest of her life, often feels herself judged and evaluated according to the size and contours of her breasts, and indeed she often is. For her and for others, her breasts are the daily visible and tangible signifier of her womanliness, and her experience is as variable as the size and shape of breasts themselves. A woman's chest, much more than a man's, is in question in this society, up for judgment, and whatever the verdict, she has not escaped the condition of being problematic.

In this essay I explore some aspects of the cultural construction of breasts in our male-dominated society and seek a positive women's voice for breasted experience. First I discuss the dominant culture's objectification of breasts. Relying on Irigaray's suggestive ideas about women's sexuality and an alternative metaphysics not constructed around the

---

of immediate affective experience of the self in the world; see "The Forms of Spatiality," in *Phenomenological Psychology* (New York: Basic Books, 1966), 22–27. Seymour Fischer finds heart awareness an important variable in body consciousness; see *Body Experience in Fantasy and Behavior* (New York: Appleton-Century Crofts, 1970), especially chapter 27.

2. See Barbara Ann Brenna, *Hands of Light* (New York: Bantam Books, 1987), 132–35.

3. One of the women interviewed by Ayalah and Weinstock relies on the ideas of yoga to suggest that her sense of herself and her relation to her breasts influenced her entire being in the world as either tight or relaxed in the chest.

4. Many of the women interviewed by Ayalah and Weinstock trace significant aspects of their adult personalities to their adolescent experiences of breast development.

concept of object, I express an experience of breast movement and sensitivity from the point of view of the female subject. I ask how women's breasts might be experienced in the absence of an objectifying male gaze, and I discuss how breasts are a scandal for patriarchy because they disrupt the border between motherhood and sexuality. Finally, I return to the question of objectification by reflecting on a woman's encounter with the surgeon's knife at her breast.

I. Breasts as Objects

I used to stand before the mirror with two Spalding balls under my shirt, longing to be a grown woman with the big tits of Marilyn Monroe and Elizabeth Taylor. They are called boobs, knockers, knobs; they are toys to be grabbed, squeezed, handled. In the total scheme of the objectification of women, breasts are the primary things.

A fetish is an object that stands in for the phallus—the phallus as the one and only measure and symbol of desire, the representation of sexuality. This culture fetishizes breasts. Breasts are the symbol of feminine sexuality, so the "best" breasts are like the phallus: high, hard, and pointy. Thirty years ago it was de rigueur to encase them in wire, rubber, and elastic armor that lifted them and pointed them straight out. Today fashion has loosened up a bit, but the foundational contours remain; some figures are better than others, and the ideal breasts look like a Barbie's.

We experience our objectification as a function of the look of the other, the male gaze that judges and dominates from afar.[5] We experience our position as established and fixed by a subject who stands afar, who has looked and made his judgment before he ever makes me aware of his admiration or disgust. When a girl blossoms into adolescence and sallies forth, chest out boldly to the world, she experiences herself as being looked at in a different way than before. People, especially boys, notice her breasts or her lack of them; they may stare at her chest and remark on her. If her energy radiates from her chest, she too often finds the rays deflected by the gaze that positions her from outside, evaluating her according to standards that she had no part in establishing and that remain outside her control. She may enjoy the attention and learn to draw the gaze to her bosom with a sense of sexual power. She may loathe and fear the gaze that fixes her in shock or mockery, and she may take pains to hide her chest behind baggy clothes and bowed shoulders. She may for the most part ignore the objectifying gaze, retaining never-

5. See Sandra Bartky, "On Psychological Oppression," in *Philosophy and Women*, ed. Sharon Bishop and Marjorie Weinzweig (Belmont, Calif.: Wadsworth Publishing Co., 1979), 33–41; and E. Ann Kaplan, "Is the Gaze Male?" in *Women and Film: Both Sides of the Camera* (New York: Methuen, 1983), 23–35.

theless edges of ambiguity and uncertainty about her body. The way women respond to the evaluating gaze on their chests is surely as variable as the size and character of the breasts themselves, but few women in our society escape having to take some attitude toward the potentially objectifying regard of the Other on her breasts.

Being does not have to be conceptualized in terms of objects. The ontology of objects is a specifically Western construct that can be traced to the Platonic-Aristotelian doctrines of reason and substance but has its more recent and continuous relation to modern conceptualization beginning in Cartesian egology.[6]

So what is an object? The correlate and construct of a self-identical subject, outside nature, detached and originary. The subject, outside all objects, fixes the object in its gaze, mastering and knowing it with unambiguous certainty. The object is determinate and definable, with clear boundaries, separated from other objects. It is what it is, does not derive its being from its surrounding context, and does not change its nature from one context to another.[7] The object is passive, inert matter, having no self-moving capacity, its movement all externally and mechanically caused. The object is what can be handled, manipulated, constructed, built up and broken down, with clear accountability of matter gained and lost. The essential properties of the object are thus all quantities: extension, location, velocity, weight.

Practically, the object is property. The object is what is had, owned, with clear boundaries of right. Objects are precisely countable, so that owners can keep accounts of their property. They attain their full weight as commodities, objects for exchange on the market, in a circulation of power where precise accounting of equivalents and contract is the source and locus of power.[8]

Breasts are the most visible sign of a woman's femininity, the signal of her sexuality. In phallocentric culture sexuality is oriented to the man and modeled on male desire. Capitalist, patriarchal American media-dominated culture objectifies breasts before a distancing gaze that freezes and masters. The fetishized breasts are valued as objects, things; they must be solid, easy to handle. Subject to the logic of phallocratic domination of nature, their value, her value as a sexual being, appears in their measurement. Is she a B-cup or a C-cup? Even when sleek athletic

6. See Martin Heidegger, *What Is a Thing?*, trans. W. B. Barton and Vera Deutsch (Chicago: Henry Regnery Co., 1967).

7. Carolyn Merchant takes "context independence" to be one of the defining characteristics of the materialist mechanical view of nature, which triumphed over an organic view of nature in the seventeenth century. See *The Death of Nature* (Berkeley: University of California Press, 1980), chapter 9.

8. I am thinking of Irigaray's attention to the property and commodity basis of objecthood; "Women on the Market," in *This Sex Which Is Not One* (Ithaca, N.Y.: Cornell University Press, 1985), 170–91.

fashions were current, breasts were often still prominent. And today the news is that the big bosom is back.[9]

What matters is the look of them, how they measure up before the normalizing gaze. There is one perfect shape and proportion for breasts: round, sitting high on the chest, large but not bulbous, with the look of firmness. The norm is contradictory, of course. If breasts are large, their weight will tend to pull them down; if they are large and round, they will tend to be floppy rather than firm. In its image of the solid object this norm suppresses the fleshy materiality of breasts, this least muscular, softest body part.[10] Magazines construct and parade these perfect breasts. They present tricks for how to acquire and maintain our own— through rigorous exercise or $50 creams (neither of which generally produces the desired effect), or tricks of what to wear and how to stand so as to appear to have them.

Like most norms of femininity, the normalized breast hardly describes an "average" around which real women's breasts cluster. It is an ideal that only very few women's bodies even approximate; given the power of the dominant media, however, the norm is ubiquitous, and most of us internalize it to some degree, making our self-abnegation almost inevitable.[11] Even those women whose breasts do approximate the ideal can do so only for a short period in their lives. It is a pubescent norm from which most women deviate increasingly with each passing year. Whatever her age, if she has given birth her breasts sag away from the ideal; perhaps they have lost some of their prepartum fullness and roundness, and her nipples protrude. Whether a woman is a mother or not, gravity does its work, quickly defining a woman's body as old because it is no longer adolescent. The truly old woman's body thereby moves beyond the pale. Flat, wrinkled, greatly sagging, the old woman's breasts signify for the ageist dominant culture a woman no longer useful for sex or reproduction, a woman used up. Yet there is nothing natural about such a decline in value. Some other cultures venerate the woman with wrinkled, sagging breasts; they are signs of much mothering and the wisdom

9. "Forget Hemlines: The Bosomy Look Is Big Fashion News," *Wall Street Journal* (December 2, 1988); Jeremy Weir Alderson, "Breast Frenzy," *Self* (December 1988), 83–89.

10. Susan Bordo suggests that achievement society takes Western culture's denial of the body and fleshiness to extremes, projecting norms of tightness and hardness for all bodies. This is the particular contemporary cultural meaning of the demand for slenderness in both men and women, but especially in women. Bordo does not mention breasts specifically in this discussion, but clearly this analysis helps us understand why media norms of breasts make this impossible demand for a "firm" breast. See Bordo, "Reading the Slender Body," in *Body/Politics: Women and the Discourses of Science,* ed. Mary Jacobus, Evelyn Fox Keller, and Sally Shuttleworth (New York: Routledge Chapman and Hall, 1989), 83–112.

11. See Sandra Bartky, "Foucault, Femininity, and the Modernization of Patriarchal Power," in *Feminism and Foucault: Reflections on Resistance,* ed. Irene Diamond and Lee Quinby (Boston: Northeastern University Press, 1988).

of experience. From their point of view an obsession with firm, high breasts would be considered to express a desire to be immature.[12]

II. Woman-Centered Meaning

However alienated male-dominated culture makes us from our bodies, however much it gives us instruments of self-hatred and oppression, still our bodies are ourselves. We move and act in this flesh and these sinews and live our pleasures and pains in our bodies. If we love ourselves at all, we love our bodies. And many women identify their breasts as themselves, living their embodied experience at some distance from the hard norms of the magazine gaze. However much the patriarchy may wish us to, we do not live our breasts only as the objects of male desire, but as our own, the sproutings of a specifically female desire.

But male-dominated society tends not to think of a woman's breasts as hers. Woman is a natural territory; her breasts belong to others—her husband, her lover, her baby. It's hard to imagine a woman's breasts as her own, from her own point of view, to imagine their value apart from measurement and exchange. I do not pretend to discover a woman-centered breast experience. My conceptualization of a woman-centered experience of breasts is a construction, an imagining, that I will locate in the theme of a desubstantialization. If we move from the male gaze in which woman is the Other, the object, solid and definite, to imagine the woman's point of view, the breasted body becomes blurry, mushy, indefinite, multiple, and without clear identity. The project of giving voice to a specifically female desire is an important one for feminism, I think, but it does not exist somewhere underlying phallocentric desire as a pure and authentic female core. It must be made up, and its making is itself a political strategy.

A metaphysic generated from feminine desire, Luce Irigaray suggests, might conceptualize being as fluid rather than as solid substances, or things. Fluids, unlike objects, have no definite borders; they are unstable, which does not mean they are without pattern. Fluids surge and move, and a metaphysic that thinks being as fluid would tend to privilege the living, moving, pulsing over the inert dead matter of the Cartesian worldview.[13] This is, simply, a process metaphysics, in which movement and energy is ontologically prior to thingness and

12. Comment of Fran, in Ayalah and Weinstock, *Breasts*, 136.

13. Luce Irigaray, "The Mechanics of Fluids," in *This Sex Which Is Not One*, trans. Catherine Porter (Ithaca, N.Y.: Cornell University Press, 1985). Compare Jeffner Allen, "An Introduction to Patriarchal Existentialism," in *The Thinking Muse: Feminism and Modern French Philosophy*, ed. Allen and Iris Marion Young, (Bloomington: Indiana University Press, 1989), especially 81–83; and Allen, "The Naming of Difference: Truth and Female Friendship," in *Lesbian Philosophy: Explorations* (Palo Alto, Calif.: Institute of Lesbian Studies), especially 104–6.

the nature of things takes its being from the organic context in which they are embedded.

I know that I am not making a popular move when I appeal to a metaphysics of fluids in constructing a woman-centered experiential voice. Irigaray's idea that women are specially linked to the aqueous is the subject of much ridicule, which sometimes makes me wonder whether there is a fear going on even among feminists, a fear of the loss of "something to hold on to." As far as I am concerned, it is not at all a matter of making a claim about women's biology or bodies, for conceptualized in a radically different way, men's bodies are at least as fluid as women's. The point is that a metaphysics of self-identical objects has clear ties to the domination of nature in which the domination of women has been implicated because culture has projected onto us identification with the abject body. It makes a difference how we think about beings in the world, and we can make choices about it that seem to have political implications. A process metaphysics, a metaphysics of fluids, where the being of any location depends on its surrounding and where we cannot delineate clearly what is inside and outside, is a better way to think about the world from an ecological point of view. Inasmuch as women's oppression derives to a significant degree from literal and figurative objectification, I am suggesting, subverting the metaphysics of objects can also be liberating for women.

An epistemology spoken from a feminine subjectivity might privilege touch rather than sight.[14] Unlike the gazer, the one who touches cannot be at a distance from what she knows in touch. While active, touch is simultaneously passive. The gazer can see without being seen, and as Foucault has pointed out, this possibility is a major source of modern disciplinary powers. But the toucher cannot touch the happenings she knows without also being touched by them. The act of touching is also necessarily an experience of being touched; touching cannot happen without a touching back, and thus there can be no clear opposition between subject and object, because the two positions constantly turn into each other. With touch as the model of experience of the world, moreover, dividing the world into objects with definite borders makes much less sense. Touch differentiates—indeed, takes pleasure in—the subtlest difference of texture or softness, but inasmuch as the things touched also touch each other, the borders are not firm. Without a place outside the world to stand, touching also steps down from the clouds of universalism; a knowledge that is in touch with things knows them in their concreteness, and not merely as the instances of general laws imagined by a mathematical mind.

14. The ontology of the later Merleau-Ponty is the closest there is to an epistemology based on touch. See "The Intertwining—The Chiasm," in *The Visible and the Invisible*, trans. Alphonso Lingis (Evanston, Ill.: Northwestern University Press, 1968); Irigaray comments on this text in *Ethique de la Différence Sexuelle* (Paris: Editions de Minuit, 1984), 143–72.

From the position of the female subject, what matters most about her breasts is their feeling and sensitivity rather than how they look. The size or age of her breasts does not matter for the sensitivity of her nipples, which often seem to have a will of their own, popping out at the smallest touch, change of temperature, or embarrassment. For many women breasts are a multiple and fluid zone of deep pleasure quite independent of intercourse, though sometimes not independent of orgasm. For a phallic sexuality this is a scandal. A woman does not always experience the feeling of her breasts positively; if they are large she often feels them pulling uncomfortably on her neck and back. Her breasts also give a feeling of bodily change. She often experiences literal growing pains as her body moves from girl to woman. When she becomes pregnant, she often knows this first through changes in the feeling of her breasts, and many women have breast sensitivity associated with menstruation. When she is lactating, she feels the pull of milk letting down, which may be activated by a touch, or a cry, or even a thought.

Breasts stand as a primary badge of sexual specificity, the irreducibility of sexual difference to a common measure. Yet phallocentric sexuality tries to orient the sexual around its one and only sexual object. Active sexuality is the erect penis, which rises in its potency and penetrates the passive female receptacle. Intercourse is the true sex act, and nonphallic pleasures are either deviant or preparatory. Touching and kissing the breasts is "foreplay," a pleasant prelude after which the couple goes on to the real Thing. But in her own experience of sexuality there is a scandal: she can derive the deepest pleasure from these dark points on her chest, a pleasure maybe greater than he can provide in intercourse. Phallocentric heterosexist norms try to construct female sexuality as simply a complement to male sexuality, its mirror, or the hole—lack that he fills. But her pleasure is different, a pleasure he can only imagine. To the degree that he can experience anything like it, it's only a faint copy of female potency. Imagine constructing the model of sexual power in breasts rather than penises. Men's nipples would have to be constructed as puny copies, just as men have constructed women's clitorises as puny copies of the penis. Of course this all presumes constructing sexuality by a common measure. Phallocentered construction of sexuality denies and represses the sensitivity of breasts.

> For what male "organ" will be set forth in derision like the clitoris?—that penis too tiny for comparison to entail anything but total devaluation, complete decathexization. Of course, there are the breasts. But they are to be classed among the secondary, or so-called secondary, characteristics. Which no doubt justifies the fact that there is so little questioning of the effects of breast atrophy in the male. Wrongly, of course.[15]

15. Luce Irigaray, *Speculum of the Other Woman* (Ithaca, N.Y.: Cornell University Press, 1985), 22–23.

Both gay men and lesbians often defy this niggardly attitude toward nipple sexuality. Gay men often explore the erotic possibilities of one another's breasts, and lesbians often derive a particular pleasure from the mutual touching of breasts.

The breasts, for many women, are places of independent pleasure. Deconstructing the hierarchical privilege of heterosexual complementarity, giving equal value to feelings of the breast diffuses the identity of sex. Our sex is not one but, as Irigaray says, plural and heterogeneous; we have sex organs all over our bodies, in many places, and perhaps none is privileged. We experience eroticism as flowing, multiple, unlocatable, not identical or in the same place.[16]

The brassiere functions partly as a barrier to touch. Without it, every movement can produce a stroking of cloth across her nipples, which she may find pleasurable or distracting, as the case may be. But if the chest is a center of a person's being-in-the-world, her mode of being surely differs depending on whether her chest is open to touch, moving in the world, or confined and bordered.

Without a bra, a woman's breasts are also deobjectified, desubstantialized. Without a bra, most women's breasts do not have the high, hard, pointy look that phallic culture posits as the norm. They droop and sag and gather their bulk at the bottom. Without a bra, the fluid being of breasts is more apparent. They are not objects with one definite shape but radically change their shape with body position and movements. Hand over the head, lying on one's back or side, bending over in front—all produce very different breast shapes. Many women's breasts are much more like a fluid than a solid; in movement, they sway, jiggle, bounce, ripple even when the movement is small.

Women never gathered in a ritual of bra burning, but the image stuck. We did, though, shed the bra—hundreds of thousands, millions of us. I was no feminist when, young and impetuous, I shoved the bras back in the drawer and dared to step outside with nothing on my chest but a shirt. It was an ambiguous time in 1969. I had a wondrous sense of freedom and a little bit of defiance. I never threw the bras away; they were there to be worn on occasions when propriety and delicacy required them. Why was burning the bra the ultimate image of the radical subversion of the male-dominated order?[17] Because unbound breasts show their fluid and changing shape; they do not remain the firm and stable objects that phallocratic fetishism desires. Because unbound breasts make a mockery of the ideal of a "perfect" breast. The bra normalizes the breasts, lifting and curving the breasts to approximate the one and only breast ideal.

16. See "This Sex Which Is Not One," in the volume of the same title, 23–33.

17. Susan Brownmiller suggests that women going braless evoke shock and anger because men implicitly think that they own breasts and that only they should remove bras. See *Femininity* (New York: Linden Press, Simon and Schuster, 1984), 45.

But most scandalous of all, without a bra, the nipples show. Nipples are indecent. Cleavage is good—the more, the better—and we can wear bikinis that barely cover the breasts, but the nipples must be carefully obscured. Even go-go dancers wear pasties. Nipples are no-nos, for they show the breasts to be active and independent zones of sensitivity and eroticism.

What would a positive experience of ourselves as breasted be in the absence of the male gaze? There are times and places where women in American society can experience hints of such an experience. In lesbian-dominated women's spaces where women can be confident that the male gaze will not invade, I have found a unique experience of women's bodies. In such women's spaces women frequently walk around, do their chores, sit around and chat, naked from the waist up. Such a context deobjectifies the breasts. A woman not used to such a womanspace might at first stare, treating the breasts as objects. But the everydayness, the constant engagement of this bare-breasted body in activity dereifies them. But they do not thereby recede, as they might when clothed. On the contrary, women's breasts are interesting. In a womanspace with many women walking around bare-breasted, the variability and individuality of breasts becomes salient. I would like to say that in a womanspace, without the male gaze, a woman's breasts become almost like part of her face. Like her nose or her mouth, a woman's breasts are distinctive, one sign by which one might recognize her. Like her mouth or her eyes, their aspect changes with her movement and her mood; the movement of her breasts is part of the expressiveness of her body.

III. Motherhood and Sexuality

The woman is young and timeless, clothed in blue, a scarf over her head, which is bowed over the child at her breast, discreetly exposed by her hand that draws aside her covering, and the baby's hand rests on the round flesh. This is the Christian image of peace and wholeness, the perfect circle of generation.[18] With hundreds of variations, from Florentine frescoes to the covers of dozens of books at Borders, this is a primary image of power, female power. To be purity and goodness itself, the origin of life, the source to which the living man owes his substance—this is an awesome power. For centuries identification with that power has bonded women to the patriarchal order, and while today its

18. For an interesting discussion of the meaning of this image in the Renaissance, see Margaret R. Miles, "The Virgin's One Bare Breast: Female Nudity and Religious Meaning in Tuscan Early Renaissance Culture," in *The Female Body in Western Culture*, ed. Susan Rubin Suleiman (Cambridge, Mass.: Harvard University Press, 1985), 193–208.

seductive hold on us is loosening, it still provides women a unique position with which to identify.[19]

But it is bought at the cost of sexuality. The Madonna must be a virgin mother. The logic of identity that constructs being as objects also constructs categories whose borders are clear and exclusive: essence/accident, mind/body, good/bad. The logic of such oppositions includes everything, and they exclude one another by defining the other as excluded by their oneness or essence. In Western logic woman is the seat of such oppositional categorization, for patriarchal logic defines an exclusive border between motherhood and sexuality. The virgin or the whore, the pure or the impure, the nurturer or the seducer is either asexual mother or sexualized beauty, but one precludes the other.

Thus psychoanalysis, for example, regards motherhood as a substitute for sexuality. The woman desires a child as her stand-in for the penis, as her way of appropriating the forbidden father. Happily, her desires are passive, and she devotes herself completely to giving. Helene Deutch, for example, identifies normal motherhood with feminine masochism; the true woman is one who gets pleasure from self-sacrifice, the abnegation of pleasure.[20]

Barbara Sichtermann discusses this separation of motherhood and sexuality:

> Basically, women were only admitted to the realm of sexuality as guests to be dispatched off towards their "true" vocation as agents of reproduction. And reproduction was something which happened outside the realm of pleasure, it was God's curse on Eve. Women have to cover the longest part of the road to reproduction with their bodies and yet in this way they became beings existing outside sexuality, outside the delights of orgiastic release, they became asexual mothers, the bearers of unborn children and the bearers of suffering. Breast-feeding too was of course part of this tamed, pleasureless, domesticated world of "maternal duties."[21]

The gender logic of Western culture still operative in our society depends on this border between motherhood and sexuality. In our lives and desires it keeps women divided from ourselves, in having to identify with one or another image of womanly power—the nurturing, competent, selfless mother, always sacrificing, the soul of goodness; or the fiery, voluptuous vamp with the power of attraction, leading victims down

19. Kristeva, "Sabat Mater" in Suleiman, *The Female Body in Western Culture;* see also Susan Rubin Suleiman, "Writing and Motherhood," in *The (M)other Tongue: Essays in Feminist Psychoanalytical Interpretation,* ed. Shirley Nelson Garner, Claire Kahane, and Madelon Sprengnether (Ithaca, N. Y.: Cornell University Press, 1985), 352–77.

20. Helene Deutch, *Psychology of Women,* vol. 2, cited in Suleiman, *The Female Body in Western Culture,* 356.

21. Barbara Sichtermann, "The Lost Eroticism of the Breasts," in *Femininity: The Politics of the Personal* (Minneapolis: University of Minnesota Press), 57.

the road of pleasure, sin, and danger. Why does the gender code require such a division between motherhood and sexuality? This is perhaps one of the most overdetermined dichotomies in our culture; accordingly, I have several answers to this question.

In the terms in which Kristeva puts it, for both sexes entrance into the symbolic requires repressing the original jouissance of attachment to the mother's body.[22] A baby's body is saturated with feeling, which it experiences as undifferentiated from the caretaking body it touches; repeated pains break the connection, but its pleasure is global and multiple. Eroticism must be made compatible with civilization, submission to the law, and thus adult experience of sexuality must repress memory of this infantile jouissance. Adult meanings of eroticism thus must be divorced from mothers. Even though for both genders, sexual desire and pleasure are informed by presymbolic jouissance, this must be repressed in the particular cultural configuration that emphasizes rationality as unity, identity, thematic reference.

The dichotomy of motherhood and sexuality, I said, maps onto a dichotomy of good/bad, pure/impure. These dichotomies play in with the repression of the body itself. One kind of attachment, love, is "good" because it is entirely defleshed, spiritual. Mother love and the love of the child for the mother represent the perfection of love—eroticism entirely sublimated. Fleshy eroticism, on the other hand, goes on the other side of the border, where lies the despised body, bad, impure. The separation of motherhood and sexuality thus instantiates the culture's denial of the body and the consignment of fleshy desires to fearful temptation.

The incest taboo also accounts for the separation, as even classical Freudianism suggests. Such patriarchal propriety in women's bodies may be unconsciously motivated by a desire to gain control over himself by mastering the mother. But sexual desire for the mother must be repressed in order to prepare the man for separation from femininity and entrance into the male bond through which women are exchanged. As Dorothy Dinnerstein suggests, repression of desire for the mother is also necessary to defend his masculinity against the vulnerability and mortality of the human condition.[23]

Now to some explanations more directly related to masculinist interests. By separating motherhood and sexuality, men/husbands do not have to perceive themselves as sharing female sexuality with their children. The oedipal triangle has three nodes, and there are issues for the father as well as the child. The Law of the Father establishes ownership

22. See, for example, Kristeva, "The Father, Love, and Banishment," in *Desire in Language* (New York: Columbia University Press, 1980), 148–58.

23. Dorothy Dinnerstein, *The Mermaid and the Minotaur* (New York: Harper and Row, 1977), chapter 6.

of female sexuality. The satisfactions of masculinity are in having her to minister to his ego, the complement to his desire; he has private ownership of her affections.[24] Her function as either the phallic object or the mirror to his desire cannot be maintained if her mother love is the same as her sex love. They need to be projected onto different people or thought of as different kinds of relationships.

The separation between motherhood and sexuality within a woman's own existence seems to ensure her dependence on the man for pleasure. If motherhood is sexual, the mother and child can be a circuit of pleasure for the mother, then the man may lose her allegiance and attachment. So she must repress her eroticism with her child, and with it her own particular return to her repressed experience of jouissance, and maintain a specific connection with the man. If she experiences motherhood as sexual, she may find him dispensable. This shows another reason for repressing a connection between motherhood and sexuality in women. A woman's infantile eroticism in relation to her mother must be broken in order to awaken in her a heterosexual desire. Lesbian mothering may be the ultimate affront to masculine privilege, for it involves a double displacement of an erotic relation of a woman to a man.

Without the separation of motherhood and sexuality, finally, there can be no image of a love that is all give and no take. I take this as perhaps the most important point. The ideal mother defines herself as giver and feeder, taking her existence and sense of purpose entirely from giving. Such a mother-giver establishes a foundation for the self-absorbed ego, the subject of modern philosophy, which many feminists have uncovered as being happily male.[25] Thus motherhood must be separated from her sexuality, her desire. She cannot have sexual desire in her mothering because this is a need, a want, and she cannot be perfectly giving if she is wanting or selfish.

The sex/gender system as we know it, then, enacts a border between motherhood and sexuality. Woman is both, essentially—the repository of the body, the flesh that he desires, owns and masters, tames and controls; and the nurturing source of his life and ego. Both are necessary functions, bolstering male ego, which cannot be served if they are together—hence the border, their reification into the hierarchical opposition of good/bad, pure/impure. The separation often splits mothers; it is

24. Carole Pateman makes a forceful and scholarly argument that modern patriarchal ideology implicitly supports a view of men as owning women through the marriage contract and the prostitution contract. See *The Sexual Contract* (Stanford, Calif.: Stanford University Press, 1988), chapters 5–7.

25. See Naomi Schemen, "Individualism and the Objects of Psychology," and Jane Flax, "Political Philosophy and the Patriarchal Unconscious: A Psychoanalytic Perspective on Epistemology and Metaphysics," both in *Discovering Reality: Feminist Perspectives on Epistemology, Metaphysics, Methodology and Philosophy of Science,* ed. Sandra Harding and Merrill B. Hintikka (Dordrecht: D. Reidel Publishing Co., 1983).

in our bodies that the sacrifice that creates and sustains patriarchy is reenacted repeatedly.[26] Freedom for women involves dissolving this separation.

The border between motherhood and sexuality is lived out in the way women experience their breasts and in the cultural marking of breasts. To be understood as sexual, the feeding function of the breasts must be suppressed, and when the breasts are nursing they are desexualized. A great many women in this culture that fetishizes breasts are reluctant to breast-feed because they perceive that they will lose their sexuality. They believe that nursing will alter their breasts and make them ugly and undesirable. They fear that their men will find their milky breasts unattractive or will be jealous of the babies who take their bodies. Some women who decide to breast-feed report that they themselves are uninterested in sex during that period or that they cease to think of their breasts as sexual and to take sexual pleasure in their breasts while they are nursing.[27]

Breasts are a scandal because they shatter the border between motherhood and sexuality. Nipples are taboo because they are quite literally, physically, functionally undecidable in the split between motherhood and sexuality. One of the most subversive things feminism can do is affirm this undecidability of motherhood and sexuality.

When I began nursing I sat stiff in a chair, holding the baby in the crook of my arm, discreetly lifting my shirt and draping it over my breast. This was mother work, and I was efficient and gentle, and watched the time. After some weeks, drowsy during the morning feeding, I went to bed with my baby. I felt that I had crossed a forbidden river as I moved toward the bed, stretched her legs out alongside my reclining torso, me lying on my side like a cat or a mare while my baby suckled. This was pleasure, not work. I lay there as she made love to me, snuggling her legs up to my stomach, her hand stroking my breast, my chest. She lay

26. Ann Ferguson discusses a "double consciousness" created in mothers by the enactment of this split between motherhood and sexuality in their lives; see "On Conceiving Motherhood and Sexuality: A Feminist Materialist Approach," in *Mothering: Essays in Feminist Theory,* ed. Joyce Trebilcot (Totowa, N.J.: Rowman and Allenheld, 1983), especially 162–65. Kristeva talks about women as essentially sacrificed in the male social contract. See, for example, "Women's Time," Alice Jardine and Harry Blake, trans., *Signs: Journal of Women in Culture and Society* 7.1 (Autumn 1981), 13–59.

27. Women's attitudes toward breast-feeding and its relation or lack of it to sexuality are, of course, extremely variable. Teenage mothers, for example, have a great deal more difficulty than do older mothers with the idea of breast-feeding, probably because they are more insecure about their sexuality. See Lorie Yoos, "Developmental Issues and the Choice of Feeding Method of Adolescent Mothers," *Journal of Obstetrical and Gynecological Nursing* (January–February 1985), 68–72. Ayalah and Weinstock interview many mothers specifically about their attitudes toward and experiences in breast-feeding. The reactions are quite variable, from women who report the experience of breast-feeding as being nearly religious to women who say they could not consider doing it because they thought it was too disgusting.

between me and my lover, and she and I were a couple. From then on I looked forward with happy pleasure to our early-morning intercourse, she sucking at my hard fullness, relieving and warming me, while her father slept.

I do not mean to romanticize motherhood, to suggest by means of a perverted feminist reversal that through motherhood, women achieve their access to the divine or the moral. Nor would I deny that there are dangers in the eroticization of mothering—dangers to children, in particular, that derive from the facts of power more than sexuality. Mothers must not abuse their power, but this has always been so. Certainly I do not wish to suggest that all women should be mothers; there is much that would be trying about mothering even under ideal circumstances, and certainly there is much about it in our society that is oppressive. But in the experience of many women we may find some means for challenging patriarchal divisions that seek to repress and silence those experiences.

Some feminist discourse criticizes the sexual objectification of women and proposes that feminists dissociate women from the fetishized female body and promote instead an image of women as representing caring, nurturing, soothing values. American cultural feminism exhibits this move: women will retreat from and reject patriarchal definitions of sexuality and project motherly images of strength, wisdom, and nurturance as feminist virtues, or even redefine the erotic as like mother love.[28] Much French feminism is also in danger of a mere revaluation that retains this dichotomy between motherhood and sexuality, rather than exploding received definitions of motherhood.[29]

A more radical move would be to shatter the border between motherhood and sexuality. What can this mean? Most concretely, it means pointing to and celebrating breast-feeding as a sexual interaction for both the mother and the infant.[30] It means letting women speak in public about the pleasure that many report they derive from their babies and about the fact that weaning is often a loss for them.[31] But there is a more general meaning to shattering the border, which applies even to mothers

28. In the feminist sexuality debate, some sexual libertarians accuse those with whom they debate of holding a kind of desexualized, spiritualized, or nurturant eroticism. See Ann Ferguson, *Blood at the Root* (London: Pandora Press, 1989), chapter 7, for an important discussion of the way out of this debate. I do not here wish to take sides in this debate, which I hope is more or less over. The debate certainly reveals, however, the strength of a good/bad opposition around eroticism as it plays out in our culture. Ferguson suggests that the debate sets up an opposition between pleasure and love, which is an unhelpful polarity.

29. See Donma Stanton, "Difference on Trial: A Critique of the Maternal Metaphor in Cixous, Irigaray, and Kristeva," in Allen and Young, *The Thinking Muse.*

30. This is the main point of Sichtermann's "Lost Eroticism of the Breasts."

31. See Harriet H. Myers and Paul S. Siegel, "Motivation to Breastfeed: A Fit to the Opponent-Process Theory?" *Journal of Personality and Social Psychology* 49.1 (July 1985): 188–93.

who do not breast-feed and even to women who are not mothers. Crash-
ing the border means affirming that women, all women, can "have it
all." It means creating and affirming a kind of love in which a woman
does not have to choose between pursuing her own selfish, insatiable
desire and giving pleasure and sustenance to another close to her, a nurturance that gives and also takes for itself. Whether they are mothers or
not, women today are still too often cast in the nurturant role, whatever
their occupation or location. This nurturant position is that of the self-
sacrificing listener and stroker, the one who turns toward the wounded,
needful ego that uses her as mirror and enclosing womb, giving nothing
to her, and she of course is polite enough not to ask. As feminists we
should affirm the value of nurturing; an ethic of caring does indeed hold
promise for a more human justice, and political values guided by such
an ethic would change the character of the public for the better. But we
must also insist that nurturers need, that love is partly selfish, and that
a woman deserves her own irreducible pleasures.

IV. The Knife at the Breast

Masculinist culture, I have said, constructs breasts as objects, the correlate of the objectifying male gaze. What matters most is how breasts
look and measure, their conformity with a norm, the impossible aesthetic of round, large, and high on the chest. These objectifying constructions are clearly manifest in surgical medicine's angle on the breast.

Plastic surgeons cut into breasts more than into any other body part.
In 1986 alone women reportedly had a total of 159,300 enlargements,
lifts, or reductions; 93,500 of these were enlargements.[32] Breast surgery
is not something to be taken lightly. For one thing, it is expensive. An
augmentation operation may cost anywhere from $3,000 to $6,000.
One writer suggests that breast enlargement has become another sign of
yuppie success in the consumer culture, where what you can buy is a
major measure of your worth.[33] Like other operations, moreover, breast
enlargements and reductions can cause considerable pain and bruising,
and sometimes require special drains and incisions; often the healing
process takes many months.[34] In some cases sensitivity in the breasts
may be temporarily or permanently reduced.

---

32. Jeremy Weir Alderson, "Breast Obsessed," *Self* (December 1988); also "Whose
Breasts Are They, Anyway?" *Mademoiselle* (August 1987), 70.

33. Alderson, "Breast Obsessed."

34. Ayalah and Weinstock report on a woman who had breast-reduction surgery that
caused pain, bruising, and, for a while, no feeling in the breasts (see 52). Another woman
gives an excruciating account of her experience with breast enlargement and its pain and
loss of feeling (110–11).

Popular culture much touts the possibilities of the plastic body.[35] You can have the body you choose, ads and magazine articles suggest; you don't have to be stuck with your given body. But these messages do not give us a choice of the variety of real possible bodies. No, the idea that we can have the body we choose is that we can choose to take the body we have—with its particular lumps, folds, bone structure, and round spots—and make it over into the one and only good body, the slender but voluptuous glamour body that haunts the look, the scene, the pictures viewed. So cosmetic surgery, once the hidden instrument of assimilation or youthfulness, now is openly discussed by doctors, patients, and celebrities. There is little choice of what body to value; the normalized body is reinforced by the transformative possibilities of medical technology. Why wouldn't a woman "choose" perfect breasts when the opportunity is there?

Though this operation sometimes results in some temporary or permanent loss of feeling and sometimes leaves prominent scars, breast reduction appears to carry fewer risks than does augmentation. Some women with very large breasts experience back or neck pain, and some women even risk debilitating damage to their posture and bone structure from very large breasts. Breast-reduction surgery is much less commonly performed than is augmentation. As a feminist, I am less uncomfortable with reduction than with augmentation because it appears that most women who have reductions do so for the sake of comfort or because there are medical indications that they risk back damage. I find augmentation more questionable in its implications.

A phallocentric construction of breasts, I suggested earlier, privileges the look, their shape and size and "normalcy." From a woman's point of view, their feeling, sensitivity, and erogenous possibilities are more important—factors unrelated to their size or the way they look. Breast augmentation has as its purpose only looks: to enhance a woman's presentation on stage or in magazine photos, to make her look more normal or sexy, to better fill out the look of her clothes. Few people are fooled by the feel of an enlarged breast—it is firmer and harder than one made only of flesh. As for the woman's own feeling, the healing time can be long and painful, and in a few women the pain is never quite gone. And while she may look sexier, she may lose some sexual sensitivity in her breasts as a result of the surgery.

I also said that phallocentric culture objectifies the breasts. Breast augmentation often actually makes women's breasts more like objects.

35. Susan Bordo argues persuasively that twentieth-century advanced capitalist consumer culture has gone beyond the Cartesian mechanistic metaphysics and its correlate mechanical understanding of the body, to a view of the body as plastic, moldable, completely transformable and controllable, according to a variety of possibilities. See "Material Girl: Postmodern Culture, Gender, and the Body," unpublished manuscript, Le Moyne College, May 1989.

They take on that stability and firmness implicit in the Barbie ideal; some women report that it becomes painful for them to lie on their stomachs because the mass of their breasts pushes into their flesh. Others report reluctance to lie on their backs on the beach because their breasts do not flop with the pull of gravity, the way other women's do.[36] In as many as one-third of cases, the tissue around the implant becomes literally rock-hard, causing unwelcome shape and pain, and usually requiring its removal or replacement. Implants filled with saltwater can deflate, while those filled with silicone may slowly leak their contents into the body. Medical journals have published reports of such postsurgical possibilities as future immune-system problems and toxic-shock syndrome. Since very little research has been done on these questions, no risks are confirmed. As more and more women opt for breast surgery, more research must be done. Perhaps the most disturbing risk that may be associated with breast surgery is cancer. Some physicians worry that breast implants can make it more difficult to discover a tumor early, whether by hand or through a mammogram.[37] A study by Dow Corning Corporation found that breast implants caused cancer in some laboratory rats.[38]

In this society that fetishizes breasts more than any other part of a woman's body, and also because a woman's breasts are bound up in some ways with her sense of herself, a woman with small breasts often suffers embarrassment, humiliation, or a sense of inadequacy. She often hears subtle or not-so-subtle comments on her flat chest, especially in her adolescence. Especially when the popular magazines they read offer them the ease of the plastic body, it is little wonder that many women seek augmentation.[39] For some women, moreover, bigger breasts are a condition of career success. Many women models and entertainers undergo augmentation operations, if not as a condition of employment, still at the suggestion of employers.[40]

Given the frequency of breast-augmentation surgery, I believe that much of it must be frivolous and unnecessary, like diamonds or furs. But my criticism is not of women who elect augmentation surgery. Their decisions may be rational responses to the particular constraints of their lives, their emotional needs, the social pressures they are under, and so on. The extent to which it can be said, however, that women are exercis-

36. See S. Beale, G. Hambert, H. O. Lisper, L. Ohlsen, and B. Palm, "Augmentation Mammoplasty: The Surgical and Psychological Effects of the Operation and Prediction of the Result," *Annals of Plastic Surgery* 13.4 (October 1984): 279–97, for reports of these sorts of complaints.

37. Alderson, "Breast Obsessed."

38. "Forget Hemlines," *Wall Street Journal.*

39. One study reports that 57 percent of women seeking augmentation surgery were influenced by popular magazines in their views of breasts, compared with only 15 percent of those in a control group. See Ohlsen et al., "Augmentation Mammoplasty."

40. Ayalah and Weinstock interview several women who had augmentation surgery because of their jobs.

ing choice when they elect augmentation, however, is questionable. Phallocentric norms do not value a variety of breast forms but rather elevate a standard; women are presented culturally with no choice but to regard our given breasts as inferior, puny, deflated, floppy. While most plastic surgeons do present the facts about possible risks and consequences of the surgery, many women nevertheless report surprise at the pain, the length of healing, their lack of feeling, how comparatively little their breasts have been enlarged. Thus it is not clear how well informed many of them really are. For the most part, augmentation surgery seems to fall within the great category of disciplinary practices in which women feel that they must engage in order to achieve and maintain femininity.[41] Like dieting and much exercise, surgery can be understood as a self-punishment necessary to bring her body into line.

Cancer is the other occasion for a knife at the breast. Here, in the center of my being, in these pleasurable orbs in which so much value is invested—theirs and mine—can lurk the dark home of malignancy. Until recently the undisputed normal therapy for breast cancer was a mastectomy—removal of the breast, often together with lymph nodes and pectoral muscles. Research recently has suggested that removal of the cancerous lump, together with intensive chemotherapy, is as effective in many cases.[42] But a great many women diagnosed with breast cancer still lose a breast through surgery.

There is little doubt that in many cases of breast cancer, mastectomy is either the only or the best therapy. Still, many medical professionals seem not to be sensitive to the deep identity issues that many women face with breast loss. More research and education must be done to provide alternative therapies so that mastectomy will be a last resort, and more genuinely supportive services should be provided for women who still must undergo breast loss.

A number of studies have documented that many women suffer serious emotional distress with breast loss, sometimes for years. This distress is often not detected by health professionals, let alone treated.[43] That breast loss is a trauma should come as no surprise. As I have said, for many, if not most, women, breasts are an important aspect of identity. While their feelings about their breasts often have been multiple and ambivalent, nevertheless they are a central element in their bodily

41. See Bartky, "Foucault, Femininity, and the Modernization of Patriarchal Power," and Bordo, "Reading the Slender Body."

42. Boston Women's Health Collective, *Our Bodies, Ourselves* (New York: Simon and Schuster, 1976; 2nd edition, 1983).

43. See Taylor, Lichtman, Wood, Bluming, Dosik, and Liebowitz, "Illness-Related and Treatment-Related Factors in Psychological Adjustment to Breast Cancer," *Cancer* 55.10 (May 1985): 2506–13; Collette Ray, Janet Grover, H. V. Cert, and Tom Misniewski, "Nurses' Perceptions of Early Breast Cancer, and Their Psychological Implications, and of the Role of Health Professionals in Providing Support," *International Journal of Nursing Studies* 21.2 (1981): 101–11.

self-image. Phenomenologically, the chest is a center of a person's being-in-the-world and the way she presents herself in the world, so breasts cannot fail to be an aspect of her bodily habitus. For many women, breasts are a source of sexual pleasure or bodily pride. Many women emotionally locate important episodes in their life history—such as coming to adulthood or having children—in their breasts.

My reading about women's experiences with mastectomy leads me to think that frequently, the integration of breasts with a woman's self is seriously denied in the events of mastectomy. In conformity with Western medicine's tendency to objectify the body and to treat the body as a conglomerate of fixable or replaceable parts, a woman's breast is considered to be detachable, dispensable. A lack of sensitivity to how important a woman's breast is to her identity probably accounts for the fact that for so long, radical mastectomy was the only accepted therapy for breast cancer.[44]

People often seem to take the attitude toward breast loss that after all, breasts are really not functional, only decorative. They doll you up, make you beautiful and sexy, but you don't need them in the same way you do legs or hands. If the woman is middle-aged or old, her breasts may be perceived as being even more dispensable, since she will have no more children and her sexuality is usually denied. The woman who expresses feelings of rage or depression at the idea and actuality of breast loss is often made to feel that she is unacceptably vain. She is encouraged to become detached and to "take it like a man." To the degree that people sympathize with the emotional trauma of breast loss, it is most often from a male-identified point of view. They assume that a woman's major emotional problem is in relation to her husband or male lover, that she worries how he will love her body; and the popular literature about breast loss is full of stories of the selfless and magnanimous men who stand by their women, insisting that they love her and not her breasts.

That she in an important sense is her breasts is denied, and thus she is not allowed to be public and honest in her fear and grief. Then, when she has lost her breast, the culture's message is clear and unambiguous: She must adjust by learning to hide her deformity. Above all, she must return to daily life looking and behaving as though nothing has happened. She replaces her breast with a prosthesis, which finally achieves the objectified attributes of the phallicized breast: it is firm, does not jiggle, points just right (except when it slips), and usually has no nipple. Or today, women can opt for the ultimate in breast objectification: sur-

---

44. See Rose Kushner, *Breast Cancer: A Personal History and Investigative Report* (New York: Harcourt Brace Jovanovich, 1975), 302–10. Kushner also suggests that the prevalence of mastectomy may derive from the predominance of men over female medicine.

gical reconstruction. Fulfilling the dream of replaceable parts, for a fee and through additional pain, a woman can be "as good as new." Or so the hope is held out to her, even though many women find themselves surprised and disappointed by how little a reconstructed breast looks and feels like the lost breast.[45]

Whether she wears a prosthesis or a surgically constructed artificial breast, she certainly cannot feel the same. Both objects serve to hide and deny her loss of feeling and sensitivity, both sexual and also the simple daily feeling of being in the world with these breasts. Prosthesis and reconstruction give primacy to the look, to the visual constitution of a woman's body. Her trauma is constructed not as the severance of her self and her loss of feeling, but as her becoming visually deformed, repulsive to look at. She must protect others from viewing her deformity and herself from the gaze of repulsion. So of course most women will wear a prosthesis and cannot be criticized for doing so.

Audre Lorde points out a crucial consequence of this culture's enslavement to a woman's looking "normal" after breast loss. Besides making it difficult or impossible for a woman to come to terms with her new body, it also makes it difficult or impossible for one-breasted women to identify one another. It renders a woman's experience completely invisible not only to those who do not wish to think about cancer and breast loss, but also to those who have experienced them. Given the frightening frequency of breast cancer among women in American society, this primacy of the normalizing look completely silences and isolates a huge number of women.

> Prosthesis offers the empty comfort of "Nobody will know the difference." But it is that very difference which I wish to affirm, because I have lived it, and survived it, and wish to share that strength with other women. If we are to translate the silence surrounding breast cancer into language and action against this scourge, then the first step is that women with mastectomies must become visible to each other. For silence and invisibility go hand in hand with powerlessness. By accepting the mask of prosthesis, one-breasted women proclaim ourselves as insufficients dependent upon pretense. We reinforce our own isolation and invisibility from each other, as well as the false complacency of a society which would rather not face the results of its own insanities.[46]

The opportunity thus does not offer itself to her to transform her body identity into a one-breasted woman, an Amazon. In a differently constructed culture, she might reconstitute her body identity and learn

---

45. See Karen Berger and John Bostwick, *A Woman's Decision* (New York: C. V. Mosby Co., 1984); the authors are advocates of breast reconstruction, but they report that some women are disappointed that their new breasts do not look like the old ones.

46. Audre Lorde, *The Cancer Journals* (Trumansburg, N.Y.: The Crossing Press, 1980), 61.

to love herself with one breast. Women's body histories are fluid and changing; it would be possible for her to form a new and positive body identity. She adjusted to being breasted when she was a teenager; if she had children, she adjusted to radical changes in her body form when she was pregnant. Only among lesbians is there an effort to affirm in public the possibility of a positive one-breasted woman, and even in such woman-centered communities the success is often ambiguous.

6

Menstrual Meditations

In a sexually equalitarian society, woman would regard menstruation simply as her special way of reaching adult life; the human body in both men and women has other more disagreeable needs to be taken care of, but they are easily adjusted to because, being common to all, they do not represent blemishes for anyone; the menses inspire horror in the adolescent girl because they throw her into an inferior and defective category. This sense of being declassed will weigh heavily upon her. She would retain her pride in her bleeding body if she did not lose her pride in being human.

—Simone de Beauvoir, *The Second Sex*

My original plan for an essay describing women's menstrual experience and reflecting on the ontological and moral implication of such experience assumed that I would follow the form of the essays on pregnancy, clothing, breasted experience, and home that appear in this volume. First I would proffer an account of the devaluation and oppression associated with femininity, told from the social experience of male domination, and thus with a critical voice. Then I would switch to a more woman-centered account of the positive resources in this specifically female experience that can be used to refigure social values. There is a positive female experience of the processes and meanings of menstruation, I supposed, covered over by patriarchal biases and interests.

We can learn many things from reflecting on menstrual experience, I will suggest here, but a transvaluation of values is not likely. The social status of women has improved significantly in many societies. Even in those where women might be considered most free, however, there are many socially caused discomforts and oppressions associated with the experience of menstruation. This essay devotes most of its space to uncovering and reflecting on the social oppression of women as menstruators, in two major forms: the shame associated with menstruation that

I am grateful to the following people for helpful comments on an earlier version of this essay: David Alexander, Morgen Alexander-Young, Sandra Bartky, Deborah Bergoffen, Mary Anne Case, Sonia Kruks, and Elizabeth Wilson. Thanks to Keisha Lindsay for research assistance.

compels girls and women to conceal their menstrual events, and the misfit between women and public places such as schools and workplaces, which often refuse to accommodate women's social and physical needs. If we imagine away these injustices, we find underneath not a glorious experience, but rather a personal bodily process that causes many women some discomfort or annoyance some of the time. The process nevertheless carries emotional meaning for many women. The descriptions and data on which I rely come mostly from the United States, although some are from Britain and a few other societies. I will frame this analysis of unfairness associated with social response to menstruation in the first section with accounts of women's experience of menstruation derived from Simone de Beauvoir and contemporary feminist research, and in the last section with some exploration of mood and memory as menstrual events mark a woman's self-narrative.

Before I begin, however, let me call attention to something this essay does not do. I reflect very little on medical theory and practice related to menstruation. From a feminist perspective there is much to say about how physicians, medical textbooks, nurses, and other representatives of medical institutions articulate menstrual processes and position girls at puberty, adult menstruating women, and the processes of menopause and postmenopausal women. Feminist criticism has been important in questioning a label like premenstrual "syndrome" or the assumptions behind routine prescription of hormone replacement therapy at menopause. I have chosen to say little about the medical system's treatment of menstruation, because there is more feminist writing about these issues than about the social and personal experience of menstruation in women's lives.

I. Experience: Beauvoir and Contemporary Feminism

December 1978. At a mostly male conference I hug, chat, eat, drink, listen with my sisters in philosophy. My body avalanches from its recent maternal swellings to the plateaus of a folded uterus, milkless breasts. I left my baby daughter in Chicago, who used to suckle for ninety minutes at a time while I read *The Women's Room*. For the first time in fifteen months that warm red flow moves through my clitoral canals. No quiet transition, but a body revolution throbbing my back and neck . . .

That night in my restless sleep, I dream. A ballroom filled with women, hundreds under the chandeliers, a reception after business at the Society for Women in Philosophy. I flit from one group of women to another in smiling comfort. As I turn to find another friend I see her tall figure across the room, as though overlooking the sisterly crowd: Simone de Beauvoir.- Then, just before I wake, a single object, shimmering: a glass of milk.[1]

1. Iris Marion Young, "Humanism, Gynocentrism, and Feminist Politics," first published in *Women's Studies International Forum* 8.3 (1985): 173.

Twenty years ago I wrote those paragraphs to introduce an essay criticizing Simone de Beauvoir's stubborn humanism, her commitment to an
ideal in which sexual difference no longer matters for the status of human dignity and women have the same opportunities as men in all human endeavors. Influenced by more recent French feminist thought, in
the persons of Luce Irigaray and Julia Kristeva, as well as by U.S. feminist arguments that women's equality should not mean that we are expected to measure up to a male-biased standard of character and
achievement, I argued then that Beauvoir's feminism too much deni-
grates the female body. I criticized her analytic framework, which distinguishes human freedom as transcendence from the immanence of the
body that chains all of us, but women more so, to the species, to sickness
and death. Following Beauvoir with such a dichotomy between transcendence and immanence, I argued, implies continued devaluation of the
specificity of women's experience.

In preparing to write this essay, I read *The Second Sex* again. The
experience was like coming home to learn that your mother is wiser
than you thought in your younger days of rebellion. It still seems to me
that Beauvoir holds up ideals of human achievement derived from male-
dominated experience of art, politics, and commerce. A feminism that
aims to convert sexual difference from a liability to a virtue, moreover,
seems beyond her imagination. After thirty years of concentrated and
diverse feminist social criticism, it is easy to have such critical reactions.
The Second Sex remains a feminist classic, however, not only because it
is beautifully written and began so many lines of feminist inquiry. Beauvoir describes the embodied experience of being a girl, adult woman,
and an old woman, with unparalleled depth of detail and tenderness
that continues to inspire young and not-so-young women with recognition. The book contains still unmined resources for understanding female experience and performing social criticism.

Most feminist treatises are silent about the experience and social significance of menstruation. Not Beauvoir's. She reflects systematically on
menarche and its implications for the emerging women's ambivalence
about her place in society. She discusses the everyday difficulties most
women have at some point in their lives accommodating their cycling
bodies to the demands of expected activity and modesty. Most admira-
bly, Beauvoir presents the postmenopausal woman as a solid person,
rather than the ghost of a woman that popular culture tends to portray.
There remain elements of Beauvoir's reflections on women's bodily experience and its implications for freedom that are open to criticism. For
example, her reflections on menstruation vacillate between arguing that
the sense of discomfort and devaluation that many women experience
about menstruation has its source entirely in social relations, on the one
hand, and claiming that women's nature as reproducers chains them to
species being in a way to which we must simply resign ourselves. The
thoroughness of her treatment of these experiences, which she describes

from a woman-centered point of view, however, makes these passages unique and vivid.

Beauvoir describes the onset of menstruation as a *crisis* for the girl, for which she is not well prepared, and about which she feels fear, shame, disgust, ambivalence, but also sometimes pride at becoming a woman.

> Sometimes the girl does not yet feel ashamed of her body, in what may be called the stage of prepuberty, before the appearance of the menses; she is proud of becoming a woman and watches the maturing of her bosom with satisfaction, padding her dress with handkerchiefs and taking pride in it before her elders; she does not yet grasp the significance of what is taking place in her. Her first menstruation reveals this meaning, and her feelings of shame appear. If they were already present, they are strengthened and exaggerated from this time on. All the evidence agrees in showing that whether the child has been forewarned or not, the event always seems to her repugnant and humiliating.[2]
>
> And though the first surprise is over, the monthly annoyance is not similarly effaced; at each recurrence the girl feels again the same disgust at this flat and stagnant odor emanating from her—an odor of the swamp, of wilted violets—disgust at this blood, less red, more dubious, than that which flowed from her childish abrasions. Day and night she must think of making her changes, must keep watch of her underwear, her sheets, must solve a thousand little practical and repugnant problems. (315)

A source of this shame and disgust, according to Beauvoir, is a reluctance to assume the feminine status that the girl knows is subordinate. The physical limitations that menstruation brings by nature or convention symbolize the relatively constricted life that is a woman's in a male-dominated society. To be sure, there are positive moments for some, the women who enjoy the power of their sexuality or who throw themselves happily into motherhood. The stance of most girls toward feminine maturation, however, is ambivalence: affirming and denying themselves as women, split and alienated.

Beauvoir's depiction of a woman's experience of menstruation is dramatic and evocative. A feminist reading passages such as these today might be inclined to judge them idiosyncratic or anachronistic or both. Surely most women don't feel so negative as this; surely the changes in women's status and opportunities in France or England or the United States have mitigated our sense of alienation or annoyance with this most normal and regular bodily process. My inexhaustive survey of contemporary expressions of women's experiences and attitudes appears to

---

2. Simone de Beauvoir, *The Second Sex*, trans. H. M. Parshey (New York: Random House, 1952). Page numbers from Vintage edition (New York: Vintage, 1989), 309–10; subsequent citations of this work appear in parentheses in the text.

confirm that Beauvoir's is a common attitude that has changed little in the intervening half-century.[3]

Studies of girls who have recently begun menstruating, as well as interviews with older women remembering menarche, give an impression similar to Beauvoir's about the negativity and ambivalence of the experience. While some of the young people are happy to pass from the status of girls to grown women, even many of them at the same time feel anxiety.[4] Both popular media, educational and medical pamphlets, and communications from adults tend to send them mixed messages about menstruation.[5] On the one hand, girls should take pride in becoming women, with the sexual and reproductive powers that this entails. On the other hand, they must take care to hide evidence of their bleeding from family members, schoolmates, and even strangers on the street. Girls typically regard menstruation with annoyance and discomfort, and a sense that they themselves are distant from the process.

These feelings of disgust and alienation often remain even as the woman matures. Midlife women typically speak of menstrual processes as dirty, messy, disruptive, annoying, something to dread.[6] Emily Martin reports that the women she interviewed tend to express a sense of distance between their selves and their menstruating bodies. Menstruation is an annoying fact that they must deal with and manage but is not an aspect of their being as subjects.[7] Many girls and women report varying degrees of physical pain, discomfort, mood changes, or energy changes associated with their body cycles. According to some studies, however, most women reject labeling themselves as subject to premenstrual syndrome, because they understand this label as naming a physical or psychological disorder.[8]

Some educators and medical writers worry about whether girls and women have sufficient knowledge of the menstrual process. For many

3. I have searched for research in the English language only. Thus most of the experience reported here is of women in the United States, Canada, Britain, or Australia.

4. See Janet Lee and Jennifer Sasser-Coen, *Blood Stories: Menarche and the Politics of the Female Body in Contemporary U.S. Society* (New York: Routledge, 1996), 31–34; Koff, Rierdon, and Jacobson, "The Personal and Interpersonal Significance of Menarch," *American Academy of Child Psychiatry*: 148–58; T. Sevier, "The First Menstruation: Bodily Memories of Finnish and Russian Women," in *Women's Voices in Russia Today*, ed. Anna Rotkirch and Elina Haavir-Mannila (Aldershot, England: Dartmouth, 1996), 88–106.

5. See Docial Charlesworth, "Paradoxical Constructions of Self: Educating Young Women about Menstruation," *Women and Language* 24.2 (Fall 2001), 13–20.

6. Lee and Sasser-Coen, *Blood Stories*, 146–47.

7. Emily Martin, *The Woman in the Body: A Cultural Analysis of Reproduction* (Boston: Beacon Press, 1987), 78–79.

8. P. Y. L. Choi and S. McKeown, "What Are Young Undergraduate Women's Qualitative Experiences of the Menstrual Cycle?" *Journal of Psychosomatic Obstetrical Gynecology*, 18 (1997): 259–65.

of these, "knowledge" refers to an understanding of the physiological processes of the reproductive system that cause ovulation, the build-up of fluids on the uterine wall, and the monthly discharge. Researchers who study the question often find that girls around the age of menarche have a very sketchy understanding of reproductive biology, often carry and disseminate among themselves misinformation about the causes of the normal discharge, and have little or distorted understanding of the connection of menstruation to the possibility of pregnancy.[9] Often they fill in the mystery with myths that fuel fears and anxieties associated with menstruating.

Even when biological understanding is more accurate, it may nevertheless add to rather than reduce a sense of alienation from one's body. Martin argues that medical discourse in the twentieth century represents menstruation as failed production. Textbooks depict reproductive processes in mechanical terms and imagine the telos of reproductive biology as the production of a baby. Within this framework, each menstrual event is a sign of failure to conceive; Beauvoir herself discusses menstrual processes in similar terms, without any apparent self-consciousness about positioning the processes as failed production.

> It is during her periods that she feels her body most painfully as an ob-scure, alien thing; it is, indeed, the prey of a stubborn and foreign life that each month constructs and then tears down a cradle within it; each month all things are made ready for a child and then aborted in the crimson flow. Woman, like man, *is* her body, but her body is something other than herself. (29)

Many of the experts who write about girls' and women's experience of menstruation, even when they assert feminist commitments, seem to assume without question that women *ought* to have an accurate and complete understanding of the physiology of menstruation.[10] To the extent that they do not, these writers seem to assume the educational system has failed. But should we accept this assumption? Few of us, both men and women, have a very accurate or complete understanding of the physiology of other internal bodily processes—digestion, for example, or the production of sperm. This assumption that menstrual "knowledge" is equivalent to medical science may itself contribute to a sense of alienation women have from the process. Certainly we need some reassuring account of why we are bleeding, but to have such does not imply being able to give a textbook description of reproductive biology.

Martin suggests that women who express less sophisticated techni-

---

9. Susan M. Moore, "Girls' Understanding and Social Constructions of Menarche," *Journal of Adolescence* 18.1 (February 1995): 87–104.

10. See, for example, Elissa Koff and Jill Riersdon, "Early Adolescent Girls' Understanding of Menstruation," *Women and Health* 22.4 (1995): 1–19.

cal knowledge of the menstrual process tend to speak about menstruation more in terms of their lived experience of bodily change and management of discharge in relation to themselves and others. While such a less objectified and mechanized representation apparently does not render the experience joyful for most women, in this experiential language they nevertheless express less alienation from their bodies.[11]

Interviews and focus groups with teenage girls, as well as recollections of older women of their early menstruating years, seem to indicate that the knowledge girls crave is not scientific but practical. They want to know how to "solve a thousand little practical and repugnant problems," as Beauvoir puts it, that the process brings into their everyday lives. What's the difference between maxi- and minipads, how do I insert tampons, how often should I change? How do I keep from staining my clothes, sheets, or the chairs I sit on? How can I carry pads or tampons to the bathroom without detection? How can I ensure that I am able to get to a bathroom as often I need to? While some girls get answers to these urgent questions from mothers, teachers, or tampon manufacturers' pamphlets, many get their answers from other girls.[12] In contemporary advanced industrial capitalist societies, moreover, much of what we learn is how to consume "hygiene" products.

Joan Brumberg argues that the meaning of menstruation changed significantly in the lives of pubescent girls and women in early-twentieth-century America. Nineteenth-century medical and popular culture tended to reduce the behavior and attributes of women to their sexual and reproductive functioning in ways that legitimated the subordination and exclusion of women from many public activities and opportunities. In this context, menstruation was monitored as a symptom of reproductive health or pathology, and experts recommended that women not tax themselves. Feminist struggles to open public spaces and opportunities to women and to disengage the personhood of women from their biology contributed to a changing view of menstruation that regards it as a normal and incidental process that is not debilitating. At the same time, a revolution in consumer culture in the early twentieth century extended to ready-made products for managing menstrual flow.[13] Advertising campaigns by companies like Kotex replace the view of menstruation as debilitating with an understanding of menstruation as a healthy process that is nevertheless dirty, presenting a hygiene problem that needs managing with their products. This consumer packaging of menstrual experience has increased in the intervening century. Women in North America can now avail themselves of a dizzying array of thick or thin pads, with

11. Martin, *The Woman in the Body*, chapter 6.

12. Elizabeth Arveda Killing, "Bleeding Out Loud: Communication about Menstruation," *Feminism and Psychology* 6.4 (1996): 481–504.

13. Joan Brumberg, *The Body Project: An Intimate History of American Girls* (New York: Random House, 1997), chapter 6.

or without wings, scented or unscented; dozens of tampon choices; and a plethora of douches, sprays, soaps, and creams. If we keep our bodies clean, fresh, and well-scented, we can conceal our periods and be carefree.[14]

Despite the liberating implications of this shift in the cultural inter-pretation of menstruation from a confining condition to a normal pro-cess, Brumberg argues that twentieth-century American culture pro-duced a new alienation for girls and women from their bodily processes. We do not have a socially sanctioned opportunity as girls and women to reflect on the meaning of sexuality and reproduction. Whereas some other societies mark moments of menarche and menstruation with cos-mic ritual, contemporary sexual egalitarian and consumer society level the process to just another form of dirt to be disposed of. Brumberg suggests that women need shared meanings to give their menstrual expe-rience reflective significance. While I don't know quite what this might mean in practice, Brumberg's account raises an important question.

Lee-Sasser and Coen also suggest that the ambivalence that many girls have when they begin to menstruate may arise partly from the lack of cultural recognition and well defined rituals surrounding it.[15] Martin also notes that adding symbolic significance to menstrual events along-side or instead of medical explanation might make many girls and women less alienated from their menstruating bodies.[16]

No doubt, as women mature, menstrual events become more routine and an accepted part of their lives. They are less a focus for women bonding and more private, in many cases. We surge with positive or negative emotion at the appearance or nonappearance of the menses in connection with our desires to avoid or become pregnant. Whether we have wanted our pregnancies or not, we feel something monumental about the return of our periods. The monthly bleeding punctuates our lives, marking significant events, and it is also routine. According to Lee and Sasser-Coen, however, women throughout their lives continue to speak with some negativity about the process. Many continue to find periods annoying and disruptive. Many describe periods as "something to dread," "a mess," "a pain in the neck," and they continue to report a kind of body alienation in which they feel that the physical and emo-tional menstrual process is out of their control.[17]

Simone de Beauvoir constructs the experience of menopause in vary-ing, even contradictory ways. On the one hand, Beauvoir describes a sense of loss and despair that menopause may bring for women who

14. Joyce Rutter Kaye, "Sanitary Chic," *Rockville* 55.4 (July–August 2001): 62–67; Shelley Park, "From Sanitation to Liberation: The Modern and Postmodern Marketing of Menstrual Products," *Journal of Popular Culture* 30.2 (Fall 1996): 149–68.

15. Lee and Sasser-Coen, *Blood Stories*.

16. Martin, *The Woman in the Body*, 111.

17. Lee and Sasser-Coen, *Blood Stories*, 146–47.

have derived self-esteem from society's valuation of feminine sexuality and reproductive capacity.

> Whereas man grows old gradually, woman is suddenly deprived of her femininity; she is still relatively young when she loses the erotic attractiveness and the fertility which, in the view of society and in her own, provide the justification of her existence and her opportunity for happiness. With no future, she sill has about one half of her adult life to live. (575)

Beauvoir suggests that some women respond to this grim circumstance with a sort of mysticism. Because menopause rudely divides her life into before and after, when she is no longer truly a woman in the eyes of society the postmenopausal woman may construct herself as entering a transcendent new life. "She is dead and risen again, she views the world with an eye that has penetrated the secrets of the beyond, and she thinks she is about to take flight for peaks hitherto unreached" (581). Beauvoir here indulges in her own flights of literary fancy, it seems to me, in a soap opera vein.

On the other hand, earlier in her text, Beauvoir describes a woman's attitude toward menopause in less negative or less extravagant terms. She says that with menopause a woman at last "escapes the iron grasp of the species" (31). When menstruation ceases, a woman regains unity with her body. "Woman is now delivered from the servitude imposed by her female nature, but she is not to be likened to a eunuch, for her vitality is unimpaired. And what is more, she is no longer the prey of overwhelming forces; she is herself, she and her body are one" (31).

The first of Beauvoir's attitudes I have quoted does indeed seem to correspond to the dominant popular image of the post-menopausal woman in youth-oriented consumer society. Women's magazines and pharmaceutical companies warn women that menopause brings depression, hot flashes, volatile emotions, brittle bones, facial hair, loss of sexual desire, and generally, the end of womanly life. Some women do indeed suffer various forms of physical or emotional distress at or after menopause, and some no doubt feel some loss of status or identity.

Interviews with women about their experience of and feelings about menopause and being postmenopausal, however, seem more to confirm Beauvoir's third, more matter-of-fact and holistic picture. Both Martin and Lee and Sasser-Coen report that the vast majority of women they interviewed found going through menopause "no big deal," and that they are happy to have menstrual annoyances behind them. On the whole, they do not feel diminished as persons, and indeed many report their postmenstrual energy, ambition, sexual desire, and approach to the world as some of the most positive of their lives.[18]

---

18. Lee and Sasser-Coen, *Blood Stories*, chapter 6; Martin, *The Woman in the Body*, chapter 10; see also Patricia A. Kaufert, "Menstruation and Menstrual Change: Women in Midlife," in *Culture, Society, and Menstruation*, ed. Virginia L. Olesen and Nancy Fugate Woods (Washington: Hemisphere Publishing Co., 1986), 63–76.

Beauvoir wrote mostly about the menstrual experience of women in mid-twentieth-century France. Her descriptions of shame, everyday practical problems, fantasies, comfort with one's body, and ambivalent movement among all these stances corresponds remarkably to reports of the experiences of North American and British women thirty years later. I do not know to what extent the differing cultural and commercial context of women in Asia, Africa, or Latin America, as well as the very different living conditions from relatively affluent urban consumer society, imply different menstrual experiences for women in these contexts.[19] My guess is that women often experience greater problems around menstruation in settings of greater poverty and sexual inequality.[20] Despite the vibrancy and insight of Beauvoir's descriptions, which resonate with that of others, I find in her text a tone of resignation to the ambivalent feelings and practical problems women experience, largely because of fraught social attitudes about women. Perhaps we can be a bit more resistant to this fate.

II. In the Menstrual Closet

In the late twentieth and early twenty-first century in societies that claim to respect women as the social equals of men, our social position as menstruators appears contradictory. On the one hand, for a culture of meritocratic achievement, menstruation is nothing other than a healthy biological process that should not be thought to distinguish women and men in our capacities and behavior. Women have demonstrated that there is no womanly nature that prevents us from achieving what men achieve. We can do anything we choose while menstruating—go to work, play ball, wear skimpy swimsuits, enjoy vaginal sex with another person. Such a degree of freedom and equality for women was only a hope for Beauvoir and her contemporaries.

On the other hand, from our earliest awareness of menstruation until the day we stop, we are mindful of the imperative to *conceal* our menstrual processes. We follow a multitude of practical rules. Do not discuss your menstruation with anyone but your mother, your doctor, and your very best girlfriends; perhaps you may discuss your periods with a long-term male partner, but that all depends on how he feels about it. Keep the signs of your menstruation hidden—leave no bloodstains on the floor, towels, sheets, or chairs. Make sure that your bloody flow does

19. For one example of very different understandings and practices associated with menstruation, among a group of women indigenous in Australia, see Elizabeth Povinelli, "Native Sex: Sex Rites, Land Rights, and the Meaning of Aboriginal Civic Culture," in *Gender Ironies of Nationalism*, ed. Tamar Mayer (London: Routledge, 2000).

20. See Renart, "Of Diapers and Tampons: Women and the Earthquake," *WIN Magazine* no. 25A, 1999.

not visibly leak through your clothes, and do not let the outline of a sanitary pad show. Menstruation is dirty, disgusting, defiling, and thus must be hidden. In everyday life these requirements of concealment create enormous anxiety and practical difficulties for women, and are a major source of our annoyance with the monthly event.

Is this a paradox? We receive the message and believe that as women we can and should participate in the same way as men in social and physical activities; menstruation is completely acceptable and unremarkable. Yet at the same time strong social pressures and our own internalized sense of decency tell us that we must vigilantly guard against revelation of our bleeding, especially in public and to strangers. While there is an apparent friction between them, in fact these two messages easily cohere. The message that a menstruating woman is perfectly normal *entails* that she hide the signs of her menstruation. The normal body, the default body, the body that every body is assumed to be, is a body not bleeding from the vagina. Thus to *be* normal and to be taken as normal, the menstruating woman must not speak about her bleeding and must conceal evidence of it. The message that the menstruating woman is normal makes her deviant, a deviance that each month puts her on the other side of a fear of disorder, or the subversion of what is right and proper. It seems apt, then, in this normatively masculine, supposedly gender-egalitarian society, to say that the menstruating woman is queer. As with other queers, the price of a woman's acceptance as normal is that she stay in the closet as a menstruator.

Eve Sedgwick suggests that the closet experience of those deviating from heterosexual norms has come to stand for wider and diverse experiences of normalization.

> I want to argue that a lot of the energy of attention and demarcation that has swirled around issues of homosexuality since the end of the nineteenth century, in Europe and the United States, has been impelled by the distinctively indicative relation of homosexuality to wider mappings of society and disclosure, and of the private and the public, that were and are crucially problematical for the gender, sexual, and economic structures of heterosexist culture at large, mappings whose enabling but dangerous incoherence has become oppressively, durably condensed in certain figures of homosexuality. "The closet" and "coming out," now verging on all-purpose phrases for the potent crossing and recrossing of almost any politically charged lines of representation, have been the gravest and most magnetic of those figures.[21]

Sedgwick nevertheless rightly insists that the image of the closet "is indicative for homophobia in a way it cannot be for other oppressions" (75). Unlike many other oppressions, including racial oppression and the oppressions of many people with disabilities, no physical markers

---

21. Eve Kosofsky Sedgwick, *Epistemology of the Closet* (Berkeley: University of California Press, 1990), 71.

signal to others the right to label others "homosexual." Perhaps more important, as Sedgwick points out in comparing the hiding and revelation of Jewish identity with the hiding and revelation of sexual orientation, unique ambiguities, uncertainties, and dangers to the lives of others attend coming out of the homosexual closet. An ethnic or religious identity formerly hidden and now revealed is not usually in question as an identity in the way that sexual experience is. Rarely do other comings-out threaten the sense of self of those who witness them, moreover, whereas coming out of a homosexual closet often puts in question the desires and self-understandings of many of those related to the revealer.[22]

By aligning my analysis with queer theory I do not mean to erase the difference between the stigma attached to sexual being and action that deviates from normative heterosexuality, on the one hand, and women's experience of menstrual constraint and shame. In the end, for many women, the latter may be less damaging to our dignity and self-esteem than the former is for those stigmatized as fags, dykes, or other buggers, some of them women. A queer perspective teaches that the multitude of ways that persons are made ashamed or positioned as odd ought not to be understood as a consequence of their being or actions, but that the trouble is with the idea of normal. Michael Warner details the dilemmas that entrap a gay movement that aspires to normalcy according to the standards of a clean and proper culture.[23] I wish to explore here some of the tensions and personal shames that capture women who aim to be normal human beings in a somatophobic culture that finds menstrual processes dirty and even frightening.

By bringing menstruation under the metaphor of the closet, I aim to assert a connection between this particular aspect of the stigma attached to women and that borne by those reviled for their sexuality. At the same time, it is important to notice the distinctive structural positions and experience of each. There are large differences in the situation of the two groups. In an obvious sense, menstruators can never be closeted in the way that those who challenge heterosexual norms can. Most of us are visibly and viscerally women to those who encounter us. Consequently, the menstrual closet does not afford the same sort of safety as the homosexual closet, but neither does coming out of it carry the same threat of job loss or violence. Because the homosexual closet renders the identity it hides more invisible, moreover, it also opens greater space for development of a counterculture for those who know one another as in it than does keeping menstruation hidden. Despite these important differences, the menstrual closet shares with others a normative enforcement that produces shame.

22. Sedgwick, *Epistemology of the Closet*, 76–80.
23. Michael Warner, *The Trouble with Normal: Sex, Politics, and the Ethics of Queer Life* (New York: Free Press, 1999).

I will explore the oppression of the menstrual closet in two respects. First is the experience of knowing oneself as shameful, as an abject existence that is messy and disgusting. Women as menstruators live through a split subjectivity insofar as we claim the pubic face of normalcy and a fear of exposure of the private fluidity of our flesh. Given the dominant disembodied norms of clean and proper, it is difficult for me not to experience my being as defiled and out of control.

Second, menstruating women must monthly deal with a misfit between our needs and the public institutions that afford our main access to social benefits and recognition. I will restrict my attention to schools and workplaces. In modern, supposedly sexually egalitarian societies these claim to include women equally with men. As such they assume public norms that generally fail to accommodate the particular needs of menstruating women, both physical and social. This failure of public acceptance increases a woman's sense of shame, and can disadvantage her in the distribution of benefits.

A. The Existential-Ontological Problem

Recent feminist theory offers several possible and not incompatible frameworks for giving an account of the ontological and emotional issues that might be at stake in the imperative to hide menstruation. Julia Kristeva's theory of abjection offers one such interpretive framework. The abject denotes a correlate to the subject that lies just on the other side of the border of its identity and threatens to dissolve that border. Human substances ejected from the body most especially evoke reactions of disgust or loathing—vomit, pus, piss, shit, the corpse itself as the limit case of the disintegration of the self. These substances whose origin is in the body challenge the affective investment in our sense of impermeable and solid body boundaries.

The horror of abjection, according to Kristeva, has two paradigms, the excremental and the menstrual.

> Excrement and its equivalents (decay, infection, disease, corpse, etc.) stand for the danger to identity that comes from without: the ego threatened by the non-ego, the society threatened by its outside, life by death. Menstrual blood, on the contrary, stands for the danger issuing from within the identity (social or sexual); it threatens the relationship between the sexes within a social aggregate and, through internalization, the identity of each sex in the face of sexual difference.[24]

The meaning of menstrual blood is overdetermined. As the main marker of sexual difference, its semiotics help secure the border of the sexualized self. Menstrual blood reminds every subject of her origins

24. Julia Kristeva, *Powers of Horror* (New York: Columbia University Press, 1982), 71.

inside a female body and her own ejection through vaginal canals; abjection is the fear of losing the border between self and other we have constructed in our infant struggle to separate from the warm and nurturing mother. Menstrual blood is a fluid and olfactory substance that itself defies boundaries and fixity.

Men and women both experience menstruation as abject for these reasons. If this sort of account is plausible, then it may be too much to expect a reversal of values that would interpret menstruation as glorious and a badge of public honor. Both men and women, however, could accept the menstrual in a less sensationalist way as a fact of bodily life, the way we accept earwax or runny noses. That is to say, we could just live with this fear of falling back into fusion with the maternal that haunts our selves, instead of denying it or building rigid walls around our vulnerable selves.

Instead, this modest and proper civilization tries to throw the burden onto women alone. Kristeva says that modern society tends to conflate the feminine and the maternal. As Kelly Oliver puts it, "Without a secular discourse of myth of motherhood that absorbs abjection, abjection is misplaced onto women. Although women and mothers are in fact distinct, without a way of conceiving the mother that allows us to abject her and come to terms with that abjection, we abject all women."[25]

Elizabeth Grosz builds on this sort of account to interpret menstruation as paradigmatic of body fluids that permeate the borders of self. As other to the Western ontological valuation of solid objects and a correlative position of the subject as controlling both those objects and itself, woman as other becomes linked to what is out of control. Menstruation, Grosz suggests, comes to stand in for this status as fluid other: "For the girl, menstruation, associated as it is with blood, with injury and wound, with a mess that does not dry invisibly, that leaks uncontrollably, not in sleep, in dreams, but whenever it occurs, indicates the beginning of an out of control status that she was led to believe ends with childhood."[26]

On a variation of the horrific, Christine Battersby theorizes the female subject position as "monstrous" in relation to the dominant construction of subjects. On her account, social institutions and hegemonic discourses give to male bodies and masculine styles of behavior and comportment a normative status. When female bodies and comportment deviate in significant ways from these norms, as in being a pregnant body, or menstruating, "the female subject has to negotiate the monstrous, the inconsistent and the anomalous."[27] Battersby's philosophical

25. Kelly Oliver, *Reading Kristeva: Unraveling the Double-Bind* (Bloomington: Indiana University Press, 1993), 161.

26. Elizabeth Grosz, *Volatile Bodies* (Bloomington: Indiana University Press, 1994), 205.

27. Christine Battersby, *Phenomenal Woman*, 39.

project calls for imagining ontological categories for which female bodies would serve as the norm.

These are three variants of an account of a cultural construction of secure identity that privilege a notion of a clean and proper body coded as male. Other variants no doubt are possible. Several recent feminist writers concerned with the social meaning of menstruation refer to Mary Douglas's conceptualization of purity as border drawing, for example, and Kristeva's account itself draws on Douglas.[28] Let me summarize the general points for my purposes.

As menstruators, women threaten psychic security systems because female processes challenge the distinctions between inside and outside, solid and fluid, self-identical and changing. Both men and women experience menstruation as abject or monstrous, because both harbor anxieties about a dissolution of self and merging with the ghost of a mother. One way of holding this anxiety at bay is to separate the feminine from the clean and proper masculine. Thus, either menstruating women must be separated from others, especially men, and isolated in a distinct space; or women may be allowed to roam free among men but must keep signs of their menstruation hidden. In either case, women every month carry the burden of abjection, the monstrous, the stigma of birth and death, as a practical and enforced shame.[29] She is in a menstrual closet. If a woman wishes to walk among men while she bleeds, if she wishes to lay claim to the rights and privileges of a solid self who stands forth and achieves, then she had better keep her private fluidity secret. Thus she must observe the practices of what Sophie Laws calls menstrual *etiquette*.[30]

B. Menstrual Etiquette

With this term Laws denotes an intricate set of rules governing interactions between men and women, and between women and women, negotiating the material manifestations and cultural meanings of menstruation. Menstrual etiquette concerns who can say what to whom about menstruation, what sort of language is appropriate, and what should not be spoken. The rules of menstrual etiquette recommend the use of certain equipment and products, how they should be acquired, carried, stored, disposed of, and referred to in conversation. Above all, menstrual etiquette rules govern the comportment of menstruating women

28. Mary Douglas, *Purity and Danger: An Analysis of Concepts of Pollution and Taboo* (London: Routledge, 1966).

29. Glenda Koutroulis, "Soiled Identity: Memory-Work Narratives of Menstruation," *Health* 5.2 (2001): 187–205.

30. Sophie Laws, *Issues of Blood: The Politics of Menstruation* (London: MacMillan, 1990).

to ensure that the facts of our menstruation remain hidden from nearly everyone each month.

The idea of menstrual etiquette differs from more commonly stated ideas of taboos associated with menstruation. While Laws alludes to this difference, she does not develop it explicitly. As I understand it, the concept of a taboo belongs to societies or social practices that make a strong distinction between the sacred and the profane. This is a spiritual or metaphysical distinction that aligns human behavior and social practices with cosmic distinctions and consequences. Purity, in such a cosmological system, usually requires preservation of spatial and practical borders, and a taboo generates rules against crossing the borders.

Rules of etiquette, by contrast, appear in social systems drained of this cosmological significance in social interaction. There is something more minute and even trivial about manners than the taboos associated with sacred spaces and events; etiquette involves a micromanagement of behavior, whereas taboos invoke major fault lines of the social system. When there are menstrual taboos, the whole woman must be confined, closeted, or kept away from certain people, processes, or substances. The system of menstrual etiquette, on the other hand, does not constrain the woman herself from involvement in spaces and activities also involving nonmenstruating persons. Rather, it concerns a self-discipline she must apply in those settings.

Menstrual etiquette creates an emotional and disciplinary burden for girls and women. By the repeated enforcement of these rules of etiquette, we girls and women know that we are shameful, not because of anything that we have done, but just by being what we are.[31] The shock of having to bear the burden of shame is what Beauvoir invokes as the wound to a girl's confidence when she comes to puberty. Adolescent girls frequently stand in solidarity with one another by aiding one another's efforts to conceal their periods. "Look at the back of my skirt, is anything showing?" "Here, take my sweater and tie it around your waist, I'll walk behind you." "Can you pass me a tampon in your algebra book?" We dwell in the delicious space of shared secrets and protect one another from ridicule.

But isn't it an exaggeration to refer to these disciplines as oppressive? A decent society depends on a certain bodily modesty and self-discipline on the part of its members, does it not? Surely the rules of menstrual etiquette are no more oppressive than norms of body covering in public or expectations of control, concealment, and cleanliness associated with other excretions. Am I arguing that we all ought to let everything about

31. On shame culturally enforced on women, see Sonia Kruks, "Panopticism and Shame: Foucault, Beauvoir, and Feminism," in *Retrieving Experience: Subjectivity and Recognition in Feminist Politics* (Ithaca, N.Y.: Cornell University Press, 2001); and Sandra Lee Bartky, "Shame and Gender," in *Femininity and Domination: Studies in the Phenomenology of Oppression* (New York: Routledge, 1990), 83–98.

our bodies and their processes hang out for all to see? If not, then what's such a big deal about menstrual concealment, and why do I and other feminists suggest that its norms are symptomatic of an unjust subordinate status for women?[32]

I have largely answered these questions already. The jokes and judgments of disgust associated with menstruation are a stronger manifestation of abjection than are many other such expressions. The expectation that girls and women control their bodies to conceal this process seems especially unjust because this excretion is not controllable. There is nothing a woman can do to stall or temporarily stop the flow, in the way most people can hold back urination, for example. Indeed, as I discussed in referring to Elizabeth Grosz, women come to occupy the position of the abject because we are identified as out of control. Social relations of somatophobia and misogyny continue to hold over women in some circumstances the threat of being "outed" as menstruators, sometimes with serious consequences to their self-esteem or opportunities for benefits. As I will now detail, all these small harms and liabilities are exacerbated by institutional settings that poorly support a woman's physical and social need to take care of herself and conceal her menstrual processes.

C. Institutional Nonacceptance

I began this section by noting an apparent paradox: dominant norms in advanced industrial societies affirm that women should have the opportunities to do anything that men do, but at the same time force women to conceal their menstruation. This paradox resolves, I suggested, when we recognize that the affirmation of equality for women comes under a process of normalization; all opportunities are open to women to try to conform to the standards of achievement in public life that first have been set for men. This normative humanism must thereby suppress deviant facts such as the physical and social implications of menstruation.

This suppression has potentially disadvantaging consequences for women, I will now argue, because menstruating produces some special needs in the context of public institutions such as schools and workplaces. Schools, workplaces, and other public institutions of bureaucratic equality assume a standard body with standard needs, and that body does not menstruate. This assumption of equality as sameness often unfairly discomforts and disadvantages menstruating women and threatens us with embarrassment and shame. I find three forms of such unfairness. First, schools and workplaces often fail to make provision

32. I am raising objections that I think some who argue for public norms of concealment and privacy would raise. See, for example, Thomas Nagel, "Concealment and Exposure," in Nagel, *Concealment and Exposure and Other Essays* (Oxford: Oxford University Press, 2002), 3–26.

for the physical and social needs of menstruating women. Second, they often ignore or punish the temporary unwellness some women suffer before or during menstruation. Third, the sexually indifferent institutional norms make women vulnerable to being "outed" by others in public settings in ways potentially damaging to the respect and reward we hope for in achievement oriented institutions.[33]

1. Schools and public workplaces, the two sorts of settings where girls and women aiming to be normal must show themselves as good as the boys and men, often fail to provide the time, space, and equipment necessary for girls and women to manage the menstrual process to keep themselves comfortable and conceal the process from others. We have special needs as menstruators, needs constructed by the intersection of the bodily process and the rules of menstrual etiquette. We need to go to the bathroom often to change our pads or tampons, especially on heavy days. We need ways of disposing of used ones and ways of acquiring new ones. We need to proceed from our workstations to the changing space without detection of our purpose. We need time to take care of these management matters without punishment for lateness. While menstruating, we spend much of our emotional energy anxious about meeting these needs.

Schools and most workplaces are disciplinary institutions that give space for going to the bathroom according to their own imperatives of regularity and efficiency. Disciplinary institutions nearly always restrict time in the bathroom, and often themselves set the time at which students or workers can use the toilet, rather than accommodating the needs of each body. In one case that hit the courts, female assembly-line workers at Nabisco Foods in Oxnard, California, sued the employer for sex discrimination, saying that they were allowed only three bathroom breaks a day, during which two hundred women had to compete for twelve toilets. They said that the men, who generally were non–assembly line workers, were permitted to use the bathroom at any time.[34]

As in this case, employers usually cite productivity as the reason for such restriction. If this is plausible, then it reveals the degrading instrumentalism of employer attitudes to workers. A more important reason, many students and workers think, is to make and keep students and workers subordinate. The institutions wish to keep the students and

---

33. For a beautifully written study of these issues in a particular context, see B. M. Thuren, "Opening Doors and Getting Rid of Shame: Experiences of First Menstruation in Valencia," *Women's Studies International Forum* 17.2/3 (1994): 217–28.

34. Nina Schuyler, "No Rest Room for the Weary," *Working Women* 20.7 (1995): 13–14. Compare Marc Linder and Ingrid Nygaard, *Void Where Prohibited: Rest Breaks and the Right to Urinate on Company Time* (Ithaca, N.Y.: Cornell University Press, 1998). Linder and Nygaard discuss the fact that many workers of both sexes have no or few paid bathroom breaks; attempts legally to challenge equal bathroom time for men and women, on grounds that women need more time, have been invalidated by most American courts.

workers under supervision as much as possible; the bathroom, as a place of relative privacy, can also be a subversive place. These disciplines oppress all students and workers with needs or conditions that require more than minimal bathroom use in a given day.

Part of the problem is the presence of a particular set of norms held as the standard against which all individuals should be measured. When equality is understood as sameness, then the requirements of equal respect and equal treatment have been met when all workers or students have the same number of bathroom breaks or days off. But even some state legislators have begun to admit that this is a sham notion of equality in the face of bodily difference and need and have passed laws enlarging bathroom space or time for women as a requirement of equality. While courts have found such gender-based public toilet legislation consistent with principles of nondiscrimination, on the whole they refuse to support legislative efforts to mandate rest periods for women.[35] I would agree that what we need may be not special treatment for women, but rather a shift in the norm for equal treatment.

Too often women are caught unprepared by our periods, or the flow on a particular day is greater than we predicted. We have not anticipated our needs for pads or tampons, and we are in a spot. It's a joke among women that machines in public bathrooms that claim to dispense these products are always empty or jammed. In many women's bathrooms it's easier to buy a condom or comb than a tampon. The ubiquity of this problem, even in well-resourced universities or factories, leads one to find institutions guilty of denial and wanton indifference about these simple ways that women might be helped to be comfortable and to conform to social expectations of concealment.[36]

2. Not all menstruating women suffer physical discomfort or emotional distress around the times of their periods. Many do, however, at least during some years of their lives. Some women report physical symptoms such as headache, backache, abdominal cramps, and cervical pain. Some women experience volatile emotions and moods that can interfere with their ability to concentrate. Few employers recognize menstrual distress as a small disability they ought to accommodate. Sometimes they punish women who take time off or ask for lighter work during their periods because they experience discomfort. In one case, for example, a former employee of the Des Moines Metropolitan Transit Authority brought action alleging sex discrimination against the MTA

35. Linder and Nygaard, *Void Where Prohibited*, 154–55.

36. Robin Harvey, "'That Time of Month' Still a Taboo Subject—Most Employers Don't View Menstruation as Their Problem," *Toronto Star*, October 9, 1998. Women who work in jobs where they have to stand often have special problems when menstruating. Companies with scheduled washroom breaks make it difficult for menstruating women. There are no formal employment policies to recognize the needs of menstruating women; Sophie Laws found that the men she interviewed flatly disbelieve that women suffer any discomfort during their periods; *Issues of Blood*, chapter 8.

and her former union. The woman had a condition that produced painful menstruation, which caused her to stay home from work. She was dismissed for excessive absenteeism, even though men who also violated the attendance standards as a result of medical or personal problems were not similarly terminated for excessive absenteeism.[37]

While physical and emotional symptoms disable some women from working, most can and do carry on with their normal work activities in spite of strain and discomfort. Although many people think that women take off more sick days than men due to their periods, studies show that the most common reason for female absence from work is a sick child.[38] Most women who experience physical and/or emotional discomfort before or during their periods, that is, try hard to work at their highest level and to conceal from coworkers and supervisors that menstruation makes working more difficult for them. I think that it is unfair to expect us to do this.

The default norm of the public person as in a male body creates numerous problems for many women that public institutions on the whole fail to recognize as sources of disadvantage. The rules of menstrual etiquette require us to conceal our condition, yet we often lack access to the private spaces that would allow us to do so. As workers and students we are expected to perform at the same level when menstruating as when not, and we are compared with men, even though the capacities of some of us are impaired during these days. Menstrual etiquette, moreover, forbids complaining of being unwell, even though our nonmenstruating neighbors are free to admit that a cold is slowing them down. Most women do their best to meet expectations under trying circumstances: we take special measures to keep the evidence of menstruation out of sight and smell, bear silently its strains and discomforts unless they are severe, and we expect in return to earn an equal place among those who command respect.

3. No matter how hard she works to conceal this fact of her womanliness, however, others, especially men, always have it as a switch to beat her with, a stigma with which to mark her as deviant, a threat of exposure with which to harass and humiliate her. When a woman becomes angry, impatient, or easily hurt in workplace interaction, some of her coworkers may attribute her behavior to hormones, in complete ignorance of her current menstrual state. There is little research that aims to document male attitudes to menstruation. I think it is plausible that the attitudes expressed by the men in the focus groups that Sophie Laws conducted are typical. She found that men express and report interac-

37. *Iowa Employment Law Letter* 3.2 (1996).

38. Marie Annette Brown and Phyllis Arn Zimmer, "Help-Seeking for Premenstrual Symptomology: A Description of Women's Experiences," in *Culture, Society, and Menstruation*, ed. Virginia L. Olesen and Nancy Fugate Woods (Washington: Hemisphere Publishing Co., 1986).

tions with other men where menstruation jokes importantly figure.[39] A woman in the workplace is liable to suffer anything from mild teasing to serious harassment to abject humiliation under the gaze of joking or malicious men.[40] This creates enormous possibility for emotional cruelty. Precisely because her womanliness is always visible, a woman is always liable to being "outed" as one who menstruates. The harm here is that of producing shame and stigma by others revealing what the dominant norms say should be hidden. Leaving an apparently bloodstained maxi-pad at a woman's workstation can be construed as a very threatening act. I have heard reports that in countries where women workers have a legal right to special treatment on account of menstruation—days off, or extra bathroom time, for example—it sometimes happens that male supervisors demand that a woman give evidence to support her claim to them or male physicians by means of a humiliating vaginal exam.[41]

What would it mean to diminish these difficulties, inequalities, and shames women face as menstruators in contemporary supposedly sexually egalitarian societies? It would mean publicly accepting menstruation as an ordinary and unremarkable, if still bothersome, process. Even in twenty-first-century consumer societies where so much about sexuality has become more public and discussed, this is a radical goal, for it means demoting women's bodies from the abject or monstrous to the merely different, and this entails acknowledging that all our bodies are fluid, messy, requiring public accommodation to our needs. Many men would benefit along with most women if our public and private institutions assumed no bodily norms and simply accommodated individual variation and need. While we might continue to expect a kind of body modesty that allows us to concentrate on issues other than our bodies and their processes in many settings, the exposure of female body processes would not be a cause of shame.

III. Moody Times

Mood cycles in both men and women appear to correlate more with the social cycle of the workweek than with physiological processes such as menstruation. Many people hit an emotional low point in midweek and an upswing on the weekend; some people's emotional lows, on the other

---

39. Laws, *Issues of Blood*, chapter 4.

40. Alan Feuer, "Sexual Harassment Suit Filed," *New York Times*, August 3, 2001. Three female construction workers filed suit again Tratoros Construction company saying they experienced sexual harassment from male supervisors that included making humiliating allusions to menstruation. The complaint accused one of the supervisors of telling his male colleagues to leave the women alone "because they had cramps" and ordered the women to "change their Pampers."

41. Such stories were relayed by a group of observers who lived for some months in a neighborhood of Jakarta, Indonesia.

hand, tend to happen on their days off.[42] Most people are not aware of these socially triggered mood changes, however, or their recurrence; only the systematic recording of their affective experience in journals and the researcher's aggregation of a large number of such reflections reveals these mood swings.

Both cultural stereotype and personal experience, on the other hand, associate menstruation consciously with moodiness. When asked, most women report experience of premenstrual tension, irritability or agitation, though this disrupts the lives of only a minority.[43] At the same time, however, most distinguish such experience from stereotypes of premenstrual syndrome that would classify their symptoms as a physical or emotional disorder. They wish both to express their experience of mood change and anxiety around the time of menstruation, and to understand such emotional states as normal.

The stereotypes of the bitchy female "on the rag" accompany the construction of women as abject, monstrous, out of control. We are oversensitive, unpredictable, verbally unpleasant because of our womanly natures; we are most likely to erupt, so the imagery goes, at that time of the month. As I detailed in the previous section, these judgments can be and often are used against us as women whether we are menstruating at any given moment or not. Coworkers may dismiss a woman's anger or impatience as just a symptom of her hormones, and thus not to be taken seriously and addressed. In the face of such denigration, many women suppress their feelings and try to keep even and cool so as to appear properly professional or cheerful in their public interactions. We try to conform to a modern norm of dispassionate reasons and proper niceness, a norm that allows the expression of emotion only in a narrow range.

Negative emotions are especially forbidden in this system of public reason and optimism; we abjure expressions of anger, frustration, despair, depression, dread, anxiety, or melancholy. Yet these vague feelings of discomfort and uncertainty that shadow the everyday lives of most of us, female or male, especially when we are trying to accomplish difficult tasks or endeavoring to win recognition from others. We are haunted by self-imposed threats of failure or inadequacy; we have countless little reasons to feel sadness or regret.

Since others often impose on us the status of being moody and out of control, and since many of us experience a heightened awareness of mood change around the time of our periods, we have the opportunity to embrace rather than suppress these affective experiences. Some-

42. See Alice Rossi and Peter Rossi, "Body Time and Social Time: Mood Patterns in Menstrual Cycle Phase and the Day of the Week," *Social Science Research* 6 (1977): 273–308.

43. Brown and Zimmer, "Help-Seeking for Premenstrual Symptomology."

times we allow ourselves to *give over* to our moods, feeling a heightened sensitivity to ourselves in menstruating. We can retreat temporarily from the stiff demands of smooth interaction and getting things done efficiently in order to brood. We close in on ourselves for a couple of days a month and reflect on our lives, often with a sense of melancholy or wistfulness. We experience our moodiness as coming from nowhere, and we feel it dissipate just as much without our willing or steering it.

Here I am not generalizing about women's emotional states in menstruation, but rather gesturing toward a possibility the experience offers that some of us take up some of the time. This female body experience does not offer the possibility of transvaluing the values of a commodified, efficiency-oriented, rationalist culture. It can, however, speak to all of us about the reflective possibilities of moody meditation, if we listen.

Can moodiness be transformed from a condition to be avoided or suppressed to a state of reflective insight? There is probably less philosophical reflection on the significance of mood than on the lived body. Indeed, Martin Heidegger's *Being and Time* is one of the few philosophical works in which mood figures centrally to the analysis of Being. Heidegger himself would no doubt be shocked to have his lofty text appropriated for the sake of revealing human possibilities in unspeakable menstrual experiences. That fashioning such an association may be slightly naughty only adds to the lesson, it seems to me.

The project of *Being and Time* is to articulate the categories and dialectic that describe the meaning of Being as the ground of the possibility of things and actions in a meaningful world. Heidegger refers to this project as fundamental ontology. Basic to his analysis is a distinction between the ontic and the ontological. Most of us most of the time experience ourselves, other people, things, institutions, at the level of the ontic. Particular things and events occupy our attention as embedded in the practical projects we set out on. They presuppose a historical and social background of meanings and relations constituted themselves through this process of being-in-the-world, but which we rarely bring to the foreground. The ontological, on the other hand, consists in a level of understanding that brings these background structures that constitute our world into view.

Being in a mood is something very different from having an emotion. Emotions have objects, they are pointed and directed. I am angry at, joyful about, delighted with, afraid of, in a determinate way. Emotions belong to the ontic, in Heidegger's terms. They accompany and vary with my engaged action. Mood, on the other hand, is ontological. A mood pervades, it influences the way I experience everything while I am in it.

Heidegger says that mood is primordial. Mood is prior to both the knowledge of things and the formation of goals and actions of my own.

Mood first discloses the world, but in the mode of an evasive turning away. Often we ignore or try to shake off moods that surround us. We throw ourselves into the details of our projects or let ourselves be distracted from the mood's revelatory potential by attending to momentary experiences that we find interesting or amusing.[44]

But sometimes we allow ourselves to sink into our moods. Then we transit from the inauthenticity of everydayness to the authentic experience of our own Being. The mood assails us. It arises neither from within our own agency, as does an image we conjure, nor from some perceived external cause, like the breeze on our skin. In this sense of coming from nowhere the mood reveals us, in Heidegger's terms, as "thrown." "Having a mood brings Dasein face to face with its thrownness in such as manner that this thrownness is not known as such, but disclosed far more primordially in 'how one is.' . . . My mood represents whatever may be the way in which I am primarily the entity that has been thrown" (389).

To exist is to experience ourselves as always already having been thrown there in the world. Before there are particular perceptions of entities in the world and projects to form with them, mood makes it possible to be open to the world. The primary discovery of the world, Heidegger says, is left to bare mood (177). The ontological structure of being-in-the-world, according to this text, is time.

Mood not only makes it possible to be open to a world, it also reveals the temporality of existence; the self exists through the three ecstasies of temporarlity, as Care. In Heidegger's infelicitous formulation, Care consists in "ahead of itself Being already (in the world) as Being alongside entities encountered in the world" (237). This formula shows temporalization as involving future, past, and present mutually constituting one another. I am open to the world as a set of possibilities for myself that appear in relation to the entities I encounter there in the world as one who has already been thrown there. The existentially basic character of moods consists in bringing us back to this thrownness of our having been not as in the past, but as the ongoing pastness of my existence whose future remains open.

Heidegger locates dread, or anxiety, as the primary mood for ontology. This mood brings us back to existence as such, as unconditioned, contingent, finite, and open to possibility. Mood here sets the tone of everything and itself cannot be grasped or brought before consciousness. It is what we *are*, not as an attribute or fact, but as one for whom there are possibilities.

To the extent that women use menstrual moods to come to ourselves

---

44. Martin Heidegger, *Being and Time*, trans. John Macquarrie and Edward Robinson (New York: Harper and Row, 1962), 175. Further citations to this work appear in parentheses in the text; page numbers refer to the English edition.

and renew an openness to the world, then we find in this turning toward our bodies a possibility of meditation available to any of us at all times, but in which we usually decide we are too busy to indulge, or from which we are blocked by the exigencies of pain, suffering, and survival. As located on the edges of propriety, and in a closet, the menstruating woman can sometimes take a distance and reflect on how things are going with us. "A mood makes manifest 'how one is, and how one is faring'" (173). Performing this ontological function, living through the mood will have a certain weightiness that we name with terms like *blue*, or *sad*, or *melancholy*. Even anxiety hovers at the edges. In these menstrual moods we often say that we are upset for "no reason" that "nothing" has brought it on.

The stereotypical association of menstruation with time can supplement this reflective possibility. Just because the event returns monthly, it affords an experienced discontinuity that prompts gathering oneself to look back and forward. The monthly flow mundanely organizes our everyday adult memory. Without meaning to, I find myself remembering which event occurred before which according to my last period. Sometimes we feel we should schedule our appointments around anticipation of our periods, or rather, their absence. I try not to meet that special lover when I am menstruating. I arrange to travel to places where managing menstrual secrecy is difficult during times when I hope I will not be menstruating.

Beauvoir suggests that events associated with menstruation give a unique temporal shape to a woman's life.

> The individual life history of women—because she is still bound up in her female functions—depends in much greater degree than that of man upon her physiological destiny; and the curve of this destiny is much more uneven, more discontinuous, than the masculine curve. Each period in the life of woman is uniform and monotonous; but the transitions from one stage to another are dangerously abrupt; they are manifested in crisis—much more decisive than in the male. (545)

As she too often does, Beauvoir exaggerates here; a woman's life is not uniform and monotonous between major physiological changes. Still, Beauvoir captures an important aspect of many women's experience. Because menstrual moments punctuate our lives, they easily orient our self-narrative. Many women remember vividly the onset of menses not necessarily because the event itself was so dramatic, but because we experience ourselves in a major transition from child to woman in this process. We remember our excitement at the thought of growing up, wearing stockings, having sex, leaping forward into responsibility. At the same time, we look regretfully over the bleeding wall that separates us from our childhood with a little bit of loss, a sense of the real world having crashed in on us too soon.

This can perhaps make sense of Julia Kristeva's cryptic and slightly mystical claim that women's time is *monumental*.[45] Menstrual events produce large markers that differentiate everything before and after. I probably become aware of my pregnancy first by the absence of the flow. As in the narrative of my own life that I quoted at the beginning of this essay, the return of my periods after months of pregnancy, childbirth, and nursing marks another kind of new beginning, which a woman may greet with a mixture of familiarity and annoyance.

The time of menopause, however, may be the most monumental. We call it the change of life. Another door that closes behind us on a past to which there is no return except in our dreams. It does not close on most of us all at once, but rather slowly creaks on its hinges, sometimes swaying back and forth, affording us the opportunity to step in and out of reflection on who we have been and want to be. Most of us are glad to have the messy body business done with. For the most part, we do not feel as Beauvoir attributes to us in a passage I quoted earlier, "With no future, she still has about one half of her adult life to live" (757). We more likely experience, as in the other passage I cited, "a health, a balance, a vigor (we) lacked before" (31). We have plenty of future, and we make plans for projects bigger than we have hitherto undertaken. At the same time this turning point gives us a long view of our past as a having been that we remain.

In another of her existentialist masterpieces, *La Viellesse,* translated as *The Coming of Age* in English, Beauvoir takes some issue with the Sartrean account of temporality, which he derives from Heidegger. To exist as human, on this Sartrean account, means that the future is always equally open. However long and burdened with habit one's life, one is always equally free to take up a different direction or attitude. In one sense this is certainly true; one can say definitively who a person is only after his or her death.

Considered from another point of view, however, this is a strangely ethereal image of human life. It does not take proper account of the embodied person, whose memory grows thicker at the same time as her waist. Remembering her own younger bodily self and capacities as well as a sedimented set of events of her life, the older person brings to her future more layers of meaning than the younger.[46] Shifting the significance of menstruation from the monstrous to something mundane and revealing can reinforce this truth for all of us, women and men.

45. Julia Kristeva, "Women's Time," trans. Alice Jardine and Harry Blake, *Signs: A Journal of Women in Culture and Society* 7.1 (Autumn 1981): 13–59. See also Tina Chanter, "Female Temporality and the Future of Feminism," in *Abjection, Melancholia and Love,* ed. John Fletcher and Andrew Benjamin (London: Routledge, 1990).

46. Beauvoir, *The Coming of Age* (New York: Warner Books, 1978), 535–37.

7

House and Home:

Feminist Variations on a Theme

For millennia the image of Penelope sitting by the hearth and weaving, saving and preserving the home while her man roams the earth in daring adventures, has defined one of Western culture's basic ideas of womanhood. Many other cultures historically and today equate women with home, expecting women to serve men at home and sometimes preventing them from leaving the house. If house and home mean the confinement of women for the sake of nourishing male projects, then feminists have good reason to reject home as a value. But it is difficult even for feminists to exorcise a positive valence to the idea of home. We often look forward to going home and invite others to make themselves at home. House and home are deeply ambivalent values.

In this essay I sort through this ambivalence. On the one hand, I agree with feminist critics such as Luce Irigaray and Simone de Beauvoir that the comforts and supports of house and home historically come at women's expense. Women serve, nurture, and maintain so that the bodies and souls of men and children gain confidence and expansive subjectivity to make their mark on the world. This homey role deprives women of support for their own identity and projects. Along with several feminist critics, furthermore, I question the yearning for a whole and stable identity that the idea of home often represents. Unlike these critics, however, I am not ready to toss the idea of home out of the larder of feminist

I am grateful to David Alexander, Robert Beauregard, Edward Casey, Delores Hayden, Deorothea Olkowski, and Geraldine Pratt for helpful comments on earlier versions of this paper. I also benefited from a discussion of the paper at the University of Pittsburgh women's writing group, including Jean Carr, Nancy Glazener, Paula Kane, Margaret Marshall, and Marianne Novy.

values. Despite the oppressions and privileges the idea historically carries, the idea of home also carries critical liberating potential because it expresses uniquely human values. Some of these can be uncovered by exploring the meaning-making activity most typical of women in domestic work.

Instead of following one line of argument, I aim here to weave together several thematic threads. All of them wind around meanings of subjectivity or identity. I begin by noting Martin Heidegger's equation of dwelling with the way of being that is human and note his division of dwelling into moments of building and preservation. Despite his claim that these moments are equally important, Heidegger nevertheless seems to privilege building as the world-founding of an active subject, and I suggest that this privileging is male-biased.

Luce Irigaray makes explicit the maleness of Heidegger's allegedly universal ontology. Man can build and dwell in the world in patriarchal culture, she suggests, only on the basis of the materiality and nurturance of women. In the idea of "home," man projects onto woman the nostalgic longing for the lost wholeness of the original mother. To fix and keep hold of his identity, man makes a house, puts things in it, and confines there his woman, who reflects his identity to him. The price she pays for supporting his subjectivity, however, is dereliction, having no self of her own.

Irigaray writes about the association of house and home with a male longing for fixed identity in a timeless tone. The property acquisition she describes men as engaging in as a means of substituting for the lost mother, however, is probably best thought of as characteristic of bourgeois society, whose values became hegemonic in the twentieth century in the West, and increasingly in the world. Thus I explore the specific attachment of personal identity to commodified houses and their contents, in order to find another angle of critique of the longing for home.

Before entering a critique of Simone de Beauvoir's devaluation of housework, I digress to tell the story of one bad housekeeper: my mother. The purpose of this gesture is to commemorate, but also to describe in concrete terms how disciplinary standards of orderly housework and PTA motherhood continue to oppress women, especially single mothers.

Like Irigaray, Beauvoir describes women's existence as deprived of active subjectivity because their activity concentrates on serving and supporting men in the home. Unlike Irigaray, however, Beauvoir materializes this account by reflecting on the sexual division of labor. Because she accepts a dichotomy between immanence and transcendence and identifies all of women's domestic labor with immanence, however, Beauvoir misses the creatively human aspects of women's traditional household work, in activities I call preservation.

That aspect of dwelling which Heidegger devalues thus provides a turning point for revaluing home. Preservation makes and remakes home as a support for personal identity without accumulation, certainty, or fixity. While preservation, a typically feminine activity, is traditionally devalued—at least in Western conceptions of history and identity—it has crucial human value.

I next challenge a group of feminist texts whose writers all reject the idea of home as inappropriately totalizing and imperialist. Essays by Biddy Martin and Chandra Mohanty, Teresa de Lauretis, and Bonnie Honig all argue that longing for home expresses an oppressive search for certainty and attachment to privilege. Although I accept much of their analysis, I question the wholesale rejection of an ideal of home for feminism. While values of home do indeed signal privilege today, analysis of those values and commitment to their democratic enactment for all can have enormous critical political potential in today's world. In addition to preservation, those values include safety, individuation, and privacy.

Dwelling and Building

Dwelling, says Martin Heidegger, is man's mode of being. Habitual human activity reveals things as meaningful, and through dwelling among the meaningful things people have a place for themselves. Dwelling and building, Heidegger says, stand in a circular relation. Humans attain to dwelling only by means of building. We dwell by making the places and things that structure and house our activities. These places and things establish relations among each other, between themselves and dwellers, and between dwellers and the surrounding environment. But we build on the basis of already dwelling only as the beings whose mode of being is to let things be, to think and reveal them.[1]

Building has two aspects, according to Heidegger: cultivating and constructing. One mode of building consists in cherishing, protecting, preserving, and caring for, whose paradigm is agriculture, the cultivation of the soil. "Building in the sense of preserving and nurturing is not making anything" (BDT, 147). Thus to remain, to stay in place, is an important meaning of dwelling. "To dwell, to be set at peace, means to remain at peace within the free, the preserve, the free sphere that safeguards each thing in its nature. The fundamental character of dwelling is this sparing and preserving" (BDT, 149).

After introducing this duality of building as preservation and construction, Heidegger's text leaves preservation behind to focus on construction—a curious abandonment, in light of the above claim that preservation is fundamental to dwelling. To describe the human mode of being-in-the-world, Heidegger dwells on the heroic moment of place

---

1. Martin Heidegger, "Building, Dwelling, Thinking," in *Poetry, Language, Thought,* trans. Albert Hofstadter (New York: Harper and Row, 1971). Hereafter cited as BDT.

through creative activity that gathers the environment into a meaningful presence.

We can dwell only in a place. Edifices enclose areas with walls and link areas by planes, thus creating locations. Walls, roofs, columns, stairs, fences, bridges, towers, roads, and squares found the human world by making place.[2] Through building, man establishes a world and his place in the world, according to Heidegger, establishes himself as somebody, with an identity and history. People inhabit the world by erecting material supports for their routines and rituals and then see the specificity of their lives reflected in the environment, the materiality of things gathered together with historical meaning.[3] If building in this way is basic to the emergence of subjectivity, to dwelling in the world with identity and history, then it would appear that only men are subjects. On the whole, women do not build.

Even today, when women have moved into so many typically male activities, building houses and other structures remains largely a male activity in most parts of the world.[4] In building industries, a woman with a hard hat is still a rare sight. Nowhere in the world do women participate in the building trades in more than very small numbers. Perhaps even more significantly, men dominate the ranks of those who make building decisions—corporate boards of directors, architects, planners, engineers. Even in some of the most egalitarian households, the work of building and structural maintenance falls most often to men.

In many traditional societies of Africa and Asia, women were the home builders. But peasants all over the world have migrated to cities and towns because capitalism and environmental destruction have made it nearly impossible in many places to live off the land in traditional ways. Many rural and urban development projects include programs where people build the houses in which they will live. Despite the fact that poorer households in developing countries are very often headed by women, they rarely participate in these house-building projects. Either they do not have title to land on which to build because of male biases

2. Compare Edward Casey, *Getting Back into Place: Toward a Renewed Understanding of the Place-World* (Bloomington: Indiana University Press, 1993), 112. Casey also notes (176–77) that Heidegger slides into identifying dwelling with construction even though he begins with a wider scope for building.

3. Hannah Arendt also theorized building as a fundamental aspect of human meaning. She distinguishes between labor, activity useful for production and consumption of the means of living, and work, the construction of artifacts that transcend mere life because they are made to be permanent. Thus for Arendt the moment of founding is the primordial moment of action. Through the construction of edifices people create a built environment, a civilization, by means of which they emerge as thinking and speaking subjects. See Hannah Arendt, *The Human Condition* (Chicago: University of Chicago Press, 1958).

4. Aliye Pekin Celik, "Women's Participation in the Production of Shelter," and Victoria Basolo and Michelle Moraln, "Women and the Production of Housing: An Overview," both in Hemalata C. Dandekar, *Shelter, Women, and Development: First and Third World Perspectives* (Ann Arbor, Mich.: George Wahr Publishing Co., 1993).

in property laws, or the development project has simply assumed that men are more natural builders and thus have designed construction projects with men in mind. Frequently women's income and assets are so low that they cannot qualify for the credit necessary to participate in building projects.[5]

If building establishes a world, if building is the means by which a person emerges as a subject who dwells in that world, then not to build is a deprivation. Those excluded from building, who do not think of themselves as builders, perhaps have a more limited relation to the world, which they do not think of themselves as founding. Those who build dwell in the world in a different way from those who occupy the structures already built, and from those who preserve what is constructed. If building establishes a world, then it is still very much a man's world.

Women as a group are still largely excluded from the activities that erect structures to gather and reveal a meaningful world. It will be women's world as much as men's only when women participate as much in their design and founding. But the male bias of building also appears in the devaluation of that other aspect of building Heidegger discusses, preservation, a devaluation to which his own philosophy tends. For a distinction between constructing and preserving, as two aspects of building and dwelling, is implicitly gendered. Later I will pick up the thread of this concept of preservation, to argue that much of the unnoticed labor of women is this basic activity of meaning maintenance. First we shall explore further the masculinism implicit in a philosophy of existence that takes building as world founding, by way of a bridge from Heidegger to his feminist follower and critic Luce Irigaray.

Building, says, Heidegger, gathers together dispersed surroundings, which have no center apart from the artifice around which they are oriented. The house in the woods gives to the trees and lakes a placement. The bridge across the river gathers the shores, revealing a nexus of relationships, a context. But man's building, Heidegger points out, occurs on the foundation of already dwelling. Man is enveloped by being, finds himself as already having been at home in nature, which building reveals as already surrounding. This revealing of the world itself depends on a prior ground that sustains and nurtures.

With such a move Heidegger believes himself to be sublating modern Western philosophy, and its specifically technological orientation. Descartes and those who come after him have the hubris to think of man

5. Caroline O. N. Moser, "Women, Human Settlements, and Housing: A Conceptual Framework for Analysis and Policy-Making," in *Women, Human Settlements, and Housing,* ed. Caroline O. N. Moser and Linda Peake (London: Tavistock Publications, 1987); Irene Tinker, "Beyond Economics: Sheltering the Whole Woman," in *Engendering Wealth and Well-Being,* ed. Rae Lesser Blumberg et al. (Boulder, Colo.: Westview Press, 1995), 261–84.

as self-originating, the thinking subject as the master and representor of being. They have forgotten the humility of the ancients, who understand better the placement of mortals in a nature on which they depend, whose thoughtful tending and preserving is the lot of mortals. Man builds for the sake of dwelling, to make himself at home, in respect to the prior elements that envelop and nourish him, which his building gathers and reveals.

Woman as Nostalgic Home

Luce Irigaray names the gendering already present in Heidegger's world-ing of the world: Man builds for the sake of dwelling, to make himself at home, on the basis of woman as already always positioned as the enveloping nurturing presence of nature. For man, woman is always mother, from whose dark womb he emerges to build solid structures in the light of day, with whose light he returns to look in the caverns with the speculum. In lovemaking he seeks to return to the enclosing warmth of the original union with the mother. The patriarchal gender system allows man a subjectivity that depends on woman's objectification and dereliction; he has a home at the expense of her homelessness, as she serves as the ground on which he builds.

Everyone is born in loss. Ejected from the dark comfort of the moth-er's body, we are thrown into a world without walls, with no foundation to our fragile and open-ended existence. Speaking mortals must come to terms with this separation from the mother, to find and form meaning and identity for ourselves, without foundation or certainty. In patriar-chal culture, according to Irigaray, the gender system of masculinity and femininity makes it possible for man to come to terms with this loss by never really dealing with it; instead, he attempts to return to the lost home of the womb by means of woman.

Man deals with the loss by building, in order that he may recover his dwelling. He seeks to make himself a home to stand in for the lost home. Through building he gathers the amorphous and fluid elements into solid structure. Through projecting outward he makes objective works where he can see himself reflected. He makes and affirms himself as subject through building and making. In this objectifying self-reflection woman serves as material both on which to stand and out of which to build, and women likewise serve as a primary object for reflecting him-self, his mirror.

> Man's love is teleological. It aims for a target outside them. It moves to-ward the outside and the constitution, on the outside, within that which is outside themselves, of a home. Outside of the self, the tension, the inten-tion, aims for a dwelling, a thing, a production. Which also serves men as a third part and stake.

To inhabit is the fundamental trait of man's being. Even if this trait remains unconscious, unfulfilled, especially in its ethical dimension, man is forever searching for, building, creating homes for himself everywhere: caves, huts, women, cities, language, concepts, theory, and so on.[6]

Building is for the sake of dwelling, gathering together natural material and element into a determinate place. In the patriarchal gender scheme, woman serves as the construction material (ESD, 103–7), and as the place within which man dwells. His self-affirming subjectivity is possible because she supports and complements his existence as both an origin of his creativity and the product in which he can see his self reflected. She serves as the material envelope and container of his existence. "She is assigned to be place without occupying place. Through her, place would be set up for man's use but not hers. Her jouissance is meant to 'resemble' the flow of whatever is in the place that she is when she contains, contains herself" (ESD, 52).

The form of man's self-affirmation in this gender system is nostalgia, a longing for the return to a lost home. Man puts woman in her place, so that he can return to the original maternal home. Nostalgia is this recurrent desire for return, which is unsatisfiable because the loss is separation, birth, mortality, itself. Nostalgia is a flight from having to come to terms with this loss, by means of constant search for a symbolic substitute for lost home. Man yearns nostalgically for an original union with the mother within safe walls of warmth. In women men look nostalgically to return to their own lost home; thus they fail to face women as subjects with their own identities and need of covering.

He arrests his growth and repeats, endlessly, searching for the moment when the separation of memory and forgetting was lost to him. But, the more he repeats, the more he surrounds himself with envelops, containers, "houses" which prevent him from finding either the other or himself. His nostalgia for a first and last dwelling prevents him from meeting and living with the other. (ESD, 142)

Man seeks nostalgically to return to the lost home by making buildings and putting things in them that will substitute for that original home. He creates property, things he owns and controls. But because the property doesn't satisfy the longing for lost home, he is launched on an acquisitive quest for more property. In this acquisitive economy women serve as raw materials, caretakers, and goods themselves to be traded. Her role is to be the home by being at home. Her being home gives him comfort and allows him to open on the expanse of the world to build and create. For her, however, the placement is an imprisonment.

Centuries will perhaps have been needed for man to interpret the meaning of his work(s): the endless construction of a number of substitutes for his

---

6. Luce Irigaray, *Ethics of Sexual Difference* (Ithaca, N.Y.: Cornell University Press, 1992), 101. Hereafter cited as ESD.

parental home. From the depths of the earth to the highest skies? Again and again, taking from the feminine the issue or textures of spatiality. In exchange—but it isn't a real one—he buys her a house, even shuts her up in it, places limits on her that are the opposite of the unlimited site in which he unwillingly situates her. He contains or envelopes her with walls while enveloping himself and his things in her flesh. The nature of these envelopes is not the same: on the one hand, invisibly alive, but with barely visible limits; on the other, visibly limiting or sheltering, but at the risk of being prison-like or murderous if the threshold is not left open. (ESD, 11)

Since woman functions for man as the ground of his subjectivity, she has no support for her own self. She is derelict. She too must deal with the same loss as he, with the abandonment of mortality, radical freedom, and groundlessness, and the expulsion from warmth and security of the mother's body. By means of her, man makes for himself a home to substitute for this loss. He creates by holding her as his muse, he rests by having her serve his needs at home. Her only comfort is to try to derive her satisfaction from being in the home, the Other. She tries to take her subjectivity from her being-for-him. She tries to envelop herself with decoration. She covers herself with jewelry, makeup, clothing, in the attempt to make an envelope, to give herself a place. But in the end she is left homeless, derelict, with no room of her own, since he makes room for himself by using her as his envelope.

If building establishes a world, if building is the means by which a person emerges as a subject who dwells in that world, then not to build is a deprivation. In the patriarchal gender system, men are the builders and women the nurturers of builders and the ornaments placed within their creations. As homeless themselves, women are deprived of the chance to be subjects for themselves. Language, says Heidegger, is the house of being. Men not only build material shelters, temples, bridges to gather the environment into a place, masculine subjects are also the founders of civilization itself, those who name things and construct the theories and epics in which their meanings are preserved over generations. According to Irigaray, woman's place in language is a sign of her dereliction, of her inability to attain the position of subject for herself.

The question for postmodern living is whether an end to such exploitation requires rejecting entirely the project of supporting identity and subjectivity embodied in the patriarchal ideology of home. The feminist writers with whom I engage in section VI answer this question affirmatively. While I accept many of their reasons for leaving home, I wish to explore another possibility. Is it possible to retain an idea of home as supporting the individual subjectivity of the person, where the subject is understood as fluid, partial, shifting, and in relations of reciprocal support with others? This is the direction in which I find Irigaray pointing to an alternative to the desire for fixed identity that historically imprisons women. Before thematizing an alternative concept of house and home, however, I want to explore more of its questionable aspects.

Commodified Home

Irigaray's rhetoric invokes a (patriarchal) universality. Her images of women's enclosure in the house, a house in which man arranges his possessions to satisfy his desire to substitute for the lost security of the womb, presuppose a specifically modern, bourgeois conception of home. The subject that fills its existential lack by seeing itself in objects, by owning and possessing and accumulating property, is a historically specific subject of modern capitalism. Economic and psychosocial processes collude in the twentieth century in particular to encourage the expression of a subject that fulfills its desire by commodity consumption.[7] While this consumer subject is best realized in advanced industrial societies, its allure has spread around the globe. House and home occupy central places in this consumer consciousness as the core of personal property and a specific commodity-based identity.[8] Radical critics of the allure of home rightly find this link of home and identity to be a source of quietism and privilege. The commodified concept of home ties identity to a withdrawal from the public world and to the amount and status of one's belongings.

In many societies, both historically and today, people do not "live" solely in a house. There are huts and cottages reserved for certain life activities, such as sleeping, making love, and giving birth, but dwelling in a wider sense occurs outdoors and/or in collective spaces, both sheltered and not. In rural Botswana, for example, this individual private "home" is outdoor space enclosed by a fence, within which stand small houses for different family members and different activities. When the family grows they build another little house. Preparing food, cooking, eating, washing, children's and adults' amusements all usually occur outdoors. If these families move to a small apartment in the city, they often have difficulty adjusting their lives.[9]

In many societies "home" refers to the village or square, together with its houses, and dwelling takes place both in and out of doors. While few societies fail to distinguish status partly by the size and artfulness of the individual houses, in many societies houses are rather small and plain and do not function very much as status symbols. They and their contents are only minor sources of identity. In many of these societies people take their personal pride more from collective buildings, such as churches or meeting houses. They invest creative energy into erecting

7. One of the classic statements of this idea is Herbert Marcuse's *One-Dimensional Man: Studies in the Ideology of Advanced Industrial Society* (Boston: Beacon Press, 1964); see also Stuart Ewen, *Captains of Consciousness* (New York: McGraw-Hill, 1976).

8. See James S. Duncan, "From Container of Women to Status Symbol: The Impact of Social Structure on the Meaning of the House," in *Housing and Identity: Cross-Cultural Perspectives*, ed. James S. Duncan (New York: Holmes and Meier Publishers, 1982).

9. Anita Larsson, "The Importance of Housing in the Lives of Women: The Case of Botswana," in Dandekar, *Shelter, Women, and Development*, 106–15.

and decorating these buildings with carvings, columns, statues, paintings, and fine furnishings. The celebrated carvings of the Maori people,
for example, belong for the most part to the collective meetinghouses
on the *marae* of each clan. Even in modern capitalist cities some people
"live" more in their neighborhood or on their block than in their houses.
They sit in squares, on stoops, in bars and coffeehouses, going to their
houses mostly to sleep. The bourgeois sensibility of civic privatism, however, finds such street living disorderly and threatening. In "better"
neighborhoods and communities people discretely and privately sit behind their houses, leaving the streets to teenagers.

Under these modern circumstances, home tends to be restricted to
the living space of house or apartment. Personal identity is linked to
commodified home in specific ways. The house is the primary place of
consumption itself. Freedom consists in release from work and public
responsibility in activities of leisure, pleasure, and consumption. The
house or apartment is the site of many of these activities, filled with
comfortable furnishings and gadgets.

Commodified home supports identity not only as the site of consumer
freedom, but as the mark of one's social status. The size, style, and
especially location of the house, along with its landscaping and furnish-
ing, establish the individual's location in the social hierarchy. Everyone
knows which are the better houses or apartments, better streets, better
neighborhoods, better communities, and the aspiration for upward mobility is often expressed in the desire to move house from one neighborhood or community to another.

Attachment to home as status symbol and investment opportunity
creates and perpetuates a market competition in which most people are
losers. The project of maintaining good "property values," and not simply a comfortable living space, produces or exacerbates racial and class
exclusion, which condemns a majority to inferior housing while a few
reap windfall profits. To the extent that housing status is also associated
with lot size and building size, attachment to house as status also maldis-
tributes land and living space, giving too much to some people and
wrongly crowding others. The social and economic organization of commodified housing thus makes the value of home a privilege and constructs many as relatively or absolutely deprived.

In this commodified construction of personal achievement and life-
style, the house often becomes an end in itself. The goal of a dream
house sets workers working and keeps workers working, fearing job
loss, working overtime. The consumer-driven desire of civic privatism
tends to produce political quietism because people invest their commitment into their private life, which needs even greater income to fuel it.[10]
Women have entered the labor force in mass numbers partly because

10. See Jurgen Habermas, *Legitimation Crisis* (Boston: Beacon Press, 1975).

one person's income is no longer sufficient to pay for the house; ironically, all the adults now stay away from the house for most hours of the week in order to earn the money for the house in which they invest their sense of self.[11]

Fantasy feeds consumer desire that fuels this privatist identity attached to house and home. Whatever our actual living conditions, we can buy the dream of a beautiful home in magazines. Along with sex, sports, and clothes, house and home are million-dollar magazine subjects. The magazines offer countless sets on which one can imagine one's life staged. Dining rooms, airy and light, diaphanous curtains revealing a sunny garden beyond the French doors. Solid living rooms, tasteful painting on the walls, a grand piano in the corner, massive leather couches. Cozy bedrooms, fluffed with pillows, lace, and comforters. A kitchen for grand cuisine, with a double-door refrigerator, forty feet of smooth, uncluttered wooden counter, and copper cookware hanging from the ceiling. The rooms in house magazines are nearly always empty of people, thus enabling us to step into their spaces.

The house magazines often sing with nostalgia. Rustic house in the woods, old wood, antique furniture, leaded glass windows. New tiles and floorings are reminiscent of the turn of the century. The dream house often evokes the image of the cozy traditional cottage.[12] Even when the images do not explicitly evoke the past, they often are calculated to produce a longing for a way of life gone by or which might have been as nostalgic. These home images also whisper of stillness, rest.

The attachment of personal identity to commodified home is not specifically gendered. Men and women are equally prone to assess their status and self-worth according to the things they have. The commodified home does have some specific consequences for women, however. The reduction of home to living space can confine women even more than before, especially when suburban development reduces whole townships to living space. Making the house and its furnishings an indicator of personal and family status, moreover, can increase the pressure on women to be good housekeepers, not for the sake of nurturance efficiency, or hygiene, but for the sake of appearances.

Interlude: My Mother's Story

The dream of a house in the suburbs became my mother's nightmare.

My daddy left our Flushing apartment each morning in one of his three slightly different gray flannel suits and took the subway to mid-

11. See Sophie Watson, *Accommodating Inequality: Gender and Housing* (Sydney: Allen and Unwin, 1988).

12. Delores Hayden compares the suburban desire for the detached single-family home as a nostalgia for the cottage in the woods; see *Redesigning the American Dream* (New York: W. W. Norton, 1983). Carole Despres discusses how the design of homes in contem-

town Manhattan. An aspiring novelist turned insurance underwriter, he was moving slowly but steadily up the corporate ladder. I imagined his office as Dagwood's, and his boss as Mr. Dithers.

My sister and I tripped out to school each morning, in the horrid saddle shoes our mommy made us wear, and she stayed home with the little baby boy. A perfect picture of fifties family bliss, with one flaw: my mother didn't clean the house.

Our two-bedroom apartment was always dirty, cluttered, things all over the floors and piled on surfaces, clothes strewn around the bedroom, dust in the corners, in the rugs, on the bookcases; the kitchen stove wore cooked-on food. I never invited my friends into my house. If they came to the door and peered in I told them we were getting ready to move. Mostly my friends did not care, since we played in the alleys and hallways, and not in each other's houses.

My mother spent her days at home reading books, taking a correspondence course in Russian, filling papers with codes and calculations. She seemed to me an inscrutable intellectual. But she also played with us—authors, rummy, twenty questions, with gusto—and sang and sang, teaching us hymns and old army songs. Sometimes on a Saturday she hauled out the oils and sat her little girls down to model, and then let us make our own oil paintings. From my mommy I learned to value books and song and art and games and to think that housework is not important. It was 1958. My mother had to stay home with her children even though she had worked happily in a Manhattan magazine office before we were born, even though she spoke three languages and had a master's degree. I was mortified then by her weirdness, sitting in her chair reading and writing, instead of cooking, cleaning, ironing, and mending like a real mom. Later, after she died in 1978, I read her refusal to do housework as passive resistance.

Like most of the Joneses (well, more likely the Cohens) on our block, my mommy and daddy dreamed of owning a house in the suburbs. They dragged us three kids all over the state of New Jersey looking at model homes in new developments. Back in Flushing, they poured over house-plan sketches, looked at paint samples, calculated mortgage costs. Finally we settled on one of the many mid-Jersey developments built on filled-in wetlands (called swamps at that time). From the four models available, my parents chose the midpriced split-level. My sister and I chose the blue for our room and my three-year-old brother pointed to the green patch on the sample chart. Many Sundays we drove the more than hour-long trip to watch the progress of the house: foundation, frame, walls, grass.

---

porary Quebec suburbs nostalgically aims to evoke the traditional Quebecois cottage. Despres, "De la maison bourgeoise à la maison moderne. Univers domestique, esthétique et sensibilité féminine," *Recherches Féministes* 2.1 (1989): 3–18.

Finally we moved. This was happiness. We were the Cleavers. We bought a ping-pong table for the game room. My sister and I went careening on the streets on our bikes. Then my daddy died—quickly, quietly, of a brain tumor.

My mother was devastated. She relied on us for what comfort there could be in this wasteland of strangers in four types of model homes. At first the neighbors were solicitous, bringing over covered dishes, then they withdrew. The folks at church were more helpful, offering rides to the insurance office or church. My mommy drank, but never on Sunday morning. My sister and I went to school sad, my brother stayed home with our mother, who had less motive than ever to clean the house. We were not poor once the insurance and social security money came, just messy.

But one spring day a uniformed man came into my class and called my name. He escorted me to a police car where my brother and sister were already waiting. Without explanation, they drove us to a teen-reform home. No word from or about our mommy, where she was, why we were being taken away. Slowly I learned or inferred that she had been thrown in jail for child neglect. Daughters do not always defend their mothers accused of crimes. Being one to please authorities, and at eleven wanting to be knowing and adult, I believe that I told stories to confirm their self-righteousness, of how I did most of the cooking and how my mother did not keep house.

A woman alone with her children in this development of perfectly new squeaky clean suburban houses. She is traumatized by grief, and the neighbors look from behind their shutters, people talk about the disheveled way she arrives at church, her eyes red from crying. Do they help this family, needy not for food or clothes, but for support in a very hard time? A woman alone with her children is no longer a whole family, deserving like others of respectful distance. From my mother's point of view there was no difference between child-welfare agents and police. A woman alone with her children is liable to punishment, including the worst of all for her: having her children taken from her.

Neglect. The primary evidence of neglect was drinking and a messy house. We ate well enough, had clean enough clothes, and a mother's steady love, given the way she gave it: playing ping-pong, telling Bible stories, playing twenty questions. We were a family in need of support, but we children were not neglected.

After two months we were reunited, moved back to our gray split-level. My sister and I rode our bikes on the street again, played kickball and croquet with the neighbor kids. My mother was determined to prove she could manage a household by suburban standards, so she did what she thought she had to—called an agency for live-in maids.

One day a thin fourteen-year-old black girl arrived at the door, fresh from North Carolina. We gave her my brother's room and he moved in with my mommy. I felt a strange affinity with this shy and frightened person, who sobbed so quietly in her room. She was not prepared for the work of housekeeping. She and I worked together to prepare the packaged macaroni and cheese. We sorted laundry, silently sitting across from each other, for she did not know whose things were whose. We hardly talked; she told me the barest facts about her life. I see her standing on the landing in a cotton summer dress, a Cinderella figure holding a broom and wistfully sweeping. She quit within two weeks, and the house was not any cleaner.

So we glided through the summer, playing punch ball and tag with the kids in the terrace. My mother went to the city frequently to look for work. In August she took us out to buy three pairs of new shoes, for my brother would start kindergarten. School began, my mother was off to work, my twelve-year-old life seemed rosy enough.

Until one day in early fall I came home from school to find a police sign nailed to my door. A fire. A smoldering ember in my mother's slipper chair had ignited and sent out flames, the neighbors had summoned the fire department. I used their phone to call a family friend to come and get us kids—I wasn't going to any reform school again. There was not much damage to the house, they had caught the fire early, but when breaking in to douse it they had seen the papers strewn about and dust on the floor and beer cans. My mother was arrested again.

We lived with those family friends for a year. Every three months a box of clothes arrived for us from the Department of Social Services—I loved the discovery of what they thought we ought to be wearing. After they let my mommy out of jail and rehab we visited her every couple of months in an impersonal office for an hour or so. She hugged us and cried, and told us of her job in the city and the new cleaning lady, Odessa. As I plummeted into adolescence and my brother entered his seventh year, there was a crisis in our foster home: our foster father died suddenly of pneumonia. Headed now only by a woman, our foster family instantly became a bad environment for us; they shipped us back to my mother without warning. Her family reunited again, my mother wasted no time packing up and moving us all back to the safe indifference of New York City.

Waves of grief rolled up from my gut when, ten years after my mother died, I saw the movie *Housekeeping*.

Historicity, Preservation, and Identity

Beauvoir on Housework

Simone de Beauvoir's *The Second Sex* still stands as one of the most important works documenting women's oppression, because it describes the typical life and dilemmas of women so graphically. One cannot read Beauvoir's descriptions of domestic labor without appreciating how endless the work is, how oppressive.

Such work has a negative basis: cleaning is getting rid of dirt, tidying up is eliminating disorder. And under impoverished conditions no satisfaction is possible; the hovel remains a hovel in spite of women's sweat and tears: "nothing in the world can make it pretty." Legions of women have only this endless struggle without victory over the dirt. And for even the most privileged the victory is never final.

Few tasks are more like the torture of Sisyphus than housework, with its endless repetition. The clean becomes soiled, the soiled is made clean, over and over, day after day. The housewife wears herself out marking time: she makes nothing, simply perpetuates the present.[13]

Beauvoir's account of the oppressions of domestic work fits in the frame of her general account of women's situation as confined to immanence, whereas man exists as transcendence.

The fact is that every human existence involves transcendence and immanence at the same time; to go forward, each existence must be maintained, for it to expand toward the future it must integrate the past, and while intercommunicating with others it would find self-confirmation. These two elements—maintenance and progression—are implied in any living activity, and for man marriage permits precisely a happy synthesis of the two. In his occupation and in his political life he encounters change and progress, he senses his extension through time and the universe; and when he is tired of such roaming, he gets himself a home, where his wife takes care of his furnishings and children and guards the things of the past that she keeps in store. But she has no other job than to maintain and provide for life in pure unvarying generality; she perpetuates the species without change, she ensures the even rhythm of the days and the continuity of the home, seeing to it that the doors are locked. (430)

In the existentialist framework Beauvoir uses, transcendence is the expression of individual subjectivity. The subject expresses and realizes his individuality through taking on projects—building a house, organizing a strike, writing a book, winning a battle. These projects, which may be individual or collective, are determinate and particular contributions to the world of human affairs. Transcendence also expresses a mode of temporality. The living subject is future-oriented; the future is open with possibility, which generates anxiety at the same time as its openness and possibility restructure the meaning of the present and the past. Human existence is historical in this framework, in that it is structured by creative deed and always must be structured by future deeds.

In Beauvoir's scheme, immanence expresses the movement of life rather than history. Life is necessary and very demanding. Without getting food and shelter and caring for the sick and saving babies from harm there is no possibility for transcendence and history. The activities of sustaining life, however, according to Beauvoir, cannot be expressions

---

13. Simone de Beauvoir, *The Second Sex,* trans. H. M. Parshley (New York: Random House, 1952), 451.

of individuality. They are anonymous and general, as the species is general. Thus if a person's existence consists entirely or largely of activities of sustaining life, then she or he cannot be an individual subject. Women's work is largely confined to life maintenance for the sake of supporting the transcending individual projects of men and children. As in Irigaray's account, for Beauvoir man's subjectivity draws on the material support of women's work, and this work deprives her of a subjectivity of her own.

The temporality of immanence is cyclical, repetitive. As the movement of life it moves in species time unpunctuated by events of individual meaning. The cycles go around, from spring to summer to fall to winter, from birth to death and birth to death. Beauvoir describes the activity of housework as living out this cyclical time, a time with no future and no goals.

Beauvoir has an entirely negative valuation of what she constructs as woman's situation, a negative valuation of the activity of giving meaning to and maintaining home. She is surely right that much of what we call housework is drudgery, necessary but tedious, and also right that a life confined to such activity is slavery. But such a completely negative valuation flies in the face of the experience of many women, who devote themselves to caring for house and children as a meaningful human project. If Irigaray is correct, of course, many women pour their soul into the house because they have no other envelope for the self. But it seems too dismissive of women's own voices to deny entirely the value many give to "homemaking." Following Irigaray, we can reconstruct core values from the silenced meanings of traditional female activity. Because she relies on the dichotomy of transcendence and immanence to conceptualize women's oppression, Beauvoir misses the historical and individualizing character of some of the activity associated with the traditional feminine role, which in the above quotation she calls "guarding the things of the past that she keeps in store." Giving meaning to individual lives through the arrangement and preservation of things is an intrinsically valuable and irreplaceable aspect of homemaking.

Homemaking

Beauvoir is surely right that the bare acts of cleaning bathrooms, sweeping floors, and changing diapers are merely instrumental; though necessary, they cannot be invested with creativity or individuality. She is wrong, however, to reduce all or even most domestic work to immanence. Not all homemaking is housework. To understand the difference we need to reconsider the idea of home, and its relation to a person's sense of identity. Home enacts a specific mode of subjectivity and historicity that is distinct both from the creative-destructive idea of transcendence and from the ahistorical repetition of immanence.

D.J. Van Lennep suggests that we can learn what it means to inhabit a space as "home" by thinking about forms of shelter that are not home; he suggests that we consider why a hotel room is not a home. A hotel room has all the comforts one needs—heat, hot water, a comfortable bed, food and drink a phone call away. Why, then, does one not feel at home in a hotel room? Because there is nothing of one's self, one's life habits and history, that one sees displayed around the room. The arrangement is anonymous and neutral, for anyone and one no one in particular.[14]

A home, on the other hand, is personal in a visible, spatial sense. No matter how small a room or apartment, the home displays the things among which a person lives, that support his or her life activities and reflect in matter the events and values of his or her life. There are two levels in the process of the materialization of identity in the home: (1) my belongings are arranged in space as an extension of my bodily habits and as support for my routines, and (2) many of the things in the home, as well as the space itself, carry sedimented personal meaning as retainers of personal narrative.

(1) Home is the space where I keep and use the material belongings of my life. They are mine—or ours, when I live together with others—because I/we have chosen or made them, and they thus reflect my needs and tastes. Or they have found their way into my home as inheritance or gifts or perhaps even by accident, but then I have appropriated them. The home is not simply the things, however, but their arrangement in space in a way that supports the body habits and routines of those who dwell there. The arrangement of furniture in space provides pathways for habits—the reading lamp placed just here, the television just here, the particular spices on the rack placed just so in relation to this person's taste and cooking habits. Dwelling, says Lennep,

> is the continuous unfolding of ourselves in space because it is our unbroken relation with things surrounding us. It is human existence itself which constitutes space. We simply cannot do otherwise. The things which surround us present themselves in a quality of space which we ourselves are as those who live in space. The pronoun "my" in the expression "my room" does not express my possession of it, but precisely a relation between me and the room, which means that my spatial existence has come about.[15]

Edward Casey carries this insight further in his idea of the body forming "habit memories" in the process of coming to dwell in a place. One comes to feel settled at home in a place through the process of interaction between the living body's movement to enact aims and purposes

---

14. D. J. Van Lennep, "The Hotel Room," in *Phenomenological Psychology: The Dutch School*, ed. Joseph J. Kockelmans (Dordrecht: Martinus Nijhoff, 1987), 209–15.
15. Ibid., 211.

and the material things among which such activities occur. The things and their arrangement bear witness to the sedimentation of lives lived there. The home is an extension of and mirror for the living body in its everyday activity. This is the first sense in which home is the materialization of identity.

> But more than comfort is at issue in the elective affinity between houses and bodies: our very identity is at stake. For we tend to identify ourselves by—and with—the places in which we reside. Since a significant part of our personal identity depends on our exact bodily configuration, it is only to be expected that dwelling places, themselves physical in structure, will resemble our own material bodies in certain quite basic respect.[16]

(2) The process of sedimentation through which physical surroundings become home as an extension and reflection of routines also deposits meaning onto things. Material things and spaces themselves become layered with meaning and personal value as the material markers of events and relationship that make the narrative of a person or group. The meaningful things in my home often have stories, or they are characters and props in my stories. I was a little boy in Japan and I picked out that statuette on my own. Those gashes in the top of the chest show the time I got mad at my mother and went at the chest with a pair of scissors. There's our son's room, still with the trophies he won and the books he read in high school. The things among which I live acquired their meaning through events and travels of my life, layered through stories, and the wordless memories of smells, rhythms, and interactions. Their value is priceless: often worthless even on the yard-sale market, the arrangement of these things in rooms is what I would mourn with the deepest grief if they were destroyed by fire or theft.

The activities of homemaking thus give material support to the identity of those whose home it is. Personal identity in this sense is not at all fixed, but always in process. We are not the same from one moment to the next, one day to the next, one year to the next, because we dwell in the flux of interaction and history. We are not the same from one day to the next because our selves are constituted by differing relations with others. Home as the materialization of identity does not fix identity but anchors it in physical being that makes a continuity between past and present. Without such anchoring of ourselves in things, we are, literally, lost.

Preservation

Homemaking consists in the activities of endowing things with living meaning, arranging them in space in order to facilitate the life activities

---

16. Casey, *Getting Back into Place*, 120.

of those to whom they belong, and preserving them, along with their meaning. Things are made or chosen for the house—furniture, pictures, draperies. Traditionally and today women furnish and decorate houses more than men. Often a home reflects a woman's taste and sensibility, often the style and image she projects of herself and her family. The decor of a poor or modest home usually reflects this meaning—giving impulse as much as the homes of more wealthy people—she bought fabric for the window curtains that she made by hand, she painted or covered the chairs.

That is the photograph of my grandmother, who died before I was born, and it hung over the piano in every apartment and house we lived in while I was growing up; when my mother died it was the first thing I took home. The history embodied in the meaningful things of the home is often intergenerational. Traditionally women are the primary preservers of family as well as individual histories. Women trace the family lines and keep safe the trinkets, china cups, jewelry, pins, and photos of the departed ancestors, ready to tell stories about each of them. I am suggesting that a main dimension for understanding home is time and history.

Beauvoir, like Sartre, tends to associate historicity with futurity. So she considers the oppression of women to consist in our being inhibited from the creative activity of bringing new things into being.

> The male is called upon for action, his vocation is to produce, fight, create progress, to transcend himself toward the totality of the universe and the infinity of the future. But marriage does not invite the woman to transcend herself with him—it confines her to immanence, shuts her up within the circle of herself. (448)

This focus on futurity, on the unique moment when the human actor brings something new into the world, makes Beauvoir ignore the specifically human value of activities that, as she puts it, guard the things of the past and keep them in store. She implicitly collapses the activities that consist in preserving the living meanings of past history into her category of immanence. This conflation prevents her from seeing the world-making meaning in domestic work. The particular human meanings enacted in the historicality of human existence depend as much on the projection of a past as of a future.

Hannah Arendt's distinction between labor and work is similar to Beauvoir's distinction between immanence and transcendence. Labor consists in the grinding activity of doing what is necessary to meet needs and maintain life. Its temporality is repetitive and cyclical because the products of labor are always consumed by the needs of life, and thus they leave no lasting monuments. Work, on the other hand, is that individualizing activity that makes a world of permanent historical objects—temples, squares, great books, lasting political constitutions. For

Arendt too, a quintessential moment of human meaning and individuality is that of founding—erecting the city, establishing the republic.[17] But as soon as the deeds of founding are accomplished, as soon as the heroic work of the artist, statesman, or planner are recognized and celebrated, a new task comes into play: preservation.[18]

Earlier I cited Heidegger's claim that building has a dual aspect: constructing and preserving. But even his discussion of the correlation of dwelling with building drops the thread of preservation and concentrates on the creative moment of constructing. It is time to pick up the threads of preservation in order to understand the activities of homemaking. Traditional female domestic activity, which many women continue today, partly consists in preserving the objects and meanings of a home.

Homemaking consists in the activities of endowing things with living meaning, arranging them in space in order to facilitate the life activities of those to whom they belong, and preserving them, along with their meaning. Dwelling in the world means we are located among objects, artifacts, rituals, and practices that configure who we are in our particularity. Meaningful historical works that embody the particular spirit of a person or a people must be protected from the constant threat of elemental disorganization. They must be cleaned, dusted, repaired, restored; the stories of their founding and continued meaningful use must be told and retold, interpreted and reinterpreted. They must also be protected from the careless neglect or accidental damage caused by those who dwell among and use them, often hardly noticing their meaning as support for their lives. The work of preservation entails not only keeping the physical objects of particular people intact, but renewing their meaning in their lives. Thus preservation involves preparing and staging commemorations and celebrations, where those who dwell together among the things tell and retell stories of their particular lives and give and receive gifts that add to the dwelling world. The work of preservation also importantly involves teaching the children the meanings of things among which one dwells, teaching the children the stories, practices, and celebrations that keep the particular meanings alive. The preservation of the things among which one dwells gives people a context for their lives, individuates their histories, gives them items to use in making new projects, and makes them comfortable. When things and works are maintained against destruction, but not in the context of life activity, they become museum pieces.

17. Arendt, *The Human Condition.*

18. See Sara Ruddick, "Preservative Love," in *Maternal Thinkng: Toward a Politics of Peace* (New York: Ballantine Books, 1989), 65–81; Joan Tronto, *Moral Boundaries* (New York: Routledge, 1992). Both theorists focus on the preserving and protecting actions of caring persons, but both also talk about the caring for things that supports this activity. In this essay I focus on preserving meanings through things partly because this has been a less noticed aspect of domestic work than material and emotional caring for people. The two are deeply intertwined, of course.

The temporality of preservation is distinct from that of construction. As a founding construction, making is a rupture in the continuity of history. But recurrence is the temporality of preservation. Over and over the things must be dusted and cleaned. Over and over the special objects must be arranged after a move. Over and over the dirt from winter snows must be swept away from the temples and statues, the twigs and leaves removed, the winter cracks repaired. The stories must be told and retold to each new generation to keep a living, meaningful history.

It would be a mistake, however, to conceive of the identity supported through this preservation of meaning in things as fixed. There are no fixed identities, events, interactions, and the material changes of age and environment make lives fluid and shifting. The activities of preservation give some enclosing fabric to this ever changing subject by knitting together today and yesterday, integrating the new events and relationships into the narrative of a life, the biography of a person, a family, a people.

Preserving the meaningful identity of a household or family by means of the loving care of its mementos is simply a different order of activity from washing the unhealthy bacteria out of the bathroom. As Beauvoir rightly says, the latter is general, the abstract maintenance of species life. The former, however, is specific and individuated: the homemaker acts to preserve the particular meaning that these objects have in the lives of these particular people. The confusion between these acts and the level of immanence is perhaps understandable, because so many activities of domestic work are both simultaneously. The homemaker dusts the pieces in order to keep away the molds and dirts that might annoy her sinuses, but at the same time she keeps present to herself and those with whom she lives the moments in their lives or those of their forebears that the objects remember. She prepares the sauce according to her mother's recipe in order physically to nourish her children, but at the same time she keeps alive an old cuisine in a new country.

Thus the activity of preservation should be distinguished from the nostalgia accompanying fantasies of a lost home from which the subject is separated and to which he seeks to return. Preservation entails remembrance, which is quite different from nostalgia. Where nostalgia can be constructed as a longing flight from the ambiguities and disappointments of everyday life, remembrance faces the open negativity of the future by knitting a steady confidence in who one is from the pains and joys of the past retained in the things among which one dwells. Nostalgic longing is always for an elsewhere. Remembrance is the affirmation of what brought us here.[19]

We should not romanticize this activity. Preservation is ambiguous; it can be either conservative or reinterpretive. The same material things sometimes carry the valences of unique personal identity and status priv-

19. On the distinction between nostalgia and memory, see Gayle Greene, "Feminist Fiction and the Uses of Memory," *Signs* 16.2 (Winter 1991): 290–321.

ilege. By using my grandmother's china I both carry the material memory of childhood dinners and display the class position of my family history. I spoke once to a woman committed to restoring and preserving her grandmother's Victorian southwestern ranch house, fully mindful of her grandmother's passive participation in the displacement of Native Americans from the land. The house has the history whether she chooses to live in it or not. The moral and political question for her is how she constructs her own identity and tells the stories of her family to her children. Homemaking consists in preserving the things and their meaning as anchor to shifting personal and group identity. But the narratives of the history of what brought us here are not fixed, and part of the creative and moral task of preservation is to reconstruct the connection of the past to the present in light of new events, relationships, and political understandings.

Given the cruelties of the histories of persons and peoples, remembrance and preservation often consists in the renewal of grief or rage. A Jewish survivor of the Holocaust keeps safe the small and tattered mementos of her long-dead parents. A city debates whether to demolish or preserve the two-hundred-year-old slave auction block that once stood in its center; after much political struggle in which many African Americans, among others, demand its preservation, the city decides to leave it as a painful memorial of slavery. Some of the meaning preserved in things that anchor identity can be summed in the words "never again."

Preservation of the history that supports a person's identity by means of caring for and arranging things in space is the activity of homemaking still carried out primarily by women in the West, and in many other cultures as well. Such homemaking is not done exclusively by women, but to the degree that women more than men attend more to family and community ties in everyday life, the activities of preservation tend to be gender-specific. Through these same activities, moreover, as I have already begun to indicate, the identity of groups and peoples is preserved. Especially in this late modern world where public administration and corporate standardization tend to drain individualized meaning from politics, schooling, and work, home and neighborhood retain meaningful importance as primary bearers of cultural identity and differentiation. For many migrants who wish to succeed in their new land, for example, their home is the primary place of the expression of cultural identity and continuity with their native lands.[20]

In many premodern or non-Western societies, I pointed out earlier, home is not confined to houses. Often the spaces of village squares, meeting halls, or mountaintops are more the home of the people in a

---

20. See Keya Ganguly, "Migrant Identities: Personal Memory and the Construction of Selfhood," *Cultural Studies* 6.1 (January 1992): 27–49; Susan Thomason, "Suburbs of Opportunity: The Power of Home for Migrant Women," Proceedings of the Postmodern City Conference, Sydney University, 1993.

group than are their individual shelters. The activities of preservation of the meaningful things that constitute home are important here as public acts of the group: maintaining collective spaces, guarding and caring for statues and monuments. For some traditional societies this preservative work is highly regarded, the responsibility of priests and elders. Modern Western societies also perform such public acts of preservation, but they are less often noticed or valued.

Such collective preservative activities continue in the interstices of modern urban societies today in the activities of civic clubs, neighborhood organizations, and religious institutions. When cities commemorate buildings as historic landmarks and stage periodic historically tinged festivals, they are also often performing the self-sustaining actions of preservation. These projects of keeping the meaning of past events and characters by maintaining material thus are not confined to things with positive feeling. In modern Western societies these public activities of preservation are also often coded as feminine, the devalued responsibility of "preservation ladies" who drink tea and look through moldy records, and often it is women in fact who seek to maintain or recover, interpret, and reinterpret the historical meaning of places.[21]

Beauvoir is right to link her account of women's oppression with domestic work, but not entirely for the reasons she has. A sexual division of labor that removes women from participation in society's most valued and creative activities, excludes women from access to power and resources, and confines women primarily to domestic work is indeed a source of oppression. Much of typically women's work, however, is at least as fundamentally world-making and meaning-giving as typically men's work. Especially modern, future-oriented societies devalue this work, at the same time that they depend on its continued performance for the nurturance of their subjectivity and their sense of historical continuity. We should not romanticize this activity. Like the other aspects of home that I have discussed, preservation is ambiguous; it can be both conservative and reinterpretive, rigid and fluid. To the extent that it falls to women to perform this work for men and children, just as they perform the work of cooking and washing for them, without men's reciprocation, then women continue to serve as material for the subjectivities of men without receiving like support for themselves. Equality for women, then, requires revaluation of the private and public work of the preservation of meaningful things, and degendering these activities.

Contemporary Feminist Rejection of Home

I have been arguing that the value of home is ambiguous, and that feminists should try to disengage a positive from an oppressive meaning of

21. See Delores Hayden, *The Power of Place* (Cambridge: MIT Press, 1995).

home. If women are expected to confine themselves to the house and serve as selfless nurturers, and as those who automatically expand their domestic tasks when economic retrenchment rebounds on families,[22] then house and home remain oppressive patriarchal values. To the extent that both men and women seek in their homes and in the women who make them a lost unity and undisturbed comfort, moreover, the idea of home fuels a wrongful escapism. Values of homemaking, however, underlie the affirmation of personal and cultural identity, which requires material expression in meaningful objects arranged in space that must be preserved.

A chain of recent interlinked essays elaborates an argument that feminists should reject any affirmation of the value of home. Biddy Martin and Chandra Mohanty launched this discussion in their reading of Minnie Bruce Pratt's reflections on growing up as a privileged white woman in the American South.[23] Teresa de Lauretis then commented on Martin and Mohanty, enlarging their insights about the connection between home and identity.[24] Most recently Bonnie Honig criticizes what she perceives as a privileged position of withdrawal from politics that the idea of home affords, and she enlarges de Lauretis's ideas about decentered identity and feminist politics.[25]

All these essays express a deep distrust of the idea of home for feminist politics and conclude that we should give up a longing for home. Although I agree with much in their critiques, in this section I argue that while politics should not succumb to a longing for comfort and unity, the material values of home can nevertheless provide leverage for radical social critique. Following bell hooks, I shall suggest that "home" can have a political meaning as a site of dignity and resistance. To the extent that having home is currently a privilege, I argue, the values of home should be democratized rather than rejected.

All of these writers suspect a tendency they perceive among feminists to seek a home in a sisterhood with women. Home is a concept and desire that expresses a bounded and secure identity. Home is where a person can be "herself"; one is "at home" when she feels that she is with others who understand her in her particularity. The longing for home is just this longing for a settled, safe, affirmative, and bounded

22. Governments all over the world, in both developed and developing countries, have been cutting social services and allowing prices for basic foodstuffs to rise. The result is usually more domestic work for women. See Haleh Afshar and Carolyne Dennis, *Women and Adjustment Policies in the Third World* (New York: St. Martin's Press, 1993).

23. Biddy Martin and Chandra Talpade Mohanty, "Feminist Politics: What's Home Got to Do With It?" in *Feminist Studies/Cultural Studies,* ed. Teresa de Lauretis (Bloomington: Indiana University Press, 1986), 191–212.

24. Teresa de Lauretis, "Eccentric Subjects: Feminist Theory and Historical Consciousness," *Feminist Studies* 16.1 (Spring 1990): 115–50.

25. Bonnie Honig, "Difference, Dilemmas, and the Politics of Home," *Social Research* 61.3 (Fall 1994): 563–97.

identity. Thus home is often a metaphor for mutually affirming, exclusive community defined by gender, class, or race.[26]

Feminist analysis reveals that this feeling of having a home as a bounded identity is a matter of privilege. Recall Irigaray's claim: man's ability to have a home, to return to his original identity, is achieved by means of the dereliction of woman as she provides the material nurturance of the self-same identity and the envelope that gives him his sense of boundary. In the feminist texts I am exploring here, the privilege of home the writers refer to is less a specifically gender privilege, and more a class and race privilege. Martin and Mohanty interpret Pratt's text as revealing how the sense of security and comfort that Pratt experienced as a child was predicated on the exclusion of blacks and lower-class whites at the same time that they were invisibly present as workers producing the comforts of home. Bonnie Honig argues that the sense of home as a place where one is confident who one is and can fall back on a sense of integrity depends on a vast institutional structure that allows such a luxury of withdrawal, safety, and reflection for some at the expense of many others who lose out in the global transfer of benefits. Home is here constructed in opposition to the uncertainties and dangers of streets and foreign territories where various riff-raff hang out in less-than-homey conditions.

> "Being home" refers to the place where one lives within familiar, safe, protected boundaries, "not being home" is a matter of realizing that home was an illusion of coherence and safety based on the exclusion of specific histories of oppression and resistance, the repression of differences, even within oneself.[27]

In his study of the construction of modern Western imperialist culture through interaction with the culture of the places constructed as colonies, Edward Said similarly suggests that the material comfort of bourgeois home derives from the material and discursive exploitation of distant colonies. Through a reading of Jane Austen's *Mansfield Park*, Said argues that a British sense of settled bourgeois home depended quite specifically on the nationalist enterprise of empire. Austen makes it plain, says Said,

> that the values associated with such higher things as ordination, law, and property must be grounded firmly in actual rule over and possession of territory. She sees clearly that to hold and rule Mansfield Park is to hold and rule an imperial estate in close, not to say inevitable, association with

---

26. See Bernice Johnson Reagon, "Coalition Politics: Turning the Century," in *Home Girls: A Black Feminist Anthology*, ed. Barbara Smith (New York: Kitchen Table, 1983), 356–69. Reagon criticizes the attempt to seek the comforts of home in politics, but as I read her she does not reject the values of home.

27. Martin and Mohanty, "Feminist Politics," 196.

it. What assures that domestic tranquility and attractive harmony of one is the productivity and regulated discipline of the other.[28]

The women writers we are examining all conclude from these considerations that feminist politics should reject the idea of home. In giving up the idea of home, feminism is consistently postcolonial, exposing the illusion of a coherent stable self or a unified movement of women. A more honest and open attitude toward the world recognizes the plural identities of each of us and that a politics that recognizes and affirms differences cannot draw safe borders for the self.

> When the alternatives would seem to be either the enclosing, encircling, constraining circle of home, or nowhere to go, the risk is enormous. The assumption of, or desire for, another safe place like "home" is challenged by the realization that "unity"—interpersonal and well as political—is itself necessarily fragmentary, itself that which is struggled for, chosen, and hence unstable by definition; it is not based on "sameness," and there is no perfect fit.[29]

According to de Lauretis, feminism must make a shift in historical consciousness that entails

> a displacement and self-displacement: leaving or giving up a place that is safe, that is "home"—physically, emotionally, linguistically, epistemologically—for another place that is unknown and risky, that is not only emotionally but conceptually other; a place of discourse from which speaking and thinking are at best tentative, uncertain, unguaranteed.[30]

Bonnie Honig argues specifically against the use of "home" as a means of withdrawing from politics into a place of more certain principle and integrity. Feminist politics should be prepared to face dilemmas to which there are no simple responses. Longing for home is the effort to retreat into a solid unified identity at the expense of those projected and excluded as Other.

> The dream of home is dangerous, particularly in postcolonial settings, because it animates and exacerbates the inability of constituted subjects—or nations—to accept their own internal divisions, and it engenders zealotry, the will to bring the dream of unitariness or home into being. It leads the subject to project its internal differences onto external Others and then to rage against them for standing in the way of its dream—both at home and elsewhere.[31]

Martin and Mohanty, de Lauretis, and Honig are right to criticize the bourgeois-dominative meaning of home, and earlier sections of this essay have explicated why. They are also right to fear the nostalgic seduc-

---

28. Edward Said, *Culture and Imperialism* (New York: Vintage Books, 1993), 87.
29. Martin and Mohanty, "Feminist Politics," 209.
30. De Lauretis, "Eccentric Subjects," 138.
31. Honig, "Difference," 585.

tions of home as a fantasy of wholeness and certainty. Through a reading of Irigaray, I have also elaborated on this claim. They are right, finally, to suggest that the attempt to protect the personal from the political through boundaries of home more likely protects privilege from self-consciousness, and that the personal identities embodied in home inevitably have political implications. I have also explored this undecidable difference between the personal and the political in preserving the meaning of things. These writers make persuasive analyses of the depoliticizing, essentialist, and exploitative implications that the idea of home often carries.

While agreeing with much of this critique, I have also argued that home carries a core positive meaning as the material anchor for a sense of agency and a shifting and fluid identity. This concept of home does not oppose the personal and the political, but instead describes conditions that make the political possible. The identity-supporting material of home can be sources of resistance as well as privilege. To the extent that home functions today as a privilege, I will argue later, the proper response is not to reject home, but to extend its positive values to everyone.

bell hooks expresses a positive meaning of "home" for feminism. She agrees with Martin and Mohanty, de Lauretis, and Honig that "home" is associated with safety and the making of identity. She gives a positive and political meaning, however, to these functions of "home." Appealing to the historic experience of African American women, she argues that "homeplace" is the site of resistance to dominating and exploiting social structures. The ability to resist dominant social structures requires a space beyond the full reach of those structures, where different, more humane social relations can be lived and imagined. In hooks's view, homeplace uniquely provides such safe visionary space. The mutual caring and meaningful specificity provided by homeplace, moreover, enables the development of a sense of self-worth and humanity partially autonomous from dominating, exploiting, commercial or bureaucratic social structures. Thus hooks agrees with the feminist critics of "home" that home is a site of identity; whereas they criticize a search for pre-given, whole, and apolitical identity, however, hooks finds homeplace to be the site for a self-conscious constructed identity as a political project of criticism and transformation of unjust institutions and practices.

> Historically, African American people believed that the construction of a homeplace, however fragile and tenuous (the slave hut, the wooden shack), had a radical political dimension. Despite the brutal reality of racial apartheid, of domination, one's homeplace was the one site where one could freely confront the issue of humanization, where one could resist.[32]

32. bell hooks, "Homeplace: A Site of Resistance," in *Yearning: Race, Gender, and Cultural Politics* (Boston: South End Press, 1990), 42.

Thus hooks reverses the claim that having "home" is a matter of privilege. "Home" is a more universal value in her vision, one that the oppressed in particular can and have used as a vehicle for developing resistance to oppression. As long as there is a minimal freedom of home-place, there is a place to assemble apart from the privileged and talk of organizing; there is a place to preserve the specific culture of the op-pressed people. The personal sense of identity supported in the site and things of a homeplace thus enables political agency.

hooks emphasizes this political value of homeplace as the place of the preservation of the history and culture of a people, in the face of coloniz-ing forces of the larger society. This project of preservation and remem-brance, I have argued, above, is very different from the nostalgic longing for home that Martin and Mohanty, de Lauretis, and Honig rightly sus-pect. Preservation and remembrance are historical. Colonized people can project an alternative future partly on the basis of a place beyond domi-nance that is preserved in everyday life. hooks herself seeks in her essay to remember the African American mothers and grandmothers who have preserved generations of homeplace, distinct African American cultural meanings in stories, foods, songs, and artifacts.

> I want to remember these black women today. The act of remembrance is a conscious gesture honoring their struggle, their effort to keep some-thing for their own. I want us to respect and understand that this effort has been and continues to be a radically subversive political gesture. For those who dominate and oppress us benefit most when we have nothing to give our own, when they have so taken from us our dignity, our hu-manness that we have nothing left, no "homeplace" where we can recover ourselves.[33]

Home as a Critical Value

The criticisms of the idea of home I have reviewed dwell primarily on a temptation to reject or reconstruct conflict and social difference by creat-ing safe spaces in politics. Nationalism is an important and dangerous manifestation of this temptation, in romanticizing "homeland." The positive idea of home I have advocated is attached to a particular locale as an extension and expression of bodily routines. Nationalism attempts to project such a local feeling of belonging onto a huge territory and "imagined community" of millions,[34] and in so doing creates rigid dis-tinctions between "us" and "them" and suppresses the differences with-in "us." Other attempts to project an ideal of home onto large political

33. Ibid., 43.
34. Benedict Anderson, *Imagined Communities: Reflections on the Origin and Spread of Nationalism* (London: New Left Books, 1983).

units are just as damaging. A useful response to such idealizations of politics as a search for home, however, is to emphasize the radical potential of values that attend to the concrete localized experience of home, and the existential meaning of being deprived of that experience.

Having the stability and comfort of concrete home is certainly a privilege. Many millions of people in the world today do not have sufficient space of their own to live by themselves or with others in peace. They do not have the time or space to preserve much of the history and culture of their family and community, though only refugees and the most desperately destitute are unable to try. With tens of millions of refugees and other homeless people in the world, that deprivation is serious indeed. Even if people have minimal shelter of their own, moreover, they need a certain level of material comfort in their home for it to serve as a place of identity construction and the development of the spirit of resistance that hooks discusses. In this way having a home is indeed today having a privilege.

The appropriate response to this fact of privilege is not to reject the values of home, but instead to claim those values for everyone. Feminists should criticize the nostalgic use of home that offers a permanent respite from politics and conflict, and which continues to require of women that they make men and children comfortable. But at the same time, feminist politics calls for conceptualizing the positive values of home and criticizing a global society that is unable or unwilling to extend those values to everyone. There are at least four normative values of home that should be thought of as minimally accessible to all people. These stand as regulative ideals by which societies should be criticized.

(1) Safety—Everyone needs a place where they can go to be safe. Ideally, home means a safe place, where one can retreat from the dangers and hassles of collective life. It is too much to ask, perhaps even in the ideal, that everyone can be safe anywhere. The potential for violence and conflict cannot be eradicated from the world. But it is not too much to ask that everyone have a home in which they can feel physically safe and secure.

Today we are frighteningly, horribly far from this simple goal. For too many women and children, their houses do not enclose them safely but threaten them with violence from the men who live there with them. Too many poor peasants and barrio dwellers in the world cannot sleep peacefully in their homes without fear that paramilitary squads will rouse them, rape them, shoot them, or carry them away in the dark. If anything is a basic need and a basic liberty, it is personal safety and a place to be safe. Yet ensuring such safety at home is an arduous and complex matter, one that seems too daunting for the will of the late twentieth century. We must be ashamed of a world in which safety at home is a privilege and express outrage at any stated or implied suggestion that such a need and liberty is too expensive for any society to meet.

(2) Individuation—A person without a home is quite literally deprived of individual existence.[35] However minimal, home is an extension of the person's body, the space that he or she takes up, and in which he or she performs the basic activities of life—eating, sleeping, bathing, making love. These need not all be done in the same place or behind closed doors, in a house. But the individual is not allowed to be if she does not have places to live and to perform the activities of life, with basic routine and security. As I have already outlined in the concept of homemaking, moreover, people's existences entail having some space of their own in which they array around them the things that belong to them, that reflect their particular identity back to them in a material mirror. Thus basic to the idea of home is a certain meaning of ownership, not as private property in exchangeable goods, but in the sense of meaningful use and reuse for life. Even the monk has a cell of his own in the collective life of the monastery; even in crowded families with little space there is usually an effort to allocate each person a corner of his own where he can sleep and put the things he calls his own. Where this is not possible it nevertheless remains as an ideal.[36]

(3) Connected with the value of individuation is privacy. A person does not have a place of her own and things of her own if anyone can have access to them. To own a space is to have autonomy over admission to the space and its contents. Some feminists doubt the value of privacy, because they associate this idea with the "private sphere," to which women have been historically confined. But there are crucial differences in the two concepts. Privacy refers to the autonomy and control a person has to allow or not allow access to her person, information about her, and the things that are meaningfully associated with her person. The traditional "private sphere," on the other hand, confines some persons to certain realm of activity and excludes them from others. As a value, privacy says nothing about opportunities for the person to engage in activity. It only says that whatever her social activities, a person should have control over access to her living space, her meaningful things, and information about herself.[37]

Feminists have been suspicious of a value of privacy also because traditional law has sometimes appealed to a right of privacy to justify

35. Compare Jeremy Waldron, "Homelessness and the Issue of Freedom," in *Liberal Rights: Collected Papers, 1981–1991* (Cambridge: Cambridge University Press, 1993), 309–38.

36. Seyla Benhabib affirms this individuating function of home and privacy in her discussion of the need for feminists to retain a certain meaning to a distinction between public and private. See Benhabib, *The Reluctant Modernism of Hannah Arendt* (London: Sage, 1996), 213.

37. For a feminist defense of privacy as the right to inviolate personality, see Jean L. Cohen, "Democracy, Difference and the Right of Privacy," in *Democracy and Difference: Contesting the Boundaries of the Political,* ed. Seyla Benhabib (Princeton, N.J.: Princeton University Press, 1996).

not interfering with autocratic male power in the family. Because of a supposed right of privacy, the law should turn a blind eye to marital rape or battering. But perhaps the most important defense against this legitimation of patriarchal power is an insistence that privacy is a value for individuals, not simply or primarily for households. Anita Allen argues that if we insist on privacy as a value for all persons as individuals, then the extent to which women deserve privacy at home and elsewhere, and do not have it, becomes apparent.[38] The appeal to privacy as a value thus enables social criticism.

Some might claim that appeal to a value of privacy is ethnocentric, because the idea of privacy is a Western idea. Scholars disagree on the question of whether non-Western societies both historically and today have held a value of privacy. My cursory reading of that literature leads me to conclude that there is often, if not always, a form of respect for the physical person of another and for some kind of spaces associated with the person. In stratified societies, such respect may be restricted to those in the upper strata. This does not mean that such a value does not exist in the society, but rather that it is held as a privilege. I am arguing here that certain values associated with home, among them control over access to one's person and personal space, be made available to everyone: to the degree that non-Western and premodern societies, as well as modern societies, do not democratize privacy, then I am indeed criticizing them.

Thus while it seems to me that an ideal of respect for the personal space of others is not restricted to Western societies, one can argue that conceptualizing this idea in terms that we call privacy is Western. The concept of privacy is a relatively recent development of positive law based in rights. The concept of rights to privacy extends law to relations of interaction among private individuals or between private agents, as well as between the state and individuals. Thus I wish to suggest that there are long-standing ideas and practices analogous to privacy in many societies, and that to the degree that positive law and social policy have evolved in those societies, it is not a mistake today to appeal to a value of privacy.

(4) The final value of "home" that should be available to everyone I have already explicated at length in an earlier section: preservation. Home is the site of the construction and reconstruction of one's self. Crucial to that process is the activity of safeguarding the meaningful things in which one sees the stories of one's self embodied, and rituals of remembrance that reiterate those stories. I have argued that preservation in this sense is an important aspect of both individual and collective identity.

Home is a complex ideal, I have argued, with an ambiguous connection to identity and subjectivity. I agree with those critics of home who

38. Anita Allen, *Uneasy Access* (Totowa, N.J.: Rowman and Allenheld, 1988).

see it as a nostalgic longing for an impossible security and comfort, a longing bought at the expense of women and of those constructed as Others, strangers, not-home, in order to secure this fantasy of a unified identity. But I have also argued that the idea of home and the practices of home-making support personal and collective identity in a more fluid and material sense, and that recognizing this value entails also recognizing the creative value to the often unnoticed work that many women do. Despite the real dangers of romanticizing home, I think that there are also dangers in turning our backs on home.

8

A Room of One's Own:
Old Age, Extended Care, and Privacy

Theorists distinguish among several meanings of privacy. They also identify actions and guarantees that help secure the autonomy and personal integrity a value of privacy supports. In this essay I argue, however, that privacy theories have paid insufficient attention to material support for privacy in the guarantee of *personal space*. Many theories of privacy presuppose a value of personal space without thematizing this value and thus without considering common threats to its fulfillment.

Building on ideas elaborated in the previous chapter, I conceptualize personal space through a phenomenology of the value of *home*. While appeals to a notion of home can be oppressively privatizing or sentimental, reflection on ordinary acts of dwelling uncovers a material meaning of home as a necessary support for and enactment of personal identity. At least in modern societies, an important aspect of the value of privacy is the ability to have a dwelling space of one's own, to which a person is able to control access, and in which one lives among the things that help support the narrative of one's life.

Many old people who need nursing care live in residences that routinely deprive them of privacy in this sense of secure personal space where one dwells according to one's own habits with things of one's own. I argue that old people should not have to do without a home in this sense just because they have become unable to live independently, or because their relatives for whatever reason are unable or unwilling to make a home for them in their own dwellings. Services and institutions offering shelter and care to needy persons often fail to appreciate what

I am grateful to David Alexander, Judith DeCew, Robert Goodin, Hilde Nelson, Martha Nussbaum, and Anna Yeatman for comments on an earlier version of this essay.

is required for individuals not simply to stay alive, physically well, and nourished, but to have the life of a person. A room of one's own or its equivalent, I argue, should be understood not as a luxury that social services can ill afford, but rather as a basic element of the value of privacy.

The Meaning of Home

Evocation of sentiments and longings for home often reinforce domination or oppression. Many men and some women still expect and seek in women a haven from the anxieties of public life, the demands made by others on them, and even their own mortality. Consumerism encourages people to focus on the private spheres of their homes; to this extent home is a counterpart of the capitalist marketplace and a detriment to the solidarity of community and assertive public participation. Nationalism appeals to emotions of "homeland" and nostalgia for traditions associated with family and village life. Without a doubt ideas and images of home serve multiple ideological functions that ought to be criticized.

Like ideologies of freedom, independence, beauty, or countless other often vague conceptions, however, appeals to ideas of home that reinforce oppression can succeed only because they carry ideals worth uncovering for a conception of liberation and well-being.[1] The previous chapter distinguished some of the uses of an idea of home that reinforce oppression and domination from a concept of home as an important materialization of personal, and sometimes group, identity.

As I conceptualize it, "home" is a materialization of personal, and sometimes group, identity. A person's home is a space in which he or she dwells, carries out everyday activities of caring for self and others, plays, celebrates, plans, and grieves. The home is an arrangement of things in this space, according to the life habits of those who dwell in it. Many of these things are simply utilitarian, the various things needed or enjoyed in these everyday living activities. Many also have personal meaning as materializing the narrative memories of the lives of the people in it. Thus I define homemaking as the activities of endowing things with living meaning, arranging them in space in order materially to facilitate the projects of those to whom they belong, and activities of preserving these things, along with their meaning.

There are two levels in the process of the materialization of identity in the home: (1) the arrangement of things in dwelling space as an extension of the bodily habits of those who live among them, and support for

1. For a useful discussion of ideological uses of home and homeland that argues for the retention of a meaning of home as familiar locality with positive valence, see Sara Ahmed, *Strange Encounters: Embodied Others in Post-Coloniality* (New York: Routledge, 2000), chapter 4.

their routines; (2) the sedimentation of historical meaning in the things of the home, and activities of preserving those meanings as living. Let me elaborate on each of these aspects of the enactment of home.

(1) My home is a dwelling space. To dwell means to carry out activities in movement that uses things. We dwell everywhere in that sense, of course. What distinguishes home is its individualization. My home is the space in which I dwell with things that are mine. The legal sense of ownership of these things is less important than the fact that these items have meaning primarily for me, accompany my actions and only secondarily those of others. When dwelling space is shared, home is the space in which we dwell among the things that are *ours.* The shared space and shared things give us material support for living together. Even where space is shared, however, there is often a distinction between my things and our things, and each person often has spaces of his or her own for keeping the things that are hers and engaging in activities that are hers or his—my chair, my corner, my room, my clothes, my toothbrush, my guitar, my tool box.

The home is not simply or even primarily the storage place for my stuff, however, but more specifically it is the special arrangement of my and our things as a material support for and mirror of the life activity of the dwellers. The things and their arrangement in space is *personal,* in several senses: they accompany the distinctive activities of this person or these persons, they correspond to these particular bodies and capacities, they reflect the particular desires and tastes of this person or these persons, and they exhibit the routine pathways of the everyday activities that take place in them.

My things and my dwelling space support and display *who I am.* Our homes reflect our general needs for clothes, toiletries, food and cooking facilities, but these also have a stamp of particularity—according to my size, cultural norms I adhere to, and taste. The collection of things that supports my life activities will differ from that of others—some people need books and papers, others fishing poles, some people need eyeglasses or wheelchairs. Many people in the world, of course, do not have sufficient material support to do the things they need or want to do, and this diminishes.

The dweller arranges things that support the activities of living in the dwelling space, sometimes by design according to decisions of efficiency and convenience and aesthetic judgments. As roommates and life partners often discover to their dismay, these decisions and judgments are often idiosyncratic and incommensurate with others'. The arrangement of things in dwelling space, however, also occurs not through conscious decisions but in the unconscious mutual accommodation of the person's movements and the things she moves among and with.

When people inhabit a space, they accommodate their movements to its structure, until moving through it is automatic. The morning walk to the kitchen becomes familiar, a simple habit. I can walk in the dark from the bathroom to my bed, and the bed feels viscerally familiar. When I step outside my house I find familiar surroundings whose heights and distances from one another I know in my body. Part of what it means to *make myself at home* is to develop this habitual bodily accommodation to the structure of spaces.

Not only do I accommodate my body to the spaces where I dwell, but also the arrangement of things comes to reflect my or our habits and activities. The pile of bills and letters on the table reflects my idiosyncratic organization of check writing and correspondence routines. The arrangement of dishes, pans, and spices reflect our cooking and eating habits. The position of the chair displays my habit of looking out the window, the books next to it pile up in the same disorderly way even when I take pains to reorganize it periodically.

Simone de Beauvoir comments on how important these body and space habits are, especially to old people:

> But an old person who is suddenly transplanted, even if it is only to his children's home, loses his bearings; he is bewildered and often reduced to despair: when they are uprooted like this, one out of two die within a year. . . . Clinging to one's habits implies an attachment to one's possessions: the things that belong to us are as it were solidified habits—the mark of certain repetitive forms of appropriate behavior. The possession of a garden means being able to take one's walk in it every afternoon: this armchair is waiting for me to sit in it every evening. Ownership too is a guarantee of ontological security: the possessor is his possessions' reason for existence.[2]

(2) This passage brings out the second aspect of home as the material support for personal identity in a life course. The things among which I dwell carry a sedimented history which is the story of my life, and the story of our shared lives. Many of the things in my or our home are *meaningful* to me or us in a uniquely deep way. We keep with us in our dwelling space many things which time has layered with meaning and personal value as the material markers of events and relationships that make our personal and group narratives. The meaningful things in my home often have stories, or they are characters and props in stories. Many of these meaningful things are not utilitarian at all; quite the contrary, we keep them with us precisely as carrying materialized life meaning and value: photographs, letters, trinkets that belonged to loved parents or friends, mementos recalling important events. The poem my daughter wrote and framed for me when she was ten years old hangs on my wall; I shore up the tattered and boring books from my first year of college with my mother's wooden bookends. Many of the utilitarian objects among which I dwell, moreover, carry these sedimented life meanings. I have a special feeling for some of the chairs, bowls, musical

---

2. Simone de Beauvoir, *The Coming of Age* (New York: Warner Books, 1973), 698.

instruments, and wrenches because I have dwelt among them for a long time. To others they may be ugly or ungainly, but for me they have special meaning both as reflecting body habits and recalling moments of my past. The knick on the table here happened during that argument with my daughter, the chip on the bowl during that summer party years ago. The material base of memory in these ways can also be held for me in natural objects, the hills, the trees, among which I have dwelt and my experience of their changes.

Thus in the previous chapter I defined home making as both dwelling among things in ways that endow them with meanings, and also preserving the things and their meaning. We care for the meaningful things in our home and aim to preserve them from loss, breakage, or the elemental damage of water, dirt, and heat. Some we take out now and then to look at and touch, often with an audience to whom we tell their meaningful stories. Then we carefully return them to their places, where they are safely preserved in their meaning. These are the things whose loss we most mourn in case of fire or theft, because for us they are both priceless and irreplaceable.

In the previous chapter I pointed out that some societies enact home as the arrangement of meaningful things in space without enclosed rooms or in collective spaces. To the extent that personal identity in modern society is connected to individuation, however, the material supports for that identity tend to require some individuated dwelling space—if not a room, then a corner or a clearing, which persons establish as their private zone. A need for individuated personal space in this sense is perhaps historically specific, but I do not think that it is less a need on that account. Home in this phenomenological sense is a basic support for personal identity. It provides what some writers call the "ontological security" of the person. Drawing on the work of Peter Saunders, Ann Dupuis and David Thorns argue that home provides support for identity by becoming a place where people are at ease because of the routines of time-space paths, that the home evokes sedimented meanings that provide a sense of continuity, and because it provides a sense of control and privacy.[3] The deprivation we call "homelessness" concerns not only the dangers of death and illness that prolonged exposure to the elements brings, but also being stripped of a sense of self by not having a space for daily routine and to keep and enjoy certain meaningful things of one's life. For the rest of this essay I will focus on the enactment of home as such a space in which one dwells among personally meaningful things. I shall elaborate how this experience of home underlies a value of privacy, which many philosophical theories of privacy fail to notice.

3. Ann Dupuis and David C. Thorns, "Home, Home Ownership, and the Search for Ontological Security," manuscript, Department of Sociology, University of Canterbury, New Zealand.

Home, Privacy, and Old-Age Residence

Some researchers argue that the personal space of one's home becomes more important to people as they grow older. Older people move less often than younger people; many older people have dwelt for decades in the same living space. Older people spend more time in their home space than do younger people, especially when they do not go to jobs. Although many older people who live alone seem isolated and unhappy to outsiders, according to some researchers many do not express a desire for more social contact; they claim to be content at home.[4]

One study of old people's feelings of at-homeness emphasizes this embodied understanding of security in oneself as surrounded by meaningful things.[5] This sense of self and personal integrity is also linked to control. As much as other people, old people resist efforts of managers and organizers to direct their routines and activities. Home provides not only material support for habits and meaningful memories, but a zone of control over one's life to which others have limited access.[6]

If home is a major material support for personal identity and memory, then it makes sense that its meaning would become more important to a person whose days are mostly spent at home and whose personal memories reach back many decades. In modern societies old people often occupy an unjustly marginalized status. They have too few social roles that earn them recognition and respect. Often they are treated in dismissive or patronizing ways. These and similar circumstances are oppressive because they diminish a sense of self-respect, and having a home does nothing to alter these oppressions. There are many ways that institutions and practices ought to change in these societies to raise the quality of life for many old people. Under such circumstances of relative marginalization, however, home in the sense I have defined it can be an especially important value, because the old person's home may be one of the only bases for a sense of self.

My stepfather well illustrates this. For more than twenty years after my mother died, when he was sixty-eight years old, he lived alone in a

---

4. Peter Saunders, "The Meaning of 'Home' in Contemporary English Culture," *Housing Studies* 4.3 (1988); this survey's results show older people more attached to home than younger. See also Ann Dupuis and David C. Thorns, "Meanings of Home for Older Home Owners," *Housing Studies* 11.4 (1996): 485–502. Depuis and Thorns emphasize the importance of home ownership for a sense of secure self. It seems to me that legal title per se is less important than a security that the home is "mine" to decorate as I wish and that I will not be forced to leave the home by will of another. Public housing *can* meet these needs at least as well as private title.

5. Inger F. Koran, Cora Skott, and Astrid Norberg, "A Place of One's Own: The Meaning of Lived Experience as Narrated by an Elderly Woman with Severe Chronic Heart Failure, a Case Study," *Scandinavian Journal of Caring Science* 15 (2001): 60–65.

6. Pia C. Kontos, "Resisting Institutionalization: Constructing Old Age and Negotiating Home," *Journal of Aging Studies* 12.2 (1998): 167–84.

small cottage in Massachusetts. His only income came from veterans' benefits, and the Commonwealth of Massachusetts subsidized his rent. By many people's standards, my stepfather's home would have been considered cluttered and uncomfortable. The furniture was old and simple, but it served him well enough. Like most other people, my stepfather liked to position the chair just so in relation to the lamp and the television. He piled the many magazines to which he subscribed in a particular order on his table, next to the box with the magnifying glass. His favorite coffee mug was chipped and the most used saucepan dented. Also like most people, my stepfather had stored in his cottage things that contained the history of his life—canvases and drawings from his life work as a painter, photographs, letters, records and many other items accumulated over the years of travels and relationships.

When he was seventy-three my stepfather suffered kidney failure, and from then on required dialysis treatment several times a week. Despite the fact that his condition made him less mobile and able to care for himself, he was determined to continue living by himself in his cottage. A local elder-services organization helped him with transportation, delivered a daily meal, arranged shopping, housecleaning, and laundry help. His niece and stepchildren, living considerable distances away, also did what they could to make sure he was secure and content. He led a circumscribed life, but it was in a space whose arrangement reflected his movements and desires, and among the belongings he cared about, in which his life stories lay ready to be called out by looking, alone or with intimate company.

When he was eighty-six my stepfather suffered a stroke, after which his physician said that he could not live on his own. More extensive home care services that would make it possible for him to continue living in his cottage were not available. He lived for three years in an extended-care facility. Compared to many old-age residences in the United States, he lived in a "good" facility. The staff members were cheerful, and they did not seem impossibly overworked. Meals were nutritious and varied, and the facility encouraged dining in a sunny common room where volunteers sometimes played the piano. The rooms were clean and laundry delivered weekly. But my stepfather was not at home there, and could not be from his point of view, because he lacked the personal space and privacy that might have allowed him to arrange things of his own in his own way and dwell among them.

All the rooms in my stepfather's wing of the residence had three beds, and people lived in all the beds most of the time. In the years he lived in the residence my stepfather had at least ten different roommates. His personal space, and that of each of the two others in the room, consisted in the following: a bed and a curtain that could be closed around it, but usually was not; a chair; a very small end table with one drawer; one-third of a closet and one small drawer for clothes. He shared a bathroom with five other residents. In this room there was no space to walk around or place additional furniture, or even items on the floor. A few common rooms were available for his use, but he did not want to use them. His room had a door, which I never saw closed. Staff and other residents wandered in all the time.

My stepfather had no home in this place because he could not dwell in it in either of the respects I have discussed above. Neither he nor any of the other residents could arrange things around them in an individual-ized dwelling space that reflected their habit memories. There simply was not space for such arranging in their rooms. If their chairs or eating trays moved into walking spaces as a consequence of their actions of the day, the staff would put them back where they "belonged." In the com-mon rooms no resident could claim one chair as her own, nor did resi-dents leave things of their own there. Nor did the common space reflect some kind of collective dwelling choices or activities. Each day the staff would clean and rearrange the common spaces to leave no traces of any person's particular tastes, habits, or activities.

Perhaps more important, my stepfather had almost nothing around him that belonged personally to him. The things he had consisted of a few items of clothing, a brush and a comb, a radio, a magnifying glass, and the daily newspaper. He complained that even some of these things would disappear and need to be replaced. His home had been disman-tled, with those things most precious to him sent to his niece, whom he visited once a year.

He had no space in which he could array and store some of the mean-ingful things of his life. Even if he had more space, he would not have wanted his things, because he had no privacy in which to enjoy them. He did not want some of his paintings hanging on the wall across from his bed and chair, because the ever changing roommates would gaze upon them as much as he. The staff would likely come in and cheerfully start conversation about them that he would have to answer. He rejected the idea of having a locked box under his bed with some important mementos of his life, because he would not have the opportunity to look through them undisturbed. He would not have been able to share the stories they carried for his life with a few privileged visitors without allowing the strangers in his room to partake of them as well. The things that had meaning in his cottage as the materialization of his achieve-ments and relationships would have lost their meaning in such a public and anonymous space. So he preferred not to have them.

The residents in a nursing home such as this, which seems typical of "good" extended-care facilities, lack privacy in the most elementary sense. They have no way to be alone if they wish to be. They are liable to have their thoughts and actions intruded on by staff and other residents without notice. They cannot allow their habit pathways and the things they own to spread out in a space of their own, to reflect and accommo-date their routines and comfort. Their belongings are not secure from the gaze and hands of others, and thus in significant ways they are not able to keep information about themselves private. They can dress and undress privately only in the bathroom, when it is available.

Refinement of the Value of Privacy

Early philosophical concern with privacy tended to focus on issues of when and whether states or other powerful institutions have the legitimate right to limit or intrude on the privacy of individuals or groups. When, if ever, can states search personal belongings, dwellings and workstations, read mail, listen to conversations, or regulate decisions between intimates? Rights of privacy against such state interference I shall refer to as freedom from authority. When additional arguments and legal actions aim to restrict the power of other powerful agents such as employers from exercising invasive control over individuals, these arguments and legal actions have the same form as those related to government intrusion and should also be thought of as privacy in the form of freedom from authority.

Ferdinand Schoeman has conceptualized another category of privacy issues having more to do with what he calls social freedom than with freedom from authority. Social freedom refers to the sense of autonomy and comfort people have and feel in relation to the expectations and actions of others. People exert pressure on one another to conform to expected behaviors, and they want others to act in ways that further specific ends and purposes. Social actors usually welcome many of these dense interactive expectations, because they wish to cooperate in joint ventures, or desire sociability, or want to forge and maintain particular bonds with particular people. But everyday social interactions and relations have a tendency to "overreach" their appropriate limits, as Schoeman puts it, to diminish the person or endanger relationships. Individuals usually desire and ought to have means of distancing themselves from social pressures and expectations and ought to have ways of maintaining space for personal expression.[7]

Such a distinction between political and social freedom is useful for noticing the issues at stake in privacy for old people in extended-care facilities. The medicalized nursing home system, at least in the United States, addresses privacy issues more as autonomy from authority than as social freedom. Laws and professional ethics regulate the way medical, financial, and social service records are kept and access to them in ways designed to respect a value of informational privacy for residents. Legal norms of medical institutions require informed consent for procedures and have evolved complex systems of guardianship in situations of impaired decision making capacity. Such regulations aim to promote

---

7. Ferdinand Schoeman, *Privacy and Social Freedom* (Cambridge: Cambridge University Press, 1992).

decisional privacy for old people. No doubt there are significant issues of abuse and neglect of these standards of privacy rights for old people, but on the whole the issues are institutionally recognized.

There seems to be less institutional recognition, however, of the value of privacy as personal space to make a home to serve as material support for identity. Privacy of this sort concerns less the rules of access to records and decisions, and more forms of social interaction, bodily comportment, and opportunities for expression and reflection that come under the idea of social freedom. Where the rules about records and bank accounts may be abstract from the point of view of daily routines—even though their implications may be fundamental for a person's life—issues of social freedom are more concrete and immediate. They are literally embodied in space and personal interaction. Either people are aware of being generally observable, or they are comfortable in having a place where they can be unobserved. Either people treat the bodies of others with respectful distance or they do not. Either people are forced into the presence of others or they are not.

Thus far I have distinguished autonomy from authority and social freedom. Theories of privacy also distinguish several different aspects of the concept of privacy itself. Jean Cohen finds decisional privacy to be primary, which she defines as autonomy in decision making about matters within a zone of intimacy—including marriage, divorce, sexual relations, procreation, child rearing, and so on. Privacy in this decisional sense means that a person has the right to decide for herself about the nature of intimate relations she will engage in, the actions she performs and values she is committed to, without interference from the state or other people, and without having to justify her relationships, actions, and values to others. Cohen argues that decisional privacy in this sense is a fundamental support for personal identity, self-determination, and self-realization.[8]

Anita Allen agrees that decisional privacy is important, but argues that this concept lies outside the concept of privacy strictly speaking, as a concept distinct from liberty. Allen defines privacy as a condition of restricted access: "Personal privacy is a condition of inaccessibility of the person, his or her mental states, or information about the person to the sense of surveillance of others."[9]

Judith DeCew surveys a range of privacy claims and privacy theories and concludes that privacy cannot be defined as a single concept. She argues that privacy is a "cluster concept" with three distinct aspects: information, bodily integrity, and expression. Her cluster definition in-

8. Jean L. Cohen, "Democracy, Difference, and the Right of Privacy," in *Democracy and Difference: Contesting the Boundaries of the Political,* ed. Seyla Benhabib (Princeton, N.J.: Princeton University Press, 1996).

9. Anita Allen, *Uneasy Access: Privacy for Women in a Free Society* (Totowa, N.J.: Rowman and Littlefield, 1988).

cludes both restricted access and decisional privacy. Privacy restricts the access of others to one's person through sense perception, observation, or bodily contact, and limits access to the person from unwelcome disturbance or intrusion. Informational privacy restricts access to a range of information about a person. What DeCew calls expressive privacy seems to include what many call decisional privacy, though it may also extend beyond the decision concept. Expressive privacy, she says, "protects the ability to decide to continue or modify one's behavior when the activity in question helps define oneself as a person, shielded from interference, pressure, and coercion from government or from other individuals."[10]

All of these are important aspects of the meaning of privacy. The argument I have made about the importance of home, however, motivates me to add a concept of *personal space* and restricted access to this personal space, to the concept of privacy. It seems to me that most accounts of privacy do not emphasize enough such a spatial and material aspect of the value of privacy. Attention to bodily integrity, of course, entails attention to an embodied being who is necessarily *in place*. Probably because of her restricted-access concept of privacy, Allen does in fact give attention to the space of a home as an important support for privacy. In other aspects of her discussion, however, Allen, like many others, takes the idea that privacy involves a "zone" of control to be merely metaphorical.

Much theoretical discussion of privacy seems rather "virtual." By emphasizing information, mental states, decisions, and relationships, discussions of privacy often sound like the subject of privacy is largely cognitive or mental. The cognitive, information-oriented ways of thinking about privacy fail to notice sufficiently the *material bases* of privacy. Files must be stored somewhere, the signs and consequences of my intimate relationships have material presence in things that lie somewhere, and even my thoughts are fleeting unless I give them some sort of expressive embodiment—a card, a diary, a photograph.

Personal space and possessions arranged in it according to the desires and habits of the dweller are necessary conditions for the realization of many aspects of privacy. Personal space enables us to have bodily integrity and perform many activities unobserved. It enables both informational and expressive dimensions of privacy, for this space contains many of the records and artifacts that document factual and expressive meaning. Space, and the spatialization of life activity, itself first *raises the issue* of privacy, because one can enter or restrict access only to places of some kind.

Theories of privacy tend not to emphasize the importance of personal space, I suggest, because they take it for granted. Whatever the particu-

10. Judith Wagner DeCew, *In Pursuit of Privacy: Law, Ethics, and the Rise of Technology* (Ithaca, N.Y.: Cornell University Press, 1997).

lar aspect of privacy under discussion, theories conceptualize the obliga-
tions of states and individuals regarding this value as negative. The right
of privacy entails that a person be left alone in the making of decisions,
that others have restricted access to the person and information about
her, that others refrain from observing or interfering with her personally
expressive and intimate moments. Such formulation of rights of privacy
in terms of restricted access or non-interference presuppose that the subject already has a zone of privacy which can be protected from access
or interference.

These formulations of a right of privacy assume privacy's material
base. For many people, however, their primary privacy problem is that
they do not have a home, a personal space available to them to which
they can restrict access and in which they arrange the informational and
expressively meaningful things of their lives. To the extent that they do
not, they have a truncated capacity for the formation and maintenance
of a sense of personhood, at least in societies where a sense of individuality is tied to personhood. Given that the arrangement of meaningful
things in space is a material support and mirror for personhood, the
promotion of privacy entails not merely leaving people alone, but providing or enabling the constitution and maintenance of such personal
space.

Home, Privacy, and Extended-Care Facilities

My stepfather's situation is typical of old people in the United States
who live in extended-care facilities. Indeed, it seems to be typical of old
people in residences all over the developed world. Typically old people
resist giving up their homes to enter such residences, and typically family
members and friends work to prevent the need for an old person to live
in a nursing home until they are convinced that there is no alternative.
Why do the old people themselves and those close to them so often
consider living in a nursing home to be a deprivation, a sad indignity to
be avoided if possible?

In the United States one ground for this judgment lies in the fact that
abuse and neglect are routine in too many facilities.[11] Many facilities are
short-staffed by poorly trained personnel. The elderly residents in too
many facilities suffer physical or psychological abuse or are not properly
fed, or live in dirty and poorly maintained surroundings. Old people
often resist going to live even in "good" facilities, however, and those
close to them often feel sad and guilty about the fact that they allow or
encourage their move to an extended-care facility. Among the central
reasons for this resistance is the fact that in most old-age residences the

---

11. For one exposé, see Eric Bates, "The Shame of Our Nursing Homes: Millions for
Investors, Misery for the Elderly," *Nation,* March 29, 1999, 11–19.

old people are unable to have the privacy that would allow them to make a home.

Care facilities can preserve important areas of information privacy for residents by restricting access to records. They can secure residents' valuables such as money, passports, or other important documents in locked boxes. Staff who help residents bathe, dress, or perform other necessary functions can protect those they care for from the intrusion of others during these times. Only the provision of personal space in which an old person can arrange things as she wishes and to which she can control access, however, makes the sort of home that can support a sense of secure self and identity. While the situation may be improving in committed welfare states such as the Netherlands,[12] the norm in extended-care facilities seems to be that residents share space.[13] In one study of 191 residents of four different nursing homes in Sweden—where one expects one of the highest standards of care in the world—only 22 percent of residents had a room of their own, and most shared a room with three other people.[14] Those who can afford to pay for personal space, of course, are likely to have the opportunity.

When extended-care facilities do not offer private personal space to residents, the primary reasons are the cost of facility construction, efficiency of service delivery, and physical safety of residents. It also appears, however, that some designers and administrators of old people's residence do not value privacy for residents to the same extent as the residents themselves. One study of preferences for nursing home design found significant differences between residents, on the one hand, and designers and administrators, on the other, in the relative value given privacy and sociability. Designers and administrators thought it more important to design spaces that would bring people together in common areas, small groups, and in sleeping quarters; residents, by contrast, showed a marked preference for privacy and the ability of residents to be alone without intrusion if they choose.[15]

Surveys and interviews with nursing home residents express their concern with privacy. Residents who share rooms complain that they have no places to be alone, are unable to keep people from intruding in their personal area, and do not feel that they have as much control over their

12. Anke J. E. de Veer and Ada Kerkstra, "Feeling at Home in Nursing Homes," *Journal of Advanced Nursing* 35.3 (2001): 427–34.

13. J. David Huglund, *Housing for the Elderly: Privacy and Independence in Environments for the Aging* (New York: Van Nostrund Reinhold Co., 1985); Justin Keen, "Interiors: Architecture in the Lives of People with Dementia," *International Journal of Geriatric Psychiatry* 4 (1989): 255–72.

14. M. Anderson and C. G. Gottfries, "Nursing Home Care: Factors Influencing the Quality of Life in a Restricted Life Situation," *Aging* 3 (1991): 229–39.

15. Michael Duffy, S. U. Baily, Bets Back, and Donald G. Barker, "Preferences in Nursing Home Design: A Comparison of Residents, Administrators, and Designers," *Environment and Behavior* 18.2 (1986): 246–57.

lives as people who live in single-occupancy rooms.[16] Nursing home residents who share space with several other people find the nursing home an insecure place and that other people are too easily able to intrude on their lives and space.[17] Nursing home residents usually express a desire to be able to be alone when they choose and to be able to talk with others in private.[18]

Those who study a sense of being at home among old people in extended-care facilities seem to agree that when old people have their own things in their living space arranged as they wish, they have a greater sense of autonomy and personal identity.[19] Without secure spaces, however, too often old people's personal items are tampered with or stolen.[20]

It seems that most systems that care for old people consider the privacy afforded by a secure room in which to move among things as one wishes and array one's things to be a dispensable luxury. The practices of extended care sometimes implicitly recognize a need for personal space. Rooms come with curtains to separate beds or try to construct separate but spatially shared alcoves. Staff members seek to make the residents feel at home by involving them in the choice of curtains for furniture color. None of this makes a home in the sense I have described, as a support for the self. One needs at least a small room of one's own, to which one can restrict access.

Practice and Policy

Some people might argue that it is the adult relatives of old people who should enable them to have homes. Ideally, old people who need care should be cared for by their adult children or other adult relatives in the old people's own homes. Alternatively, the adult relatives should bring the old people who need care into their homes and assure them privacy, dignity, and a personal space in which they can arrange their things.

16. Wanda M. Roosa, "Territory and Privacy—Residents' Views: Findings of a Survey," *Geriatric Nursing* (July–August 1982): 214–43.

17. Ira J. Firestone, Cary M. Lechtman, and John R. Evans, "Privacy and Solidarity: Effects of Nursing Home Accommodation on Environmental Perception and Sociability Preferences," *International Journal of Aging and Human Development* 11.3 (1980): 229–41.

18. De Veer and Kerkstra, "Feeling at Home in Nursing Homes."

19. Anderson and Gottfries, "Nursing Home Care"; Edmund Sherman and Evelyn S. Newman, "The Meaning of Cherished Personal Possessions for the Elderly," *Journal of Aging and Human Development* 8.2 (1977–78): 181–92; Roosa, "Territory and Privacy"; Koran, Skott, and Norberg, "A Place of One's Own."

20. Sandra Petrorio and Samantha Kovach, "Managing Privacy Boundaries: Health Providers' Perceptions of Resident Care in Scottish Nursing Homes," *JACR* (May 1997): 115–31; Diana Harris and Michael L. Bension, "Theft in Nursing Homes: An Overlooked Form of Elder Abuse," *Journal of Elder Abuse and Neglect* 11.3 (1999): 73–99. Seventy-eight percent of residents in forty-seven nursing homes are unable to block access to their rooms and to the places were personal possessions are stored.

The majority of old people who need care are cared for by their adult relatives, in either the old people's or the relatives' homes.[21] In practice, this means that women care for frail elderly. Women represent 70 percent of all persons who care for old people privately. The women who provide unpaid care for older relatives often do so at considerable cost to themselves. Their opportunities for professional development or greater income from working more hours are circumscribed. Being on call at all hours of the day or night if the older person needs help, the caregiver has little leisure time and may suffer stress or fatigue as she combines this responsibility with her other family responsibilities. Because dominant social attitudes tend to expect that older people will be cared for by younger relatives, however, the work that these unpaid caregivers do goes largely unrecognized by the society and by those who calculate economic contributions. As with the care of young children, society depends on this work at the same time that it obscures this dependence.[22]

Many family members who care for older relatives do so out of love and compassion and a strong sense of obligation to help them keep dignity and meaning in their lives. Many of them are to be admired and praised for their hard work and devotion to frail old people. Given income limitations and the cost of housing in many metropolitan areas, however, the living arrangements of families caring for old people in their own homes are sometimes overcrowded. Some old people would prefer not to be cared for by their daughters or other relatives; they do not want to be a burden or dislike this sort of dependence on those with whom they have a history of intimacy.[23] However much we idealize family care of old people, the reality is that there is often unhappiness, bickering, and sometimes abuse or neglect behind closed doors that often afford little privacy within the household.

Both longer life spans and changes in working life, mobility, and the dispersal of family members, moreover, put increasing strains on the ability of family members to care for old people. More families depend on all their adult members earning income outside the home in order to have a decent life. Labor-market or professional forces pull many close relatives geographically apart, making daily or weekly contact between old people and their younger relatives impossible.

21. Emily K. Abel says that relatives provide 80 percent of long-term care of dependent elderly; "Adult Daughters and Care for the Elderly," in *The Other within Us: Feminist Explorations of Women and Aging,* ed. Marilyn Pearsall (Boulder, Colo.: Westview Press, 1997), 135–150; this figure is based on a 1985 date and may well have reduced, but probably not by huge proportions.

22. Martha Holstein, "Home Care, Women, and Aging: A Case Study of Injustice," in *Mother Time: Women, Aging, and Ethics,* ed. Margaret Urban Walker (Lanham, Md.: Rowman and Littlefield, 2000), 227–44.

23. Christine Oldman and Deborah Quiglas, "The Last Resort? Revisiting Ideas about Older People's Living Arrangements," *Aging and Society* 19 (1999): 363–84.

Social justice in any society requires that social provision be made for the care of old people in ways that honor and respect them. Depending on the structure of societies, this value can be realized through many practical arrangements. In twenty-first-century industrial societies committed to equal opportunity for women and freedom of movement, this value implies that the social collective ought explicitly to recognize and take up most of the organization and costs of caring for frail old people.[24] The role of family members and intimate friends is at least as central and irreplaceable in the lives of old people as for younger people. Their love and devotion usually must be supplemented by well-resourced and professional care facilities, however, for both the old people and the younger people who love them to lead quality lives. Holding our societies to such a standard means reordering the social service and public spending priorities of many of them. Especially given current trends of privatization and social service cutbacks in most advanced industrial societies, bringing about such a reordering will be difficult at best. We ought, however, to resist the widespread impulse to trim our conception of justice to fit our perception of the social policies that are immediately feasible.

A just and decent society, then, would provide frail old people and their families with decent options from which to choose so that old people can receive the care they need without giving up the social freedom afforded by privacy. Although many people lack it, personal space is a human need, not a luxury, for people of all ages. Especially the old people whose lives are limited physically or economically ought to be able to receive the care they need and at the same time have control over personal space in which they can move and arrange things as they choose, keep the things meaningful to them, hold private conversations, and to which they can restrict access by others. A just society would make a range of living arrangements possible for old people. Some might choose to live in a home with their adult children. Others might rather have a private home of their own and be cared for by personal attendants for as many hours in the day as necessary for a good life. A third option ought to be the larger-scale collective arrangement of a nursing home. A just society will have to make trade-offs among these options, cutting costs as much as possible within the limits of social duty; economics of scale therefore likely dictate a social preference for collective nursing home living arrangements over the provision of home care in the private residences of all the old people who wish it. All the more reason, then, that nursing homes should offer every resident a room of his or her own or other arrangements for a secure personal space and make every effort to make residents' physical safety compatible with this need.

24. Robert E. Goodin and Diane Gibson, "The Decasualization of Eldercare," in *The Subject of Care: Feminist Perspectives on Dependency,* ed. Eva Feder Kittay and Ellen K. Feder (New York: Rowman and Littlefield, 2002), 246–56.

Index

abjection, 109–10, 111, 113
absenteeism, 116
abuse, 166
Africa, 126
African Americans, 144, 149, 150
alienation, 55, 57–60
Allen, Anita, 153, 164, 165
ambiguous transcendence, 35, 36, 38
anatomy, 29
androgyny, 13–14
anxiety, 120, 121
Arendt, Hannah, 126n.3, 141–42
Asia, 126
Austen, Jane, 147
authority, 163, 164
autonomy, 152, 155, 163, 164
awkwardness, 34
Ayalah, Daphna, 75, 88n.27, 90n.34

Barthes, Roland, 72
Bartky, Sandra, 4, 66
bathroom breaks, 114–15
Battersby, Christine, 5–6, 110
beauty, 53, 67
Beauvoir, Simone de
  The Coming of Age, 122
  and contemporary feminism, 98–106
  existentialism, 8, 15

and feminine existence, 29, 30, 31
on house and home, 123, 124, 136–38, 143, 145
on importance of space habits to elderly, 158
on marriage, 141
on menopause, 122
on menstruation, 10, 97, 99, 101, 112, 121
The Second Sex, 99, 136
on sexual differences, 7, 29
Being and Time (Heidegger), 119
biological foundationalism, 17
biological reductionism, 17
Bodies That Matter (Butler), 15
bodily integrity, 165
body
  comportment, motility, and spatiality, 6, 27–45
  distinctive, 18
  experience, 6–7
  fashion-beauty complex, 66
  "habit memories," 139
  image, 38n.15, 76
  lived, 15–26, 31, 35, 36, 37, 58
  as object and/or subject, 38–39, 41, 44–45, 48
  positioning of, 41
  in situation, 16
  style and extension, 32, 40